Information Literacy and Information Skills Instruction

Information Literacy and Information Skills Instruction

*Applying Research to Practice in the
School Library Media Center*

2ND EDITION

Nancy Pickering Thomas

Library and Information Problem-Solving Skills Series
Paula K. Montgomery, Series Editor

LIBRARIES
U N L I M I T E D
A Member of the Greenwood Publishing Group

Westport, Connecticut • London

Library of Congress Cataloging-in-Publication Data is available at *www.loc.gov*

British Library Cataloguing in Publication Data is available.

Copyright © 2004 by Nancy Pickering Thomas

ISBN: 1–159158–081–1

First published in 2004

Libraries Unlimited, Inc., 88 Post Road West, Westport, CT 06881
A Member of the Greenwood Publishing Group, Inc.
www.lu.com

Printed in the United States of America

The paper used in this book complies with the Permanent Paper Standard issued by the National Information Standards Organization (Z39.48–1984).

10 9 8 7 6 5 4 3 2 1

For My Children and Grandchildren
and
In Memory of My Mother

Contents

Acknowledgments

I would like to acknowledge the assistance of my colleagues at Emporia State University (ESU) for their continued encouragement and support for this project.

Very special thanks go as well to Olivia Buzzard and Jason Knight, students in ESU's M.L.S. and Ph.D. programs, respectively, for their assistance with the research and illustrations for the revised edition, and to my daughters Jennifer Birch Thomas and Wendy Thomas Russell, who served as able and sensitive readers.

Introduction

The emphasis on information literacy and a concern for creating literate communities permeates the media as well as the research literature related to all types of libraries (Lingren, 1981). And it is the acceptance of a "fundamental responsibility" to provide "the largest possible number of individuals access to and delivery of the largest possible amount of information" (Ghikas, 1989, p. 124) and to support information seeking that drives user education initiatives in public, academic, and school libraries. In a very real sense, literacy programs represent an instructional continuum, which, ideally, is initiated before children enter school and reinforced through their years of formal education. It is, as Liesener (1985) suggests, the "cumulative effect" of instruction in critical thinking and problem solving "throughout the learner's school experience" that "leads to the development of a self-directed learner able and motivated for life-long learning" (p. 13).

In the literature of librarianship and education over the past three decades, information literacy has been discussed in various ways. Zurkowski (1974) defined information literacy as "the ability to use techniques and skills 'for the wide range of information tools as well as primary sources in molding information-solutions to . . . problems' " (quoted in Eisenberg & Spitzer, 1991, p. 264). A decade later, the National Commission on Excellence in Education (NCEE) explained literacy as "the skills required for new careers and citizenship" and "life-long learning" (Baumbach, 1986, p. 279). In the mid-1990s, the American Library Association's Presidential Committee on Information Literacy described a literate person as one who can "recognize when information is needed," has "the ability to locate, evaluate, and use [it] effectively" (p. 264), and has "learned how to learn" (Breivik & Senn, 1994, p. 4). Drawing on a model created by Christina Doyle (1994), the California Media and Library Educators Association (CMLEA) has characterized information literacy as "the ability to access, evaluate, and use information from a variety of sources" (2), while Breivik and Senn (1994) discuss information literacy as the "ability to acquire and evaluate whatever information is needed at any given moment" (p. 4). In their definition, Kirk, Poston-Anderson, and Yerbury (1990, cited in Todd, 1995) attempted to indicate the complexities involved by setting forth information literacy in terms of seven skill areas: "defining the tasks for which information is needed"; "locating appropriate sources of information to meet needs"; "selecting and recording relevant information from sources"; "understanding and appreciating information from several sources"; combining and organizing the information "effectively for best application"; "presenting the information learned in an appropriate way"; and "evaluating the outcomes in terms of task requirements and increases in knowledge" (p. 133).

Whereas most information literacy definitions tend to be universally applicable, Loertscher (1996) framed literacy specifically in terms of the information needs of children. Information literate students are, according to Loertscher, avid readers, critical thinkers, creative thinkers, interested learners, organized investigators, effective communicators, responsible information users, and skilled users of technological tools. Montgomery (1997) has expanded on this theme, acknowledging that *information literacy* has become an umbrella term encompassing electronic searching and information retrieval skills, library skills, media skills, research skills, reference skills, learning skills, and study skills.

The beginning of the new century has seen renewed interest in literacy skills in education and business contexts and in government initiatives and pronouncements. Particularly compelling are arguments that posit literacy skills as fundamental for success in an increasingly global economy. An appreciation for basic skills as life skills for the 19th century had been reframed, by the end of the 20th, to recognize the information explosion and the demands of "digital age" economics and technologies. The North Central Regional Educational Laboratory (NCREL), for example, lists skills, scientific literacy, technological literacy, visual literacy, cultural literacy, and global awareness to basic and information skills as frameworks for a new generation of children. By the same token, the goals of educating citizens to act responsibly in a democratic society have been expanded to include an understanding of the relationships that exist between and among nations and an appreciation of and respect for diversity in thinking and living in a world made smaller through advances in transportation and communication technologies. In addition, attention that was once focused on ensuring electronic access has shifted to an emphasis on the critical appraisal of information and information sources—skills that are sometimes referred to as "media literacy." At the same time, even in societies that like to describe themselves as information rich, there are still many communities and individuals who remain essentially information poor. And this digital divide grows apace, with each technological innovation.

Helping children and young adults make sense of information and information seeking has been the special task and achievement of school librarians. School librarians continue to cope in responsible ways with the information explosion: updating technology and technology skills, reformulating curricular goals, and seeking new strategies for teaching and learning. More and more, their responsibility in terms of student learning has come to include the planning, conducting, and assessment of curricular activities, and has made school librarians an equal and equally accountable partner with classroom teachers. In addition, in the belief that "age should not be a barrier to the ability to access, receive, and utilize information" (Hooten, 1989, p. 268), many librarians have been in the vanguard of championing the rights of youngsters to unfettered access to and use of the most advanced technologies and virtual resources. With barriers to physical access fading (Wilhelm, Carmen, & Reynolds, 2002), the critical issue has become intellectual access, translated as the ability to think critically and evaluate information and information sources selectively (McDonald, 1988). These skills are central to a digital-age literacy agenda.

In general, this book brings together the literature on information skills instruction with particular reference to models related to information seeking and the information search process as they have been explored in the research of Kuhlthau (1988a, 1988b,

1993b, 2003) and conceptualized by a number of library and information science (LIS) researchers and scholars. These include representational models, which describe the searching behavior of people in naturalistic settings—what they "do and think in searching" (Bates, 1979b, p. 280); instructional models, which help students learn the how-to's of information seeking and searching; and facilitation models, which people can use to improve their chances of success in searching.

Studies reviewed for this book include doctoral dissertations, research reports, academic and professional journal articles in LIS and related fields, and the writings of scholars and practitioners relevant to information skills curriculum. For "preservice" graduate students seeking certification or licensure in school media, the book should provide an overview of school librarianship as an area of specialization and its development over time; an introduction to the major models and approaches that guide contemporary instructional practice; and an understanding of the social aspects of instruction and service in school settings. Students and practitioners interested in bibliographic instruction (BI) in academic libraries will also find useful the overview of the development of BI provided in the first chapter, particularly the lessons learned with regard to the creation and implementation of BI curriculum. For library media specialists, the book will help to clarify issues and identify challenges encountered by others in the field and suggest research-based solutions. For principals and teachers, the book will provide an introduction to the contemporary practice of school librarianship and to the instructional activities that are part of the "package" offered by dynamic library media specialists. For LIS educators and Ph.D. students, this literature review confirms the contributions of many LIS researchers and frames the growing body of scholarly work to ground further research on information skills instruction. Taking stock of what we know may also serve as a springboard to new thinking and reveal new directions for research related to information seeking and children.

Chapter 1 provides a brief overview of the development of library curriculum as it has evolved from its beginnings in more traditional forms of reference services. Chapter 2 traces the development of school libraries as centralized facilities and the introduction of library skills as a primary focus of library instruction programs. Chapter 3 summarizes traditional and alternative approaches to information skills instruction, including the specific source approach, the pathfinder approach, and the process approach in models created by Callison (1986), Sheingold (1986), and Kuhlthau (1988a, 1988b). Special attention is given to Kuhlthau's (1993b) Information Search Process (ISP) and intervention models and to research studies that have explored the usefulness of the information search process (ISP) and its theory base. In Chapter 4, a variety of conceptual models for teaching information skills as a process are described, including the work of Ann Irving (1985), Stripling and Pitts (1988), Eisenberg and Berkowitz (1990), Joyce and Tallman (1997), Pappas and Tepe (1997), Yucht (1997, 2002), McKenzie (1997), and others. Chapter 5 provides a closer look at instruction in terms of Grover's (1993) model for diagnosing information needs and relates information needs to theories of information seeking, theories of learning, learning styles, and individual differences. In Chapter 6, the research literature related to information skills instruction is reviewed and major findings are summarized. Chapter 7 considers the impact that technology has had on the teaching of information skills, and the challenges for librarians and students posed by the "digital divide." Chapter 8 provides an overview of contemporary school reform and assessment initiatives particularly as they relate to school libraries and information skills instruction. In Chapter 9, research related to interpersonal communication within the context of the school library is presented, and the social nature of information seeking and instruction is explored. An Epilogue considers issues of professionalism, service, research directions, and leadership for school library media specialists.

Readers who seek in this review of the literature instructional shortcuts that can transform practice and raise test scores in one fell swoop are bound to be disappointed. Neither does this book offer a magic formula for success in teaching information skills, nor does it advocate the use of a single strategy that will work in all schools, among all students, at all grade levels, under all conditions, and in all situations. What it does do is acknowledge the richness of our theoretical and instructional models and consider the value that a variety of instructional approaches can have for teaching and learning. In so doing, it also brings into sharper focus the complexities of students' research tasks and the challenges students face when seeking information in traditional and electronic resources.

Information seeking for lifelong learning ultimately requires the "seekers" to create their own best ways to find, use, and evaluate information for effective problem resolution and decision making. However, the research literature reviewed here provides ample evidence that learning the skills upon which information literacy depends cannot be left to chance; these skills must be taught, and students must receive support and guidance from knowledgeable instructors as the skills are practiced within curricular tasks that have relevance, interest, and value for them. For this reason, library media specialists will continue to have important roles to play in educating youngsters capable of surviving and thriving in the "knowledge society" of the future.

School libraries are struggling to meet the challenges inherent in the move to a digital age economy, even as they continue to respond to demands for school reform and accountability. Speaking to a conference of the International Association of School Librarianship in New Zealand in 2001, Carol Kulhthau discussed the changes to the information environment in school libraries and the need for renewal of libraries to reflect these changes. Noting the shift from a deficit model of librarianship characterized by inability to obtain necessary resources to information abundant libraries, Kuhlthau reiterated the challenge for students in making sense of information—not in the sort of "predigested, carefully selected, or logically organized" libraries and textbooks but in a "vast network of resources" now available online. To prepare youth for the 21st-century workplace, Kuhlthau urged librarians to think about education more broadly and to consider "the ways technology changes the nature of work," productivity, and "our sense of community" and "everyday life" (Kuhlthau, 2001).

The importance of basing practice on understandings obtained through research cannot be overstated. As Comer (2001) tells us: "Most [educational cures] can't work, or at best, will have limited effectiveness. They all are based on flawed models. We will be able to create a successful system of education nationwide only when we base everything we do on what is known about how children and youths develop and learn."

Within the context of library and information skills instruction, this book attempts to meet Comer's challenge.

1 From Personal Assistance to Bibliographic Instruction

The Roots of Information Skills Instruction in Academic and Public Libraries

The practice of educating the library user to locate and use library resources is an outgrowth of traditional forms of reference services in public and academic libraries. Even so, programs to assist the user in accessing information in increasingly complex technological environments are largely grassroots initiatives, which have, like Topsy in *Uncle Tom's Cabin*, just "growed." Indeed, efforts to establish bibliographic instruction (BI) as an organized library activity have been launched in a number of venues over time, and interest in this aspect of academic librarianship has mushroomed since the late 1970s (Farber, quoted in Hardesty, Schmitt, & Tucker, 1986, p. 232). For example, whereas in 1979 some 24 percent of colleges required courses in the use of their libraries and library resources, by 1987 this number had grown to 65 percent (Mensching, 1989). From these statistics it would appear that, like school librarians, academic librarians view "library instruction" as an essential aspect of service. "We are not alone," Kuhlthau (1987) reminds us, but share "with other types of librarians" a "concern and commitment" for creating effective instructional approaches and programs to assist students in learning information skills (p. 23).

Approaches to Service: Origins and Development

Even though they have most often represented pragmatic rather than theoretical approaches, efforts to provide instruction in school and college libraries are not without a history. Indeed, while the incorporation of BI initiatives and information skills programs might appear to be relative newcomers in academic and school library settings (Turner, 1991), they have roots in traditions that date back almost two centuries. As chronicled by Rothstein (1955, 1994), Lubans (1974), Hardesty, Schmitt, and Tucker (1986), and others, the origins of present-day instructional practices can be found in a dedication to providing personal assistance to library users that surfaced relatively early in the psyche of American librarians. The form of such assistance, which predated the adoption of formal reference services by many decades, included provision of all the information requested by the library user and "guidance and direction in the pursuit of information" (Schiller, 1986, p. 191).

A Taxonomy of Service

The earliest models for reference services did not consist of a coherently articulated program of professional practice. Rather, service developed first within individual academic and public libraries and thus differed widely, depending upon whatever patterns of personal assistance were in vogue there (Schiller, 1986). J.I. Wyer (b. 1869) described these differences in terms of a taxonomy of service levels: conservative, moderate, and liberal (Wyer, 1930). At the conservative level, the librarian was characterized as an "intelligent guidepost" rather than an information agent, with the "self-development" of the library user as the ultimate goal of any "service" interactions. In practice, librarians espousing a conservative view considered the act of offering more than directional assistance or the "means of gathering information" a disservice in that it "deprived[d] patrons of the invaluable benefits derived from the experience of personal investigation" (Spofford, 1900, quoted in Rothstein, 1955, p. 42). The conservative model of service was reflected in the public library arena in the work of such early library notables as John Cotton Dana (1856–1929)[1] and Charles Ami Cutter (1837–1903), both of whom judged library users capable of finding the answers to their own inquiries. According to Rothstein, this service approach was based on an "a priori assumption that the library [as] an educational institution" had a responsibility to provide formal instruction in the use of its resources but that the "truly deserving university student or public library patron" would desire no more assistance than that. As Rothstein noted, "Presumably readers more egregious in their demands were to be rejected out of hand, or to be brought to realize that less aid really did them more good than more aid" (p. 44). Rothstein himself found this claim "dubious," an example of inverted logic, and contrary to popular wisdom; surely, he thought, increasing services would ultimately mean an increase in the library's popularity and community support.

However, few disputed the inherent contradictions in the "less is more" policies of the time, perhaps because, as Rothstein (1955) suggested, as a rationale it tended to fit contemporary practice. Indeed, according to Rothstein, "the 'conservative theory' never ceased to find adherents" (p. 75), particularly in academic library settings. Perhaps for this reason, the real focus of instructional attention prior to World War I was the "inexperienced library user" (p. 45), with guided tours and formalized library courses as the most commonly used instructional methods. Other, less intrusive and less interactive methods of instruction, namely, the creation of subject bibliographies and finding lists, were also standard service approaches.

Interestingly, where a conservative or limited service model characterized reference practice, it was usually invoked for both faculty and students. "Just what educational purposes were being served by denying to faculty more than minimal assistance," Rothstein (1955) suggested, were at best "seldom made clear. Tacitly, however, the policy was undoubtedly based on the old assumption that the mature scholar did not need help—or at any rate *ought* not to need it" (p. 75) and that students didn't deserve it (Schiller, 1986). In point of fact, the assumption that "the value of a study [ought to be] measured by the personal labor of its author" (Schiller, 1986, p. 87) was entirely consistent with the social values inherent in a Puritan/Protestant work ethic (Sillars, 1991) and an American preoccupation with self-reliance, characteristic of the period. According to Rothstein, direct services in the form of information provision were often saved for those he characterized as the truly "helpless": "foreigners" and the "timid" (pp. 75–76).

There were, however, other voices in academic librarianship arguing for reference librarians to assume a more active role in the information tasks of library users. For example, J. Christian Bay (1871–1962), writing in 1924, opined that librarians should "illumine" (quoted in Rothstein, 1955, p. 76) as well as recommend specific sources, an approach that Wyer (1930) would later describe as typical of a "moderate" level of service. The interpretation of information and its utilization were, however, activities thought to be the responsibility of the information seeker.

At a third or "liberal level" of Wyer's (1930) service taxonomy, the librarian was obliged to use her or his expertise to find the information sought by patrons and to provide direct assistance in establishing the relevance, authority, and authenticity of particular titles. An articulate and enthusiastic proponent for this extended service model was William E. Henry (1927), librarian at the University of Washington, who offered as a rationale his understanding that the essential task of scholarship was the creation of a thesis rather than the mechanics of identifying, searching out, and obtaining particular sources. The most immediate consequence of Wyer's "liberal service" idea was the development of academic subject specialties by reference staff, so that they could provide a more scholarly level of assistance than had previously been available or expected.

It is perhaps not surprising to note that the conservative and liberal approaches to reference service were seldom embraced with equal enthusiasm within the same institution. Indeed, across the profession there has never been anything like total agreement as to what constitutes "best practice" in the delivery of user services (Schiller, 1986). Over time, the liberal "direct provision" camp of librarians has promoted its view with eloquence and humor, often dismissing as "ludicrous" the very notion that the library should be in the business of educating users. Jesse Shera (1903–1982), for example, called on librarians to " 'forget this silly pretense of playing teacher' " (1954, quoted in Hardesty, Schmitt, & Tucker, 1986, p. 189); while Rothstein (1964, quoted in Schiller) argued that although instruction might be defensible for children and youth, adults had "no more reason to be guided in the techniques of finding out than they have in being shown how to fix a defective carburetor" (p. 193).

On a more serious note, Schiller (1986) has asserted that efforts to provide both "instruction services" and "information services" within the same institution are self-defeating because, in her view, the two approaches are inherently "antagonistic." In fact, Schiller believes that attempts to offer a dual model of service are detrimental to both library users and librarians. On the one hand, Schiller implies that maintaining two approaches to service is discriminatory, since in many cases librarians have invoked an instructional services model to justify limiting assistance to students, whom they have traditionally regarded as "undeserving." On the other hand, the duality bewilders library users because they do not know which of the two approaches they are going to encounter when they seek reference assistance. Expecting or, perhaps, fearing that they will find the reduced service model in place makes users uncertain about the legitimacy and permissibility of asking for help and often leads them to modify or abandon their requests for assistance. In situations where users hesitate to explain their information needs fully, librarians have the problematic task of reinterpreting user questions "to discover what is actually wanted" (p. 201).

Eadie (1990) has objected to bibliographic instruction on the grounds that in the long run, instructional sessions most often address location skills rather than the more challenging and useful cognitive tasks related to "making sense" of the materials located (p. 42). In addition to critiquing BI on intellectual grounds, Eadie has argued that the entire exercise is aimed at the wrong goals. Instead of saving "the time of the reader" (Ranganathan, 1957),[2] Eadie suggests that library instruction tends to be aimed at saving the time of the reference librarian. For his part, Dickinson (1981) has dismissed the creation of instructional programs at postsecondary levels because he believes that "students should enter colleges and universities already in command of most of what [bibliographic instruction] programs endeavor to impart." Indeed, Dickinson argues that the teaching of basic library skills is more "properly the responsibility of elementary and secondary school librarians, since it is only they who can deal with it in other than a remedial sense" (p. 854). Ironically, the fact that, indeed, many students do *not* possess these skills when entering the university (Goodin, 1987, 1991; Turner, 1991) has been advanced as the rationale for BI by its many proponents.

Research versus Information Seeking

Stoan (1984) has warned academic librarians against presenting "information skills" as "research skills," which, as he asserts, are not equivalent "nor bear any organic relationship to each other" (p. 105). According to Stoan, activities that academic librarians frequently refer to as "research" are more properly information seeking and "library use," while "research," within the parlance of faculty members, is a "quest for knowledge" (p. 105) entailing the systematic collection of original "uninterpreted" (p. 100) data, conducted according to methodologies consistent with particular academic disciplines. The appropriate use of library resources within the context of a research agenda, Stoan suggests, consists of footnote and citation chasing in the secondary literature to find relevant readings. Since it is through footnotes that "scholars communicate with each other," they are more useful as keys to the utility of an article in relationship to a particular topic than are access "tools" such as subject headings and descriptors, which represent a "layer" of interpretation created by "a third party" (p. 103).

Stoan (1984) has also argued against trying to teach students a single, generic research strategy, because scholarly approaches to information seeking are personal, domain specific, subjective, and intuitive. In his view, such approaches constitute an amalgam of insights, experience, and luck sparked by engagement with resources encountered (sometimes serendipitously) along the way. Furthermore, Kaplan (quoted in Stoan) has argued that researchers are often unable to describe their own methods of information seeking and frequently employ " 'logic-in-use' " (p. 102) strategies, rather than using the indexing and abstracting resources and reference "tools that librarians deem so central to the research process" (p. 101). Finally, Stoan concludes that libraries are organized for the convenience of librarians and not to facilitate research as it is conducted by scholars.

Notwithstanding the ongoing debate over the need for and the efficacy of BI, the theories, attitudes, and strategies that emerged over time in academic and public library contexts created frameworks and models for the teaching of library and information skills in the school media center. Especially important were the characterizations of libraries as intellectual centers, learning laboratories, and information bureaus; the recommendation that students rely on primary and secondary sources rather than textbooks; advocacy for increasing the accessibility of library resources; models for individualized guidance; and roles for library users as independent searchers and lifelong learners. Given the contemporary and progressive "feel" these concepts have, it is interesting to note that all had their inception in academic and public libraries in 19th-century America. The rest of this chapter will trace these ideas and practices and their development over time.

Library Instruction as an Aspect of Service in Academic Libraries

The status of the library as a cultural institution par excellence has seldom been questioned. Rather grandly, Francis Lieber (1882, quoted in Rothstein, 1955) described libraries as "the bridges over which Civilization travels from generation to generation and from country to country" (p. 11). In higher education, the affinity between the library as cultural artifact and the library as educational workplace seems to have been appreciated even in the earliest days of the Republic. Rothstein noted, for example, that although academic libraries at the beginning of the 19th century were "indifferent" to most activities other than those involved in acquiring materials, "teaching the use of books and libraries did arouse some considerable interest" (p. 14). In 1816, for example, George Ticknor (1791–1871) described the library as "the light and spirit" of the university and its "first convenience" (pp. 10–11). " 'Give me a library,' " wrote Benjamin Ide Wheeler at the end of the 19th century, " 'and I'll build a university about it' " (quoted in Rothstein, p. 11). Writing about the same time, Frederick A.P. Barnard (1883, quoted in Rothstein), the president of Columbia University, expressed his enthusiastic support for " 'instruction and aid to undergraduates as shall enable them in all their after lives to do their individual work more readily and more successfully' " (p. 14); while American historian Herbert Baxter Adams (1887, quoted in Rothstein) found highly commendable a course in "bibliographical information" taught to students " 'by the librarian of their college or university' " (p. 14). Finally, the words of Otis Robinson (quoted in Tuckett & Stoffle, 1984) reflect the sentiments of many of the more visionary 19th-century library educators:

> **Give me a library, and I'll build a university about it.**
>
> —Benjamin Ide Wheeler, quoted in Rothstein, 1955

> A librarian should be more than a keeper of books; he [*sic*] should be an educator.
> . . . No such librarian is fit for his place unless he holds himself responsible for
> the library education of his students. . . . All that is taught in college amounts to
> very little; but if we can send students out self-reliant in their investigations, we
> will have accomplished much. (p. 58)

In a very real sense, the transformation of the librarian from archivist to educator facilitated and was facilitated by the transformation of the university library from literary "sanctum" to intellectual "workshop."

Near the end of the 19th century, the development of an instructional model for service was advanced still further at Harvard University, where the "professor of books," librarian Justin Winsor (1831–1897), actively encouraged library staff and library users to provide research assistance. According to a procedure created by Winsor, information seekers could post "notes and queries" (Rothstein, 1955, p. 24) on a spindle in the reference room; anyone interested in finding the answer could post it for others to read. Winsor also advocated the preparation of book lists "in anticipation of students' essays." "If our colleges would pay more attention to the methods by which a subject is deftly attacked, and would teach the true use of encyclopedic and bibliographic helps," Winsor wrote, "they would do much to make the library more serviceable" (p. 24).

Winsor (1986) also proposed opening the university collections to individual students and faculty and providing instruction in the "use of books and libraries." Although his somewhat modest model for instruction limited library lessons to locating and accessing library materials, Winsor's vision of the library as "the grand rendezvous of the college for teacher and pupil" (p. 7) placed him well ahead of the learning curve; many college and university librarians of his time were not nearly so accommodating. Indeed, it was not until universities began to adopt the German model of lectures and seminars as vehicles for instruction that textbooks came to be replaced by materials that were housed in campus libraries. Interestingly, if perhaps not surprisingly, state universities welcomed the establishment of personally assisted reference services with more enthusiasm initially than did librarians at older and perhaps more conservative private universities.

Another 19th-century librarian who championed accessibility to collections and the amplification of services was William Frederick Poole (1821–1894). While to contemporary ears his announcement that his "office door [was] always open" to anyone seeking assistance may sound at best reactive, at the time it must have seemed positively magnanimous. Poole also favored the creation of a university course in the "scientific methods of using books" and sought faculty status for professor-librarians to whom would fall the responsibility for providing this instruction. Raymond C. Davis (1836–1919) created a course on bibliography and reference tools at the University of Michigan as early as 1881. As forward looking as these courses were, it was Melvil Dewey (1851–1931) who, at the turn of the 20th century, finally regularized reference services and established "organized personal assistance" as an integral instrument of the Columbia College's library's educational purpose. Writing as early as 1884, Dewey set forth his expectations: In addition to organizing and cataloging library materials and providing reference resources, librarians were to furnish advice and instruction so that students would gain knowledge of the best library resources and be able "to use them intelligently" and in the proper order. For Dewey, the "first and paramount duty of the Reference Librarian" was to set an example, counsel students, and train library users in the delights of the library and the "habit of hunting" information (Rothstein, 1955, p. 28).

Themes and issues contributing to the discourse surrounding the development of instruction after 1900 can also be seen in the work of William Warner Bishop (1871–1955) and Lucy Maynard Salmon (1853–1927). Noting the "deluge" of new material published each year, Bishop in 1912 recommended that students be educated in acquiring a scholar's "attitude toward the printed page" (Bishop, 1986, p. 83) through a sequential program of instruction that should begin in elementary school and continue until a student graduated from college.[3] Another contemporary-sounding insight was shared with attendees at an American Library Association (ALA) conference in 1913 when Salmon, a history professor at Vassar, argued persuasively for the incorporation of instruction in books and libraries within the context of regular college courses. Salmon believed that because the professors knew individual students and their particular research needs, they were in the best position to provide library instruction relevant to ongoing course assignments and requirements. Not only did it made good sense to "incorporate knowledge of how to use a library with the subject matter included in a particular course" (Salmon, 1986, p. 88), she opined, it would also save everyone's time. Further, the "knowledge acquired" in the course of instruction would fall "naturally into its place in connection within definite, concrete work" (p. 88) and be more easily assimilated by college students.[4]

In order to put her ideas on library instruction into play, Salmon created a course for new students that included a library tour and designed "bibliographical work" within a "definitely planned . . . systematically carried out" progression of courses directly related to the specific and individual work of every student. From time to time conferences [were] held by members of the library staff and the instructors in history and these conferences enable[d] each department to supplement and complement the work of the other and thus avoid repetition and duplication. (p. 93)

Salmon characterized the roles of the librarian as friend, counselor, guide, and ultimately, teacher.

It is often his [sic] duty not to give, but temporarily to withhold information; not to answer but to ask questions; to answer one question by asking another; to help a student answer his own question for himself, work out his own problems, and find a way out of his difficulties; to show him how to seek and find for himself the material desired; to give training rather than specific information; to be himself a teacher and to co-operate with other instructors in training the students who seek his help. (p. 94)

Academic libraries provided varying levels of reference support during the beginning and middle decades of the 20th century. Although most did not adopt one mode or level of service over another in a formal statement of library policy, they tended to operate at a moderate level of service, established not by design but on an ad hoc basis, often in response to traffic flow. However, the development of subject specialties by librarians with degrees or advanced levels of knowledge in academic domains, which became a part of the organizational pattern in many academic and public libraries during this period, held out at least the possibility that higher levels of service and increased levels of expertise would be made available to library users. However, as Farber (1995) notes, librarians tended to expend most of their efforts in acquiring resources and organizing materials to support faculty research. In many institutions this led to a sort of double standard: personal assistance for teaching and research faculty was modeled on a liberal approach to reference services, while undergraduate students were on the receiving end of minimalist or conservative service levels (Rothstein, 1994).

Of course, the qualities and qualifications that make a person proficient at library tasks are not necessarily isomorphic with those that make a good teacher; nor should the acquisition of pedagogical skills be left to chance. Charles B. Shaw addressed these important points in a speech at Drexel University in 1928. In brief, Shaw (1986) argued that librarians must learn the fundamentals of teaching and learning if their efforts at library skills instruction were to bear fruit. Indeed, Shaw called for the development of "a new species [of librarian] which will combine in one individual the librarian's knowledge of books and bibliographical procedure with the instructor's ability in teaching method and in the skilled imparting of information" (p. 109).

Another version of academic reference services was introduced at Cornell University in the 1930s. At the university library, generalists were hired to assist faculty members in identifying resources outside the scholar's area of specialization and to procure materials from other libraries when necessary. This departure from the "specialist" model of academic reference work made use of the librarian as a consultant rather than as an information provider or instructor.

The most common approaches to library instruction during the early years were library lectures, which were usually followed by some sort of assignment that required students to use the library and its array of bibliographic tools and resources. It became evident over time that the stronger programs were those in which the librarian worked closely with the college professors. In fact, the importance of professor-librarian partnerships was a central finding of research conducted within the context of liberal arts colleges by Harvie Branscomb and published in 1940 as *Teaching with Books* (Hardesty, Schmitt, & Tucker, 1986).

An interesting program launched at Stephens College (Columbia, Missouri) in the early 1930s by B. Lamar Johnson (1904–1995) is also worthy of note. Basic to the Stephens approach were clearly articulated objectives that emphasized instruction in the use of the library resources and the development of good study skills as prerequisites for learning. Through his courses, Johnson sought to place library use at the vortex of the instructional process. The fact that Johnson occupied positions as both the college librarian and the dean in charge of instruction greatly facilitated the implementation of his ideas, and he himself admitted that the adoption of his program would have been impossible had he not had the authority to impose it on both faculty and students (Hardesty, Schmitt, & Tucker, 1986).

Johnson's faith in the value of the library as the linchpin of a college education was also shared by Louis Shores (1904–1981) at Peabody College for Teachers (Nashville, Tennessee), who in the 1930s and early 1940s launched an ambitious program based on his idea that the library is the college and the college, the library. What Shores envisioned was a library college in which all the teachers would be library-trained and in charge of supervising and tutoring individual students in independently conducted reading and research projects. Among Shores's notable contributions to the discourse of academic librarianship were the idea that learning should be student-centered and interdisciplinary and that creating independent learners was the appropriate goal of education. At the time, Shores's program had little immediate impact on the practice of his contemporaries. However, his understanding that library instruction could make a valuable contribution to the achievement of the broader educational goals of the institution aided in the development of a vision for instructional programs in academic and school libraries that were implemented later in the century (Shores, 1986).

Although the explosion of scientific knowledge immediately evident in the postwar years raised concerns of many mid-century librarians about the problems this "Niagara" of information might pose for the general public and for students, little progress in user instruction was made during the next two decades (Rothstein, 1955). In fact, in spite of a burgeoning student population and expanding collections, lack of library staff, lack of "a viable conceptual framework" (Hardesty, Schmitt, & Tucker, 1986, p. 148), lack of enthusiasm, and/or lack of instructional finesse (Kirk, 1977, cited in Hardesty, Schmitt, & Tucker) together led most academic librarians to limit their instructional efforts to orientation sessions and library tours. When they were available, library education courses were typically taught in stand-alone sessions, with content decisions most frequently based on the expertise and interests of the librarians rather than the information needs of the students. As a result, instructional programs in many universities languished. Even so, insights gained through the implementation of the innovative programs championed by Dewey, Shores, Johnson, and others created frameworks for the development of instructional programs to come. (A summary of new roles and activities is provided in Table 1.1.) Especially compelling in this regard were models for librarians that modeled active participation in the process of student learning.

Table 1.1
Themes and Insights in Early Efforts at Library Use Instruction

- Roles for librarians as teachers, advisers, consultants, and information providers
- Pedagogical training as a prerequisite for "teaching" librarians
- Importance of faculty and librarian engagement in planning
- Importance of teaching library use skills in context
- Value of information use skills over locating and accessing skills
- Librarian as identifier of relevant resources
- Librarian's role in assisting with research products and evaluating the results

Knapp's Experiment

The program that rekindled the flame of interest in bibliographic instruction among academic and school librarians was created by Patricia Bryan Knapp (1914–1972) at Wayne State University (Detroit, Michigan) in the early 1960s. Convinced that "competence in library use" constituted "one of the liberal arts" (Knapp, 1986, p. 156), and recognizing the key role college faculty played in student use of library resources, Knapp (1966) launched an initiative to "instruct the instructors" in the use of the library, its resources, and its educational value by integrating library instruction into a wide variety of courses to demonstrate the applicability of library skills across the curriculum. In addition, Knapp devised a plan to implement these skills through a series of instructional experiences carried out over time, which she hoped would lead students to develop positive attitudes toward the library and an appreciation for its utility.

Featured prominently in Knapp's (1966) approach were assignments based on problem-solving activities, rather than paper-and-pencil tests or "make-work" practice assignments based loosely on course content. In this way, she hoped to emphasize the "intellectual processes involved in retrieval of information and ideas from the complex system our society uses to organize its stored record" (p. 81). And although Knapp's program was essentially librarian-initiated, the delivery of BI was truly a cooperative effort between university librarians and the teaching faculty. The program itself called for the articulation of specific objectives, which included the organizational schemes used to structure library collections, the identification of essential reference books, and the criteria that could be used to interpret and evaluate the information obtained.

It must be admitted that Knapp's (1966) dynamic instructional program was not greeted with unqualified enthusiasm by Wayne State students and faculty. However, her insights made a major contribution to the field of library and information studies in general and to school librarianship in particular. Especially influential have been Knapp's understanding that library use is a multidimensional activity involving "knowledge, skills, and attitudes" (Farber, 1995, p. 24) and that library use skills are best learned over time and when presented within the context of ongoing classroom assignments. In fact, the systematicity of the instructional program, her emphasis on

**Table 1.2
A Summary of Insights from the Knapp (1966, 1986) Project**

- Library use as a multidimensional activity involving knowledge, skills, and attitudes

- The value of teaching library use skills in context

- The value of integrating library use skills across subject domains

- The importance of systematic planning for instruction

- The importance of cooperation and coordination between librarians and teachers

- The importance of providing "authentic" activities for practicing library use skills

- The importance of evaluation in the use of information resources

"process" over "content," and her understanding of the key roles played by course instructors are now regarded as foundational for the successful implementation of instructional programming in school library media centers. Table 1.2 lists important insights anchored in Knapp's research.

Bibliographic Instruction: The Earlham College Experience

Another major contribution to the development of bibliographic instruction models was the exemplary program of library instruction created at Earlham College (Richmond, Indiana) in the mid-1960s and implemented by librarians Evan Ira Farber, Thomas B. Kirk, and James R. Kennedy. Founded on a bedrock of active cooperation between departmental scholars and college librarians, Earlham's approach to instruction featured three central principles: integration, demonstration, and gradation (Kennedy, 1986, p. 233). Integration was achieved by embedding all library instruction within courses that most often required students to use library resources. Demonstration was chosen as the central instructional strategy and included an introduction to the search process as well as to specific types of library resources. (Annotated bibliographies of course-relevant materials were also created and distributed as part of the instructional program.) Gradation was achieved through the implementation of a planned sequence of instructional sessions, which were conducted over the four years of a student's college career. Elements that librarians viewed as key to the successful implementation of the program included rapport and synergy between the librarians and the teaching faculty; the selection of appropriate courses for library skills integration and appropriate projects within the courses; small class size; and a "just in time" approach, which based decisions related to course scheduling directly on the needs of students. Kennedy (1986) identified as strategies contributing substantially to the overall success of Earlham's innovative program: the college culture, which "demands library use"; the commitment of librarians; the motivation of students; high teacher expectations; and quality and creativity in instructional techniques (see Table 1.3).

Table 1.3
Key Elements in Earlham College's Successful Bibliographic Instruction Program

- A culture that "demands" library use

- Commitment of librarians and teaching faculty to the goals of the program

- Active rapport and collaboration between librarians and the teaching faculty

- Selection of appropriate courses for library skills integration

- Selection of appropriate projects for library skills integration

- High student motivation and interest

- High teacher expectations

- Small class size

- "Just in time" scheduling of the instructional intervention

- Instructional quality and creativity

Although in many respects Earlham's experience and its success reflected the unique qualities of the institution and its librarians, the program created at Earlham resulted in a veritable explosion of interest among academic librarians in the 1970s and continues today. The first tangible evidence of this interest was the creation of an Ad Hoc Committee on Bibliographic Instruction within the Association of College and Research Libraries and the subsequent establishment of the Bibliographic Instruction Section of that organization in 1977. The founding of the Library Instruction Round Table by the ALA in 1977 and a series of conferences, newsletters, and clearinghouses for information on bibliographic instruction followed, some of which included elementary and secondary librarians (e.g., the Library Orientation Exchange).

Contemporary modes for bibliographic instruction include a variety of practices: "library sessions" by teaching faculty within the context of their regularly scheduled course offerings; stand-alone courses conducted by library staff; orientation programs and tours, which introduce students to the library facility, services, and resources; research paper seminars, organized to assist students involved in course-related reference assignments; manuals, handbooks, and workbooks for students to use independently; and point-of-use brochures and fact sheets. Automation and the proliferation of online resources have made electronic library tours, information sessions, and tutorials attractive supplements for more traditional and personalized reference services in many academic libraries. According to Farber (1995), computerized instruction is also becoming increasingly sophisticated as CAI (computer-assisted instruction) develops voice synthesis capabilities, which can be locally produced and tailored to the libraries in which they will be used. However, as Farber (1998) opines, "No matter how effective automated instruction becomes, there's no substitute for a reference librarian who can help a student shape a topic, suggest an unusual source and offer an encouraging word."

"Personal Assistance" in Public Libraries and the Library of Congress

While programs of instruction are most often considered the special province of academic and school libraries, an understanding of the contribution public libraries could make to the creation of an informed citizenry emerged in American public libraries as early as the 1820s. Although reference services provided at that time were delivered on an ad hoc rather than systematic basis and essentially consisted of individual acts of kindness, they established the practice of courteous "personal assistance," which eventually evolved into the public service orientation that guides contemporary library practice.

A pattern of reference service slightly more aggressive than the sporadic offerings of personal assistance characteristic of the early years was articulated first at the Boston Public Library in the 1850s, where "a naive faith in the efficacy of 'good' reading in the preservation of virtue' " (Rothstein, 1955, p. 16) prompted the institution to commit itself to popular education. Boston Public's vision of the public library as "a new tool for scholarship," although entirely consistent with the values of the times, did not immediately usher in a new age of library service nor inspire the creation of similar projects in other institutions. On the contrary, limited collections and low levels of funding slowed the growth in reference service delivery during the years following the Civil War. Nonetheless, it was during this period that libraries first became concerned with demonstrating their value as community resources; and it was not long before they seized on reference services as a vehicle for expanding their usefulness, their horizons, and their visibility.

Another milestone in the development of "reference" as an important aspect of library activity was a program for reading assistance devised for library users at the Worcester (Massachusetts) Free Public Library, under the guidance of Samuel Swett Green (1837–1913). Green's public advocacy of a more formal and regularized approach to reference services came in 1876, in a paper delivered at the first conference of the American Library Association. Because, Green reasoned, the people who come into the library frequently lack knowledge of library books and resources as well as the background and skills needed to use the library catalogs, it is the obligation of the library staff to lend them a hand. To this end, Green trained his staff to provide reference services to library patrons, stressing the importance of accessibility to materials and "cordiality" in addressing users' questions. According to Rothstein (1955), Green was motivated by a sort of self-righteous self-interest in that his efforts were aimed as much at improving the library's public image as they were at elevating the public's literary tastes. In short, Green hoped to curry favor with the voting public by doing "good."

Although Green's ideas for a " 'new method' " (Rothstein, 1955, p. 22) were greeted by some of his colleagues as forward looking, others were less sanguine. One librarian, for example, rejected the idea, claiming that the questions of ordinary library users were bound to be largely "frivolous" and a waste of the librarian's energy and time and that in most cases library staff lacked the expertise necessary to assist scholars in any meaningful way. Even so, Green's somewhat tentative entry into the instructional "lists" eventually gained support and with it a realization that libraries should use every means at their disposal to make their resources useful to the publics that provided their support.

By the late 1880s, evidence of the proliferation of this approach to public service was provided in Frederick Morgan Crunden's (1847–1911) study of public libraries.

One of the founders of the ALA and an early president of the association, Crunden found "a growing sentiment in favor of the provision of personal assistance by the librarian as the most effective form of aid to the reader" (Rothstein, 1955, p. 26). Within the next 10 years, what often began as "casual, intermittent help" came increasingly to be "replaced by specific administrative organization" (p. 28) of such services. Indeed, by 1891, the new service even had a formal name—"reference work"—which replaced the more ambiguous " 'aids to readers' " and "access to librarians" (Rothstein, 1994, p. 542).

Another early proponent of user education as a part of library practice was Charles Ami Cutter (1837–1903), who proposed teaching library patrons to use catalogs and book lists so that they would be able to find their own information and answer their own reference questions. Although Cutter's plan served the rather pragmatic end of keeping library users from troubling the library staff, Melvil Dewey's "concern over the library's role as an educational institution" was considerably more altruistic and proactive. For Dewey, instruction was seen as a core rather than "peripheral" activity and "central in the library's responsibilities" (Rothstein, 1955, p. 31). Because of his commitment to improving services in both academic and public library sectors, Dewey's work created a bridge between the two that facilitated the spread of his " 'modern library idea' " (quoted in Rothstein, p. 27) more generally among library professionals.

By the 1920s, most public librarians had adopted a dual service model, although most frequently librarians provided answers and information directly to library users, unless they specifically requested instruction. As libraries grew in popularity, demands for services also increased. The strain this new "traffic" placed on reference departments, and a concern to maintain both quality and service, led librarians to create a number of innovative approaches. In cities that supported multiple libraries within a single system, some directors farmed out readers' advisory services to the library's branches, while retaining responsibility for more "serious" research functioning at the central facility. Others found a solution in the creation of a separate information desk, which could handle directional inquiries expeditiously while channeling more "important" information questions to experts in the reference department. Where funding and staffing were available, reference departments were themselves divided into specialty areas (e.g., science and technology; business; history and genealogy) similar in pattern to the disciplinary specialties (e.g., science, history, social science, humanities) increasingly prevalent in academic libraries, so that librarians could provide even higher levels of service.

Another interesting innovation, and one that suggested a degree of engagement seldom encountered in other settings, was the creation of positions at the Library of Congress known as "interpretive chairs." Conceived by Herbert Putnam (1861–1955) during the 1920s, "interpretive chairs" were reference librarians trained to provide "active aid and counsel" to researchers working in the library. The "extra measure of assistance" available through these individuals included advice on relevant sources and special reference materials, suggestions on procedural and stylistic matters related to the creation of the user's manuscript, and " 'constructive criticism' " (Roberts, quoted in Rothstein, 1955, p. 92) of the final product.

More often, however, reference services in public libraries came to be characterized by a model for service that centered on answering patrons' questions and finding resources (Rothstein, 1955) rather than on organizing and conducting formal programs of library instruction. During the course of the last half century, reference services in public libraries have developed to include ready-reference or fact-finding functions undertaken by a centralized reference unit, with specialized assistance programs, such as genealogy and local history, available in separate units or departments. Many contemporary libraries have also launched aggressive programs of outreach to extend services to populations previously ignored or underserved and frequently offer "orientation to the library" sessions for new users and user groups. Finally, in libraries where homework assistance has become an important aspect of youth services, a specialized form of reference assistance to youngsters has been devised that combines information services and instruction.

Conclusion

It is apparent from this brief review that the lessons learned in academic and public library settings have contributed significantly to the development of theory and practice in school librarianship. Indeed, although school libraries have made instruction a central feature of their mission in ways seldom realized at the academic level, they owe "innovations in most phases of library instruction, including those of conceptualization, design, experimentation, implementation and evaluation" (Tucker, 1994, p. 364) to efforts of visionaries in academic and public institutions. An appreciation of these contributions, and of the insightful programs and theoretical frameworks from which they arose, provides a useful point of departure for school media specialists engaging in designing their own instructional programs for elementary and high school students.

Interestingly, discrimination by rank (faculty or student), which typified many academic approaches to service provision in the past, survives in school libraries in practices and policies that support offering direct information services to administration and staff while limiting to instruction the services offered to youngsters. However, current thinking suggests that an important aspect of information literacy and a valid option and research strategy in information seeking is recognizing and making use of the expertise available in the person of the school librarian (Goodin, 1991). It seems clear that the extent to which library users will feel free to seek assistance from library professionals may well depend on the climate of accessibility and acceptance that the librarians themselves manage to create (Radford, 1996).

Notes

1. Dana was also noted for his "12 Rules of Reading": "1. Read. 2. Read. 3. Read Some More. 4. Read Anything. 5. Read About Everything. 6. Read Enjoyable Things. 7. Read Things You Yourself Enjoy. 8. Read, and Talk About It. 9. Read Very Carefully, Some Things. 10. Read on the Run, Most Things. 11. Don't Think About Reading, But 12. Read" (Wilson, 1933, p. 821).

2. Shiyali R. Ranganathan (1872–1972), library science visionary and creator of Colon Classification, described library service in terms of Five Library Laws: "Books Are For Use; Every Book Its Reader; Every Reader His Book; Save the Time of the Reader; A Library Is a Growing Organism."

3. Essentially, William Warner Bishop (1912) blamed the lack of use college students made of library resources on the lack of grounding in basic library skills: " 'I have known boys [sic] who passed an entire four years in a college with 350,000 books in its library, and who in those four years never entered its doors' " (Bishop, 1986, p. 82).

4. Lucy Maynard Salmon wrote: " 'To use a homely illustration, an article of food, like butter, that is essential for our physical diet serves its purpose much better when distributed through other articles of food than if taken independently and by itself' " (Salmon, 1986, p. 88).

2 The Development of School Libraries

From Concept to Reality

In many respects, the publication of *Information Power: Guidelines for School Library Media Programs* by the American Association of School Librarians (AASL) and the Association for Educational Communications and Technology (AECT) in 1988 was a rite of passage, signaling to educators and librarians that the specialized field of school librarianship had come of age. At last, library media specialists had at their fingertips a blueprint that framed the complexities and the "bittiness" (Butler, 1933) of library practice and expressed a vision to guide further growth and development of the profession. The roles for school library media specialists that *Information Power* unambiguously described were information specialist, teacher, and instructional con-

> **School libraries are a powerful force in the lives of America's children.**
>
> —Lance, 2002

sultant. The unique responsibility that librarians were to assume was clearly and succinctly stated as well: "to ensure that students and staff are effective users of ideas and information" (AASL & AECT, 1988, p. 1). As best practice, *Information Power* called on school librarians to replace fixed-scheduled stand-alone lessons that are delivered in a predetermined sequence with fully integrated information skills instruction, planned in cooperation with classroom teachers. Perhaps for the first time, school librarians possessed the power to define themselves and their activities and the vocabulary to express clearly the relationship of library instruction to teaching and learning in the classroom. Indeed, in describing school library media specialists as dynamic instructional leaders, *Information Power* created a new face for school librarianship, which would help teachers, administrators, and practitioners put aside old-fashioned and frequently negative stereotypes, and gain a new understanding and appreciation for the potential represented by proactive library programming.

Information Power (1988) was also a timely reminder that earlier goals to create centralized collections, to select multimedia resources, and to hire professional staff had been reached and that it was time for the field to set new ones. Inherent, too, was the realization that providing physical access to library materials (what, in 1933, Pierce Butler described as the "communal store" of our culture) was a necessary but not sufficient precondition for supporting the personal, social, and intellectual development of children (Heeks, 1997). In the years since *Information Power*'s publication, there has been a growing sense that if all students are to achieve intellectual access to resources and information, the school library program must become more fully integrated into classroom activities at all levels, and the library media specialist must act as an equal partner in the educational enterprise. This chapter traces the development of these ideas from their beginnings and charts the evolution of instructional practices in school librarianship from a skills-based model to a dynamic, process-oriented curriculum.

Opening the Door

History students may remember DeWitt Clinton (1769–1828) as an early governor of New York State and as the father of the Erie Canal, but he should be doubly honored by school librarians for his vision in recommending, in 1827, the creation of libraries in the public schools. Nearly 100 years earlier, Benjamin Franklin's "student academies" called for creating the library as a central feature (Gillespie & Spirt, 1973). However, it was not until Clinton and the 19th-century educator Horace Mann observed Johann Pestalozzi's[1] educational innovations that Franklin's earlier dream was realized in legislation that enabled school districts to purchase library books. The idea caught the imagination of many and spread quickly in the early years, so that by 1840 school libraries had been established to supplement instruction and promote reading in New York (1835), Massachusetts (1837), Michigan (1837), Connecticut (1839), and Rhode Island (1840). Unfortunately, this early enthusiasm was short-lived. In New York, the decline of school libraries was directly related to the fact that school administrators, when given the option (in 1843), used library funds to pay teachers' salaries. In the other states, the fledgling school libraries were in a sense undermined by the success of public libraries, which were enjoying a period of rapid growth at the time (Cecil & Heaps, 1940). Moreover, initial efforts to launch school libraries and sustain the momentum necessary for their continued support were seriously compromised by a lack of identifiable standards, adequate supervision, and trained personnel. Even so, by 1876, 21 states had funding legislation in place to support school libraries as part of public education (Bowie, 1986).

As the 19th century drew to a close, interest in establishing school libraries was sustained by efforts to improve the quality of public education. Among the most influential of the reformers was the German philosopher Johann F. Herbart (1776–1841), who realized, contrary to the conventional pedagogical wisdom of the day, that ideas and intellectual development were ultimately more valuable (Cecil & Heaps, 1940) than the mastery of a specific body of knowledge. According to Cecil and Heaps, "The Herbartian movement in reading which swept this country, particularly from 1889–1897, was a large factor in the awakening of educators to the potentialities of the library in the school" (p. 50). This focus on reading as an important educational strategy to engender "a permanent interest in reading and literature" was translated almost immediately into demands "for literature materials in the classroom" (p. 49).

During this same period, there was also a good deal of public support for an idea first advanced by Charles Francis Adams, Jr. (1835–1915) that public and school libraries should be combined. Proponents argued that joining the two entities made sense in terms of "economy, convenience, and efficiency" (Carpenter, 1905, quoted in Cecil & Heaps, 1940, p. 58). They maintained that all elements in the community would be better served, as education was the essential purpose of both types of libraries. Enthusiasm for this idea was shared by Melvil Dewey and others, including Samuel Swett Green. While Green stopped far short of recreating public and school libraries as a single entity, he made overtures to the schools of Worcester (Massachu-setts) by loaning materials to students and faculty and encouraging class visits to his public library. In the meantime, many other communities experimented with various forms of interlibrary cooperation or amalgamation. For example, the staffs of some public libraries joined with principals in planning school libraries that the principals then ran by themselves. In other instances, public libraries maintained branch facilities within public schools, tailoring the collections designed to the needs of adults as well as pupils. In areas without access to public libraries, it was not uncommon for state library agencies to provide "package" libraries of preselected collections to schools (Carroll, 1981). Museums also partnered with school libraries in many areas to make their "collections" available to nearby school districts (Coleman, 1989). This kind of interagency cooperation and activity continues today.

The idea of shared library collections, which seems to have taken hold first at the high school level, spread as more and more schools came to appreciate the value of easily accessible collections of books. A number of administrative models were tried in various districts around the country. A model adopted by some cities provided for central library management of selection and acquisition activities for all the schools in the district.[2] A second model, described above, called for the public library to use high school libraries as branch sites; while a third model created independent libraries in district high schools supervised and maintained by teachers or librarians. During the same period, there was little agreement as to how best to provide and maintain resources for the primary grades. In many schools, teachers favored classroom collec-tions, arguing that immediate accessibility to grade-appropriate books would encour-age reading and the development of reading tastes. Perhaps for this reason, the concept of a centralized collection within the elementary school grew very slowly.

The potential of the library in making contributions to the educational environ-ment of the school through reading promotion and direct programs of instruction was realized quite early, especially among leaders of the educational establishment. In fact, the National Education Association (NEA), the National Council of Teachers of Eng-lish (NCTE), and the American Library Association (ALA) helped institutionalize the idea of school libraries through the creation of special "school library" departments within their organizations. Indeed, it appears that "these professional bodies had a clear vision of what school library service could become long before school libraries were a widespread reality" (Dike, 1993, p. 744). For example, advocacy for school libraries was clearly stated in the NEA's conference proceedings in 1912, which as-serted that "the school library will be the proof of the educational value of the new curriculum . . . [and] the open door to the opportunity of the present" (p. 744). The rationale for such a move was that the curriculum of contemporary high schools was now so broad that textbooks could not provide what could be offered in the "labora-tory" of the library (Hall, 1912, p. 1274, quoted in Cecil & Heaps, 1940, p. 62). The NEA also supported the creation of classroom collections of age-appropriate books as "the most satisfactory means of forming a taste for good literature" (Coleman, 1989, p. 46) among elementary school students. Although this attitude sounds rather self-evident to contemporary ears, this recommendation must have seemed almost revo-lutionary in schools where teachers relied exclusively on textbooks and grade-level readers as the primary media of instruction.

The first four decades of the 20th century saw a definite educational turn away from more repressive programs anchored in an education-as-discipline and training theory toward a child-centered theory of education based on the principles of active learning. Some educational initiatives based on these principles included the Gary Plan (derived from the experiential learning ideas of William Wirt and John Dewey), the Winetka Plan (which featured individualized curriculum), and the Dalton Laboratory Plan (created by Helen Parkhurst, which emphasized the value of individual study). In one way or another, each of these innovative programs placed the library at the center of the curriculum (Cecil & Heaps, 1940).

Still, the growth of the movement and improvements in existing facilities during the period before World War I were modest. Indeed, a survey conducted by the NCTE in 1915 indicated that most school libraries lacked adequate materials and services. The Certain Report (*Standard Library Organization and Equipment for Secondary Schools of Different Sizes*) published by the ALA five years later enumerated problems, such as lack of resources, lack of sufficient space to provide support for school populations and staff, and proliferation of clerical tasks, which kept librarians from providing instructional assistance to students and teachers. The report suggested that state committees survey school libraries and recommended the establishment of centralized facilities managed by "professionally trained librarians." In addition, the report suggested that school librarians assume responsibility for organizing and managing the schools' burgeoning collections of audio/visual equipment and resources. Somewhat prophetically, as it turned out, the report stated in no uncertain terms that to require librarians to assume clerical tasks was "wasteful of educational resources and money" (Davies, 1974, p. 364). Clearly, the school library's door to opportunity was now open even if its future was not yet assured.

While interest in public education and public libraries in the early years of the 19th century held out the promise of improving the quality of life for many Americans, a significant proportion of the population was being systematically denied access to these kinds of public services. Although education for African Americans was never supported in the South to any great degree, the institutionalization of segregation in *Plessy v. Ferguson* in 1896 ushered in an era of inequality not seen since before the Civil War. The doctrine of "separate but equal" guaranteed for black children a substandard education in the same way that literacy and Jim Crow laws had ensured the disenfranchisement of their parents. Thus, while it is safe to say that many children in the public schools of the North lacked easy access to books and resources promised by a centralized school library collection during this period, the obstacles to such access for children in segregated schools of the South and West were infinitely greater. Where any existed, library collections most often consisted of donated books and materials, usually castoffs from white schools.

The effort to create elementary school libraries was advanced with the publication of the *Elementary School Library Standards*, distributed by the ALA in 1925. However, the primary focus was not on instruction but on creating "a new department" that could " 'assemble and distribute the materials of instruction' " (NEA and ALA, quoted in Gillespie & Spirt, 1973, p. 9). These standards also "required the school librarian to be freed from clerical tasks, to work with children and teachers, and to provide guidance in the use of both informational and recreational materials" (Davies, 1974, p. 356). In light of these early reports, a number of regional organizations around the nation made school libraries the focus of their research. For example, school libraries were the subject of an entire yearbook by the NEA's Department of Elementary School Principals in 1933.

The commitment to creating school libraries expressed in published library standards received a momentary setback during the Depression years; but as the country got back on its economic feet, concern for this important aspect of public education resurfaced. Private foundations provided some support for school libraries during this period. Notable among these was the Julius Rosenwald Fund, which provided a measure of library support for black schools in the South through grants to county libraries that could demonstrate equal service for library users of both races (Cecil & Heaps, 1940).[3] According to Hanchett (1987), the Fund also provided money directly to black schools to build library collections. Even so, these gifts did little to close the enormous disparity in funding between white and black schools in the South.[4]

Progress toward Centralization of School Collections

The 1940s and 1950s saw continuous movement in many school districts toward the development of school libraries as separate, centralized facilities, sometimes to augment and sometimes to replace classroom book collections. For example, *School Libraries for Today and Tomorrow*, published by the ALA in 1945, acknowledged the library as "an essential element of the school program." In particular, it called on school librarians to provide instruction in the use of the library and library materials in addition to reading guidance. Through these activities, students would "become skillful and discriminating users of libraries and of printed and audio-visual materials" (Davies, 1974, p. 366). However, studies continued to show that one half of the nation's children did not have access to a library in their schools. An even smaller percentage had access to the services of a trained librarian. Not surprisingly, much of the research in school media undertaken during this period considered collections, facilities, and professional staffing. The launching of *Sputnik* by the Russians in 1957 changed everything. The thought of having lost the educational edge to a totalitarian regime considered by many as evil was especially galling to a nation proud of its educated workforce and an informed citizenry. For a change, national attention was trained on public education in unprecedented ways. The initial congressional response was the National Defense Education Act (NDEA) in 1958, which offered matching funds to school districts for professional development of staff and the purchase of instructional resources to support curriculum in math, science, languages, and counseling.

A policy statement created jointly by the American Association of School Librarians, the Association of College and Research Libraries (ACRL), and the Department of Audio-Visual Instruction of the NEA in response to the legislation spelled out definitively the prerequisites for librarians in creating effective library programs: an experienced teacher; a multidimensional knowledge base related to learning, curriculum, guidance, "educational administration and supervision," and "mass communications"; and specialized knowledge related to the evaluation and use of media resources. As Davies (1974) asserts, "[T]his policy statement serve[d] as the 'declaration of independence' for school librarians" in its unequivocal acknowledgment that school media specialists must be directly "involved in the teaching and learning process" (p. 368).

In 1960, AASL's *Standards for School Library Media Programs* was issued, constituting what Davies (1979) described as the "single most important document in the history of school library development." If the policy statement in 1958 amounted to a "declaration of independence" for school librarians, then the *Standards* constituted an educational "bill of rights" for students. In fact, the *Standards* explicitly recognized the importance of library resources as "the basic tools needed for the purpose of effective teaching and learning" (p. 368) and fundamental to the educational experience of all schoolchildren. The Elementary and Secondary Education Act (ESEA; Title II) followed in 1965, providing additional funding for materials and facilities. Ironically, the act lacked a provision for the hiring of qualified librarians to superintend the selection, acquisition, and organization of library purchases. Nevertheless, government funding for books and equipment throughout the 1960s, together with powerful statements of policy and direction provided by professional organizations, ultimately made it possible for school libraries to reinvent themselves as media centers.

Another major event in the 1960s, and one that contributed to the proliferation of centralized school libraries, was the Knapp School Libraries Project (1963–1968), which created demonstration libraries at 10 selected elementary and high schools. While Knapp's work was primarily aimed at the improvement of bibliographic instruction in academic settings, her ideas contributed to the development of instructional theories related to library skills instruction for school-aged children. Her insights with regard to integrating library instruction into ongoing coursework, planning experiences for learning, and providing practice and problem-solving activities directly related to classroom requirements eventually found their way into elementary and secondary library media programs (see Chapter 1). To support the rejuvenation of school libraries and to aid in the national dissemination of the contemporary thinking on the value of their instructional programs, the Knapp initiative provided funding to reimburse the traveling expenses of school teams so that they could attend demonstration sessions. Eventually this project spawned hundreds of imitators and with it the demand for certified librarians to recreate the project's programs around the country (Gillespie & Spirt, 1973).

The move to institutionalize a centralized library facility within the school received another boost in 1969 with the publication of the *Standards for School Media Programs*, which called for the unification of all library and audiovisual services under one administrative unit (Gillespie & Spirt, 1973). In fact, by 1974, studies reported that 84 percent of the public schools in the country had centralized library facilities (Carroll, 1981). Unfortunately for school libraries, economic conditions during the 1970s created an increasing concern for bottom-line issues and focused the public's attention on all types of public expenditures. Turner (1991) maintains that budgetary downsizing during this period not only put pressure on librarians to justify the value of their programs but also persuaded school districts to promote the librarian as a regular member of the teaching staff. In many cases this change in the librarians' status from support staff to teaching staff was instituted as a way to allow librarians to cover for teachers in the classroom during teacher planning periods. Ironically, however, it also paved the way for the introduction of formal programs of library instruction and the creation of library skills curricula.

Development of Library Skills Instruction

That efforts on the part of the first school librarians reflected a concern for teaching students about library use was evidenced by the volume of journal articles and library guides published between 1876 (the date of the founding of the ALA and *Library Journal*) and 1920 (Farber, 1995). These documents urged the introduction of library skills instruction in elementary and secondary school libraries. However, the first paper that dealt specifically with the instruction of schoolchildren in the use of library resources actually came from outside the field, in a speech delivered by T.J. Morgan, the principal of a State Normal School at a meeting of the NEA in Chicago in 1887 (Cecil & Heaps, 1940).

Since the major preoccupation of the early years of the 20th century was the establishment of centralized library collections, it is probably not surprising that acceptance of a teaching role for the library media specialist emerged slowly. In fact, during the 1950s and 1960s, the delivery of library skills instruction at the high school level was most frequently managed through English classes. Indeed, English textbooks usually devoted a separate chapter to study skills and the use of library resources. In cases where the English teachers felt that their lack of expertise in this area made them unequal to the task, school librarians were often recruited for the purpose of explaining the vagaries of library organization and demonstrating the use of available reference books (Carroll, 1981). For the most part, these early library lessons tended to make little, if any, use of learning theory, and they relied almost exclusively on lectures that "all too often" seemed aimed at making "miniature librarians of the students" (p. 114).

In the aftermath of the civil rights movement and the Vietnam War, the 1960s ushered in a new perspective on the role of the school and its place in the social order. An institution that had for generations been viewed as "a transmitter of the culture" came increasingly to be considered an "agent of change" (Organization for Economic Cooperation and Development, [OECD], quoted in Carroll, 1981, p. 23). As reported by the OECD, an educational shift was occurring, centered on learning how to learn, learning for a lifetime, and making the school "an extension of the community" (p. 23). In fact, educators began thinking about learning itself in new ways. The acquisition of discrete facts was thought to be a less important learning task than understanding the principles of knowledge or the developing attitudes and skills to support independent inquiry. At the same time, schools came under increasing pressure to make educational practices more equitable and "culturally relevant" (Dike, 1993). Within this context, the school library media center "was seen as offering the variety of materials required to meet individual needs" (p. 744).

During this same period, a number of educational innovations were being introduced that would have a profound influence on the development of library skills instruction during the next four decades. These included small and large group instruction, the introduction of ungraded schools and open classrooms, the concept of team teaching, the idea of continuous progress evaluation, and an expanded use of media in the delivery of instruction (Carroll, 1981). Moves to replace the single-teacher, lecture-textbook format with instructional designs that required students to use a variety of resources, and pressures to create instructional units that offered an interdisciplinary approach to curricular topics, created both opportunities and challenges for library media specialists. Collection development, which had been predicated on the public library model of creating a well-rounded collection, became increasingly a matter of acquiring resources that directly supported school curricula.

At the same time, renewed emphasis on the instructional role of the teacher was advanced in AASL's *Media Programs: District and School* (AASL & AECT 1975), which described the "media program and personnel [as including] active, direct involvement in the school's instructional program" (Coleman, 1989, p. 48). It was also during this period that administrators began to "demand more objective data to demonstrate the worth of the school library program" (Aaron, 1982, p. 231), and the concern for educational outcomes of instruction began to surface (Gillespie & Spirt, 1973). These changes also put pressure on school libraries to systematize instructional approaches by articulating goals and objectives for their programs.

In general, the overall goal of library skills instruction in the 1970s and early 1980s reflected reform initiatives related to making students self-sufficient users of information (Liesener, 1985). The format for the delivery of "learning skills instruction" in the library context took the form, in the elementary grades, of prearranged library sessions. On junior high and high school levels, the "subject" of library skills was still most frequently taught as a part of English and language arts courses. Of course, informal instruction was also provided as needed to those individual students who came to the library by themselves.

Typically, bibliographic or library skills instruction involved a series of sequentially conducted lessons, which were repeated at each level from kindergarten through twelfth grade, with increasing degrees of complexity. Students introduced to skills and resources in the elementary grades were expected to achieve mastery or competence as they progressed through their school years. The content of these library lessons generally involved the care of books and other library materials, the parts of a book, authors and illustrators, the use of specific resources and reference tools, library organization, location of items on library shelves, alphabetical order, the card catalog, and the Dewey classification system. Results of a survey by Hyland in 1978 indicated that the skills most often included in library instructional lessons involved knowledge of the physical facilities, selection of appropriate materials, use of particular types of materials, reading comprehension, and report preparation. Baumbach's (1986) study revealed that, by 1985, 64 percent—or 29—of state and territorial respondents reported that some sort of "organized curriculum in information skills" (p. 280) was in place. Of these, the overwhelming majority included research skills, resource tool skills, location skills, and literature appreciation.

But important changes in the school libraries' instructional landscape were on the horizon. Thanks in large part to fallout from the "knowledge explosion" (Dike, 1993, p. 744), a number of practitioners and scholars developed an interest in the concept of information handling and began to explore the relationship between information and learning. For example, teachers in a study by Irving (1978, cited in Carroll, 1981) identified learning from library materials or "information use" as an essential educational outcome for their students. In addition, Irving's research drew attention to task definition as one of the most important information skills that youngsters needed to learn. This emphasis on the student's ability to recognize the need for particular information and its use in the context of specific tasks seemed to echo Willson's (1965) assertion that using information for decision making was a more educationally appropriate goal for instructional intervention than simply teaching the skills necessary to locate and access that information. Indeed, Willson had also noted the fact that decision-making skills were not ordinarily a part of library skills instruction.

A number of articles published in the late 1970s and early 1980s also indicated a need to reform the library curriculum. New approaches in education and library instruction called attention to the importance of considering both the information "user" and the "cognitive environment" of his or her information tasks (Irving, 1983, p. 4). Irving (1980, cited in Carroll, 1981) recognized before many in the field that "the development of abilities and skills in thinking" (p. 121) was the ultimate and most valuable outcome of information skills instruction. Indeed, Irving suggested placing these information and study skills within a larger framework of information seeking to make them both relevant and applicable to life, as well as to school tasks. Too often, Irving argued, the student's role in learning and information seeking had been overlooked. Noting that "the depth and meaning of their learning may be rather more influenced by the way they tackle their work than by any actions of their teachers," Irving (1983) suggested that "the relationship between teaching and learning appears more complex than was previously assumed" (p. 12). This approach represented a shift in paradigmatic focus that also had been realized in other areas of library and information science, where scholars were struggling to make theoretical sense of information behavior in general and information seeking in new media (e.g., electronic resources, databases, and networks) in particular. The idea that librarians needed to help students learn rather than help them find resources to learn—and to focus on the use of library resources to meet educational goals rather than to achieve library goals—represented a significant shift in direction for many school media specialists (Carroll, 1981). This shift also made inevitable the preeminence of the librarian's role as teacher and the information skills curriculum as the centerpiece of school librarianship (Turner, 1991).

Although Irving's was one of the earliest voices proclaiming the need for a fresh approach to library skills instruction, hers was not the only one. During the same period, Mancall, Aaron, and Walker (1986) urged that thinking skills replace resource-based curriculum as a focus for library skills instruction. In addition, Kulleseid (1986) argued for the inclusion of both affective/emotional and cognitive/rational domains in aspects of the library media program, on the basis of her study of cognitive science and developmental psychology. Inherent in these initiatives was the realization that learning was not a task confined to years of formal schooling and that teaching required a commitment to students' intellectual growth as well as to skill acquisition. These were new goals, and they called for the development of new strategies and new outcomes (Turner, 1991).

The 1980s also saw a move to end or modify fixed or rigid scheduling of classes into the library media center, in favor of flexible access, which provided opportunities for students to come into the library, connect with the librarian, and receive instruction individually or in small groups as needed. Under this scheme, teachers also had access to the library and could bring their classes to the media center to work on research tasks either in partnership with the librarian or with the librarian "on call." Flexible access thus allowed teachers to capitalize on student interests and "teachable moments" and librarians to deliver "just in time" instruction—when it was most likely to extend student learning or support students' research activities.

Where it has been successfully implemented, flexible access scheduling has prompted both the integration of information skills instruction within classroom activity and the process of joint planning by teachers and librarians. Indeed, it has become increasingly apparent that the potential benefits inherent in team teaching and collaborative planning cannot be fully realized without some sort of flexible access policy in place to structure library use (Ray, 1994). Moreover, the persistence of rigid scheduling in the library is now considered a barrier to student access to information and to "point of need" instruction (Kuhlthau, 2001).

The End of an Era

Many in the profession entertained high hopes that the use of *Information Power* (ALA & AECT, 1988) as the manual, primer, and guide for school librarianship, and the new roles it identified for school librarians, would result in instructional benefits for student learning. Unfortunately, research studies conducted during the 1980s failed to prove definitively that library skills instruction contributes to student academic achievement. Professional disappointment at this turn of events and anxiety created by shrinking budgets and increasing demands for educational accountability created a sort of crisis mentality, which has, in some ways, characterized the school library profession ever since.

Librarians' consternation over the lack of studies that might justify continuing support for their programs has been exacerbated by research that seriously challenged the educational efficacy of library and information skills instruction (Kuhlthau, 1987). Anecdotal evidence from the field, which indicated that skills initially taught in elementary school had been insufficiently learned to allow their application to reference tasks in junior and senior high school levels (Shapiro, 1976, cited in Carroll, 1981), was substantiated in the LIS research in a variety of contexts. For example, Biggs reported that college freshmen "lack[ed] all but the most rudimentary library skills" (quoted in Kuhlthau, 1985, p. 35); while Dickinson (1981) found that college students lacked sophistication in their understanding of what doing research entailed and "failed to use logical progression and systematic approaches to checking sources of information" (p. 853). In her study, Goodin (1987, 1991) reported that student learning of library skills neither transferred into new settings nor was being applied to research tasks that these youngsters encountered as college students. These same conclusions were advanced by Kester (1994), whose study of 300 college freshmen revealed that although 85 percent of them "had received library instruction in high school" (p. 15), the "instruction appear[ed] to have little carry over or effect on students going on to college" (p. 17). Among skills lacking in the students in Kester's study were technical skills related to Online Public Access Catalog (OPAC) use and online searching. Perhaps even more compelling were the results of Kuhlthau's (1991) initial study, which indicated that in spite of the sincerest efforts of librarians to teach the skills necessary for students to conduct their own research projects the students themselves approached their research tasks with feelings of dread and frequently did not know what to do first.

Although exceedingly disappointing, this research provided evidence for what many librarians had suspected all along: that the scope and sequence approach to instruction and the creation of stand-alone lessons that lack follow-up activities in the library or classroom do not translate into usable information skills. Instead, they merely ensure that the same "library skills" have to be retaught year after year. But if, as seems evident, the scope and sequence approach is ineffective, what should be introduced in its place? This question has led many researchers and practitioners to consider alternatives in both content and instructional approaches. Wall (1974, quoted in Carroll, 1981), for example, suggested that students be taught the use of "elaborate resource system[s]," not just reference books. Arguing for an improvement in instructional approaches, Wall noted that " 'simply turning [students] loose with a bag of questions and a lot of resources will not do this. The teacher, the librarian, or the adult has to be actively and sensitively intervening most of the time in some way or another' " (p. 119).

Others in the field provided a veritable laundry list of weaknesses in the traditional instruction approaches. Young and Brennan (1978, cited in Carroll, 1981), for example, identified the following as problems that should be addressed: the lack of cooperation between teachers and librarians, poor teaching materials, stand-alone lessons and artificial assignments, failure to provide instruction to meet student needs, and lack of research as to how to improve practice. Davies (1974) also identified significant barriers to effective student outcomes in information skills programs. These include lack of library skills integration, limited time for planning, failure to contribute to curriculum planning or curriculum guides, and teachers' reliance on textbooks.

Not everyone in the school media field, of course, embraced the new focus on instruction or the responsibility for student learning. Liesener (1985), quoting Freiser (1963), urged librarians to "quit this [instructional] nonsense."

> [I]nstead of forcing kids to spend the majority of their time searching for information with usually poor results, we should give them the information under certain circumstances so that they do have a foundation of good information to

work with and, as a result, develop the skills and knowledge necessary to understand, use and appreciate ideas and information sources. The belief is that these skills and knowledge are not only more important but must precede the attempt to develop information seeking skills if such efforts are to be effective. (p. 16)

Although not in favor of abandoning the instructional enterprise altogether, Liesener suggested that the best solution might be to turn the entire enterprise on its head: Provide information directly to elementary students and save library skills instruction for upper-level students.

Demonstrating Value: An Enduring Dilemma

The past 25 years have witnessed an increased emphasis on substantiating both the operational efficiency and the overall effectiveness of school library media programs. The challenge to demonstrate value that L.A. Martin noted in 1984 (p. 40) has become a professional imperative: we must provide empirical substantiation for what every librarian knows intuitively: library programming makes a difference in student achievement. Liesener (1985) summed up the situation well when he wrote:

The older concepts of passive culture repositories or centers for the development of an enjoyment and appreciation for reading good books while identifying very important functions do not appear to be actively responsive to the entire range of needs identified as crucial for survival and achievement in an extremely complex, information abundant and rapidly changing world. The level of expectation that is satisfied with a nice genteel but fairly superfluous resource is no longer relevant or appropriate. (p. 13)

It has always been problematic to estimate the contribution that library skills instruction makes to student learning. A great many variables contribute to student achievement; for this reason, crediting library skills instruction for variance accounted for as measured on standardized achievement tests has proven to be a formidable task. Recent years have seen a number of estimable attempts to provide the sort of statistical evidence that administrators appreciate. Most influential to date among American studies has been the research initiated by Keith Lance and his colleagues, and a recent study by Todd and Kuhlthau (2003). Lance's (2002) findings have led him to conclude that

there is a clear consensus in the results now available for eight states: School libraries are a powerful force in the lives of America's children. The school library is one of the few factors whose contribution to academic achievement has been documented empirically, and it is a contribution that cannot be explained away by other powerful influences on student performance.

More studies will, of course, be needed to establish and understand links between instructional models and academic achievement and lifelong learning.

Interestingly, the instructional project of the school library profession has been made more complex and more exciting in recent years by increased attention to reading and libraries in the national media. The White House Conference held in 2002 cast a spotlight on school libraries and in some respects raised expectations for their programs not witnessed in many years. However, the conference's apparent failure to focus on information skills instruction as a key part of the library program seems to reinforce an outdated conceptualization of school librarianship. While books and reading indeed remain central foci of the school library media program, school librarianship offers a great deal more. Additionally, there appears to be a perception that providing electronic access to information translates to equity and parity of educational opportunity in a straightforward way. Until and unless there is an appreciation for the cognitive challenges that exist for students operating in online environments and for the complexities involved in information seeking and learning from information now available in bewildering profusion, it seems quite likely that equating information access with educational opportunity will continue.

Notes

1. Johann Pestalozzi (1746–1827) was a Swiss-born educator and pedagogical visionary who influenced educational practice in the United States and abroad in the 19th century. Believing that access to publicly supported education was the birthright of every child and fundamental to the development of democratic values in a society, Pestalozzi also recognized the importance of parental involvement and encouragement to the education of their own children. In addition, Pestalozzi pioneered the replacement of rote memorization by experiential learning and advocated the ordering of curricular content so that mastery of simple concepts preceded the presentation of abstractions. A precursor of such educational giants as Herbart and Froebel, Pestalozzi adopted a holistic approach to education that fostered the development of physical health and a sense of morality as well as intellectual achievement.

2. In some cities, public libraries also managed classroom libraries in the public schools.

3. The Julius Rosenwald Fund was founded by an Illinois philanthropist in 1917. Rosenwald, who had amassed a fortune as president and chairman of the board of Sears, Roebuck and Co., was one of a number of public-spirited citizens of the period who hoped to bring an end to racial inequity through investment in public education. In addition to the Rosenwald Fund, other major contributors to the effort were the Rockefeller General Education Board, The Anna T. Jeanes Fund, and the John F. Slater Fund, to name only a few. The general approach of these funds was to use their money to leverage local funds from white and black communities in support of black schools. Choosing to work within the social system of the segregated South rather than confronting racism directly, these groups seemed to believe that as blacks achieved parity in education, racism would fade and the white community would accept blacks as equals. Rosenwald, in collaboration with Booker T. Washington, designed and built dozens of rural schools in the South between 1917 and 1928. After that time, he turned his attention to preparing black educators and, among other projects, established scholarships for black students.

4. Hanchett (1987) writes:

> Rosenwald and his fellow philanthropists succeeded magnificently in raising the level of black education in the South. But they failed in their larger goal of promoting equality. Despite the marked improvements in conditions, in 1930 black students were even further behind whites by almost every important measure than they had been in 1915. Though black schools had improved, white boards were improving white facilities much faster.

The same was true for school library collections. Hanchett reports that the total expenditure for library books to white schools in South Carolina during the 1925–1926 school year was $26,982.89. Library budgets for black schools during this same year totaled $205.32. Of the 2,330 black elementary schools operating in South Carolina in 1933, fewer than 10 percent had any library books at all; during the same year, over 60 percent of white elementary schools had a school library.

3 From Library Skills to Information Skills Instruction

Kuhlthau's Information Search Process (ISP)

In reviewing the specific approaches to the teaching of library and information skills, Kuhlthau (1987) identified three major models being used for instruction in school library settings: the source or library tool approach; the pathfinder or search strategy approach; and the process approach. Whereas the source and pathfinder models involve teaching techniques and tools necessary for the completion of research tasks, process models seek to address the teaching of library skills in terms of strategies for thinking and problem solving.

The Source Approach

The source approach to library and information skills features lessons related to the organization of library materials in a particular setting and the location and use of specific reference books, indexes, and other resources that are available there. This "how to" approach dates from the earliest days of school libraries and is emphasized in "scope and sequence" types of library skills lessons. Because skills lessons built on this model are generally site-specific and carefully tailored to local sources and local situations, library sessions are relatively easy to plan and conduct. However, this approach has some very serious limitations. For one thing, it is often difficult to tailor lessons delivered in a preplanned sequence to the instructional needs of specific individuals or the exigencies of a specific situation. For another, such lessons are conducted in the library outside the flow of ongoing classroom activities in which students are otherwise involved; students often fail to see the relevance of what the librarian is trying to teach them. In addition, the practice sessions that ordinarily follow the demonstration of the particular reference resource and its use are basically artificial or inauthentic in that they are made up expressly for the purposes of the lesson. Finally, the source model assumes access to a static library collection of preselected print resources; the introduction of research tools in this way does little to prepare students for information seeking outside the context of the specific library or, indeed, in the absence of the specific resources upon which the lessons are based.

The Pathfinder Approach

The pathfinder model is a search strategy that requires students to move from an overview or background source, such as an encyclopedia, through a sequence of progressively more specific sources leading finally to an examination of the most and, presumably, the most pertinent resources. This approach is particularly useful for students who lack content knowledge of a topic because it forces them to investigate the topic holistically before moving on to create a specific focus or thesis statement. It is also useful conceptually, as it serves to introduce students to different kinds and levels of resources that may be directly applied to a student's project. However, as Kuhlthau (1987) notes, it is a rather rigid approach and may have limited utility outside academic tasks and school assignments. Nor does the pathfinder approach allow teachers to take account of the cognitive abilities, information needs, learning styles, and information-seeking preferences of individual students.

Process Models Approach

Both the source and pathfinder approaches represent examples of a resource-centered view of library service in that their primary focus is on texts and documents in the library. Process models, on the other hand, are specifically user-centered in that they begin with a statement of the information need as articulated by the student. A number of process models for library skills instruction were developed during the 1980s; the best-known models were created by Sheingold (1986), Callison (1986), and Kuhlthau (1987, 1988a, 1988b).

Sheingold's Inquiry Model

Sheingold's (1986) approach is an inquiry model based on educational principles derived from cognitive psychology. As such, it places the learner at the center of instructional interest and makes thinking the central outcome. More specifically, Sheingold asserts that a "child's mind is [not] an empty vase into which information is 'poured,'" nor is the library a place where children go to "get" information. Rather, the library is viewed as an "apprentice's workshop for thinking—a place where" children actively construct their own understandings through interactions with "human, physical," and "symbolic worlds" (p. 80). Within the inquiry process, students come to create meaning by relating what they read to what they already know. Sheingold also suggests that, to be meaningful, the questions that drive the inquiry process should address real-world problems.

According to Sheingold (1986), inquiry is itself a complex, nonlinear investigative, problem-solving "process that includes formulating a problem or question, searching through and/or collecting information to address the problem or question, making sense of that information, and developing an understanding of, point of view about, or 'answer' to the question" (p. 81). Within this framework, student research is a goal-oriented activity in which the learners seek solutions, solve problems, fill needs, or answer questions. The questions children create at each stage in the process serve as frames of reference for information seeking and information collection that drive inquiry forward. These questions, which are "formulated and reformulated as new information is gathered and thought about" (p. 81), later become the basis for evaluating the relevance and utility of information found and resources used.

Sheingold's (1986) inquiry model requires learners to do something with what has been learned in order to keep the knowledge "alive." Learning is thus seen as "self-motivated," "intentional," and "purposive" (p. 82). "Knowing about oneself and other people as knowers," about "the task to be undertaken," and about the "strategies to apply" as well as the monitoring of "one's own performance with respect to the task"(p. 84) are important elements as well. Citing Vygotsky's notion that a zone of proximal development creates the frame for effective instructional intervention and optimal learning, Sheingold recommends the use of social interaction to facilitate "children's cognitive development" and instructional techniques that enable the child to assume the responsibility for learning "as the child becomes able to do it" (p. 84).

Callison's Free-Inquiry Model

The "free-inquiry" model advanced by Callison (1986) features a library skills instruction plan that is fully integrated into the curriculum with the teacher and librarian acting as an instructional team. For this reason, the lessons based on this model require advanced planning and coordination. However, lesson objectives are not prepared in advance; rather, they are created on an individual basis by students and instructors acting together. Evaluation of student performance is also a responsibility shared by instructors and pupils. Based on the work of Victor (1974, cited in Callison), the elements of the "inquiry approach to teaching and learning" (p. 21) are summarized in Table 3.1.

Essentially, Callison's (1986) inquiry model attempts to move beyond instructional tasks that require the use of library resources to engage students scientifically, through activities that afford students experience in posing their own questions, finding their

Table 3.1
Elements in Callison's (1986) Free-Inquiry Model for Teaching and Learning

- Lessons are planned and taught by librarians and teachers acting together

- Objectives of the lesson are evolutionary and negotiated between student and teacher

- Students document the processes of learning and share them with others

- Content is driven by questions that students raise and answer by exploring resources in the library and beyond

- The teacher provides direction for learning, but students are encouraged to take initiatives and work independently

- Time for the learning activities is flexible

- Peer tutoring is encouraged

- Peer interaction and teaming are supported

- Projects are shared with peers and parents

- Students may choose to extend their learning

own answers, and sharing the results with peers, parents, and community members. Within this framework, information seeking itself is based on questions that students devise, and answers are sought in terms of human resources as well as informational documents and texts. Evaluation of sources, whether located inside or outside the immediate library environment, is stressed. The model emphasizes the interaction between students and librarians, students and teachers, and students and their peers. In addition, students create logs to document and record their activities and their reflections on the processes as they unfold. Finally, the model specifically encourages students to develop the skills to act independently in finding solutions to the problems posed.

Kuhlthau's Studies of the Information Search Process

The most significant contribution to the development of the process approach to teaching and learning in the library media center has been Carol C. Kuhlthau's (1988a, 1988b, 1993b) research. As it is the only theoretical model that has been empirically tested, Kuhlthau's information search process (ISP) represents a watershed in the development of new strategies for the delivery of library skills instruction. Indeed, it has served as the basis for much of the research on children's information-seeking behavior and library skills instruction undertaken since the 1990s. For this reason, it has been highlighted here and deserves special attention.

In brief, Kuhlthau's (1991, 1993a, 1993b, 1997) studies track the creation and testing of a model for inquiry-based information seeking that librarians around the world have found useful in understanding the processes involved in research tasks and information seeking. Particularly noteworthy is Kuhlthau's concern for understanding the experience of information seeking from the point of view of student learners and for sharing her findings with professional as well as academic audiences. Her purpose throughout has been to find effective ways to assist students in the information search process—the process of learning from information. Although initially Kuhlthau (1993a) did not consider the model "a formula for teaching" or a "packaged program" (p. 12) of instruction, librarians were quick to find value in the straightforward description of the ISP it provides. Students, librarians, and teachers have also found in Kuhlthau's work a vocabulary for discussing ways in which assistance and instruction can best be delivered.[1] While Kuhlthau's model of the ISP can be understood as "representational" (Bates, 1979a) of a student's thoughts, feelings, and activities related to the conduct of research assignments, the cognitive processes involved (e.g., critical thinking, decision making, problem solving) are essentially the same as those identified by scholars as necessary for the development of information literacy. For this reason, Kuhlthau's ISP model has recently found applications in a variety of informational contexts within and beyond the school library.

Kuhlthau's (1991, 1993b) ISP model was created on the basis of a series of studies conducted over a 10-year period, designed to consider the experience of information seeking from the point of view of the library user. The initial study involved observation of high school students researching topics assigned for a term paper; in subsequent studies, Kuhlthau broadened her approach to include information seeking of informants engaged in a variety of information tasks in school, academic, public, and corporate libraries. In collecting data, Kuhlthau relied on a variety of methods: observation, case studies, individual and focus group interviews, surveys, journals, and student-produced research papers.

In creating a model to fit her observations, Kuhlthau (1993b) drew from theoretical frameworks in psychology, education, information science, and communication. In particular, her research builds on the personal construct theory of George Kelly (1963), the learning theory of John Dewey (1916, 1933), the cognitive theory of Jerome Bruner (1980), information needs theories in the work of Robert Taylor (1968) and Nick Belkin (1980), and the sense-making model created by Brenda Dervin (1983). Kuhlthau (1991) originally identified six cognitive stages that information seekers pass through in their search for relevant information. Kuhlthau labeled these: Initiation, Selection, Exploration, Formulation, Collection, and Presentation. (A summary of Kuhlthau's model is provided in Figure 3.1.) In creating an instructional model, Kuhlthau (1994, 2001) added a seventh stage, assessment; at this step students are asked to reflect on what they have learned about the subject under investigation as well as about the ISP as a whole.

Although the model appears linear as drawn, Kuhlthau argues that, in practice, students engage the stages recursively, moving back and forth between them, depending on the situation. Thus, students may have to go back and undertake activities typical of the earlier steps if, for example, they find that they have insufficiently narrowed the topic or fail to find information sufficient to solve the research problem, and so on. Following Kelly, Kuhlthau was also interested in tracking students' affective or "feelings" processes as well as their cognitive or "thinking" processes. In so doing, she observed that the feelings of information seekers varied across the course of the process, from anxiety to optimism, from confusion to clarity, from uncertainty to confidence, from apprehension to satisfaction or disappointment. In her view, her research confirms the need for instructional intervention and "guidance in learning from the information they have located" (2001) and support for students far "beyond merely leading students to sources."

Figure 3.1
Kuhlthau's (1993b, 2003) Model of the ISP

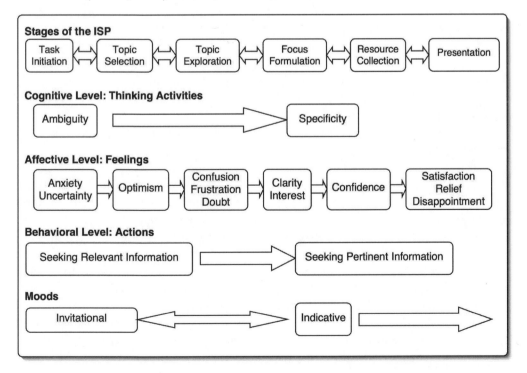

A Closer Look at Kuhlthau's ISP

Kuhlthau (1993b, 1999, 2001, 2003) characterized the first step or stage in the ISP process as *Task Initiation*. For students, this stage begins with the assignment of a research question or research project. Kuhlthau's informants indicated that many students experience this particular phase as a time of uncertainty and/or anxiety, particularly when they lack knowledge of the subject and an understanding of how to proceed. The *Selection stage* of the model is that point in the process when the students choose a question to explore or a topic in which they have an interest. Students generally experience feelings of optimism during this stage. However, Kuhlthau also found these feelings to be short-lived, fading at the *Exploration stage*, when students begin information seeking on a topic about which they know little. Feelings of confusion are typical, especially when students encounter inconsistencies and information incompatible with ideas and commonsense understandings about the topic they already possess. Part of the challenge at this stage is to make sense of new information, some of which may conflict with student's prior understandings or preconceived ideas. "As students encounter inconsistent incompatible information that does not match their expectations," Kuhlthau (1997) writes, "they commonly begin to doubt the appropriateness of the topic, the adequacy of the information sources, and their own ability to accomplish the assignment" (p. 713). Kuhlthau has characterized this drop in confidence as "the dip."

The ability to use information obtained in the exploration stage to draw some preliminary conclusions and create personal understandings enables students to create thesis statements and to formulate a personal point of view about the topic at *Focus Formulation*. It is important to note that in Kuhlthau's studies only the more successful students were observed to narrow or refine their topics in ways that provided the clarity needed to pinpoint information needs in preparation for the collection activities that followed. This focus allowed students to create thesis statements as well as to formulate a personal point of view about the topic. Kuhlthau noted that students with a clear idea of where they were headed at this stage in the search process showed an increase in interest regarding the topic and the project. During the *Collection stage* of the process, the students Kuhlthau studied went confidently about the task of gathering pertinent information; at the final or *Presentation stage*, as students prepared to organize their information, to make connections among ideas, and to present their work in the chosen format, they felt relieved that the search was over and either satisfied or dis appointed with the search results. In Kuhlthau's view, students' feelings at the end of the process were often directly related to their ability to formulate a personal focus for their projects.

Perhaps surprisingly, Kuhlthau (1993b, 1997) found that the Exploration stage was difficult for many students. Indeed, impatience with having to do the reading necessary to obtain an overall understanding of the topic sometimes caused students to jump over Exploration and Formulation stages entirely and begin collecting information. In Kuhlthau's view, taking time to relax and reflect on the information obtained through exploring the topic prepares students to create a focus at the next stage. Unfortunately, as Kuhlthau notes, most information-seeking sessions are not structured to include time for processing information in this way. In addition, many students confuse Exploration (when any topic-related information may seem relevant) with Collection (where students should concentrate on making use of information pertinent to their foci). When this happens, students can end up with too much information of a general nature, and so many notes that they have an extremely difficult time deciding what information to use and organizing the notes for presentation. Providing guidance at this stage is extremely helpful to students, especially those in middle school and junior high for whom research as a process may be an entirely novel concept. Strategies that Kuhlthau suggests include reading and reflecting and listing topic-related ideas that are of interest and importance to the information seeker.

Kuhlthau (1997) considers *Formulation* the most important task in the ISP, as it is the focus that guides students in the selection of pertinent information at the Collection phase. It is also of interest to note Kuhlthau's observation that where personal sense-making and the creation of a personal perspective are not parts of a student's process—or an expectation of the instructor—plagiarism through the appropriation of the words and thoughts of others is often the result.

Kuhlthau's (1997) research indicates, perhaps not surprisingly, that individuals move through the stages of the ISP at different rates. Studies subsequent to the first one also indicated that the confidence levels experienced by some groups were found to deviate from the model as initially proposed. For example, searchers in public library settings expressed more confidence in the initial stage of the search than those in academic and school settings. By the same token, college searchers expressed more confidence in the outcomes of these projects than did students in the high school studies. This finding suggests that the feelings experienced during the ISP may be a function of the nature of the task and the experience of the searcher.

Kuhlthau's (1991) efforts to track four of her original high school informants in a longitudinal study revealed that as more experienced information users these students noted "that interest in a topic increases as a search progresses; that a topic changes as information is gathered; [and] that a central theme evolves as information is gathered" (p. 368). It was also evident that these students felt more in control of the search process and of their projects and developed a kind of personal "sense of ownership" in the process itself as a "way to learn" above and beyond the more pragmatic goals of fulfilling a school assignment. In a very real sense, the search process became a metacognitive device, wherein the student was made aware not only of stages in the ISP but also of the evolution in his or her own thinking on the project and on the problem-solving process itself.

Kuhlthau also found that many individuals failed to formulate a personal perspective with regard to the topic at hand or to focus narrowly on the topic at all. As she suggested, this might be the result of the assigned nature of the task or students' assumptions that it is the views of the "authorities" consulted and not their own that should be expressed in presenting the finished project. Finally, Kuhlthau (1997) reports findings that suggest "that younger children experience the search process in similar holistic ways"; those "under the ages of eleven or twelve" tend to be more involved in building a knowledge base than in creating "a personal perspective" and "experience formulation less intentionally than teenagers" perhaps because they lack the developmental structures to engage in abstract thinking (p. 713).

Kuhlthau's Research "Moods"

Unique to Kuhlthau's (1991, 1993b) work is her consideration of two attitudes or "moods" exhibited by students in her studies, which she labeled "invitational" and "indicative." When information seekers are in an invitational mood, they are open to exploring their topics, and they eagerly seek and consider new ideas, information, and information sources. When students decide that they have enough information to meet their research needs, they move into an indicative mood, which allows them to end the search and proceed with the presentation and assessment phases of the process. As Kuhlthau notes, an invitational mood is especially important at Initiation and Exploration stages, when students are trying to understand their topics. Indeed, as noted above, at the outset, almost all pieces of information the student encounters may appear to have relevance. For this reason, it is important for those counseling students during the search process to encourage this invitational mood as students form their initial ideas and seek to clarify their thinking. An indicative mood, which marks the Formulation and Collection stages, helps students conclude their searches and is especially important when decisions must be made regarding the creation of a thesis. Indeed, an indicative mood is vital if students are to bring the search process to closure and organize the information gathered for presentation.

In Kuhlthau's (1997) view, it is essential that library media specialists learn to recognize student moods so that they can intercede if students sustain an invitational mood so long that they are unable to decide on a topic or end a search so early that they select a focus without the necessary reflection. An emphasis on location and access skills in information skills instruction may also serve to encourage students to close down prematurely their information-seeking activities before having explored all their options.

Implementing the ISP

In order that research projects are directly related to curricular objectives and course content, Kuhlthau (1993b) posits task initiation as the creation of open-ended questions. Ideally, these questions arise in classroom discussions and resonate with a student's own experience and interests. She also suggests identifying the audience for whom the assignment is being prepared at this stage in the process. The use of student journals is a way to help students preserve aspects of the process, particularly their thinking about possible topics and their feelings; journals can also help students keep track of their searching strategies and their notes. Guidance, coaching, and conferencing provided by teachers and librarians can help reduce student feelings of uncertainty, which frequently arise in exploring the information on a topic for the first time. Kuhlthau (1994) also believes that background reading, time for reflection, and interaction with the instructor will help students in creating a focus for their topics, constructing a personal perspective, and organizing the information for presentation. Evaluating the process, that is, assessing the use of time, "use of sources," "evidence of a focus," and "use of the library media specialist" (p. 175), is seen as an essential activity and one that requires the support of teachers and librarians.

Kuhlthau's research has contributed many insights to our understanding of the ISP and knowledge of how students learn from information. The fact that students not only need but also welcome such assistance was also one of Kuhlthau's important findings (1993b). In particular, students indicated that they need support and encouragement during the initial stages of their ISPs. But how can this intervention best be provided? When and what kinds of assistance would be most helpful? To address these questions, Kuhlthau created a "taxonomy" of assistance. The following sections of this chapter explore Kuhlthau's intervention model.

Kuhlthau's Levels of Intervention

Based on the experiences of information searchers in a variety of library settings, Kuhlthau (1993b, 1996) provides a taxonomy of assistance that can serve to guide library media specialists in providing instruction and support for their students. In this way, Kuhlthau hopes that students and librarians will come to understand that assistance is appropriate and necessary in providing intellectual as well as physical access to information resources.

Vygotsky's Zones of Proximal Development Theory

In building a model to guide instructional intervention levels in support of information seekers, Kuhlthau has drawn heavily on the work of Lev Vygotsky and his zones of proximal development (ZPD) theory. Vygotsky was a 20th-century Russian psychologist (d. 1934) whose work was largely unknown in the West until it was translated into English and published here in the 1960s. Since that time, his ideas have been extremely influential in the fields of education, psychology, and communication. Vygotsky believed that learning leads to cognitive development, not the other way around, and that, in learning, children essentially act as elaborators on information they encounter in interaction with knowledgeable others and with the environment. In short, cognitive schema are socially and interpersonally formed before they become internalized and experienced as personal thoughts or understandings. Since language is the primary tool through which interaction occurs, and since language is culturally bound, so necessarily is all understanding and learning.

In Vygotsky's (1978) view, there are certain moments in the child's development when instruction is most effective, that is, times during which the child's cognitive elaboration is most likely to occur. Vygotsky called these moments "zones of proximal development." Specifically, a zone of proximal development represents "the distance between" a child's actual "level of development as an independent problem solver and [his or her] potential level of development" (p. 86). At the lower or actual level, problem solving is achieved by the child working independently; at the upper or potential level, the child can perform more difficult tasks with assistance provided by a more knowledgeable partner.

Vygotsky (1978) believed that through careful observation of a child's present level of functioning, a perceptive teacher should be able to identify, plan, and support learning activities to match each child's proximal zone. The teacher first sets a goal and provides directions, demonstrations, and strategies that the child can use in reaching the goal, then guides the child in enacting the activity. When this initial goal is reached, the teacher offers another one at a higher or more difficult level. The central mechanism of learning, according to this approach, is the transfer of responsibility from the teacher or more knowledgeable partner to the child, as learning occurs and the task is completed. As the lesson proceeds, the teacher gradually eliminates the supportive explanations, hints, and demonstrations until, in the end, the skill is performed by the child alone. At that point, the child's newly internalized skill acquires its individual character and constitutes the new actual level of development—the foundational level for a new proximal zone. In this context, the teaching is dynamic and reciprocal, a negotiated division of labor aimed at increasing the learner's share of the burden for the attainment of the goal. Thus, in Vygotsky's view, the child does not alone possess a zone of proximal development (as, for example, a set level of achievement or an IQ score) but shares one with his or her instructor.

Kuhlthau's Intervention Model

Kuhlthau (1993b, 2003) has suggested five roles for library media specialists, based on a taxonomy of five levels of intervention. These roles and levels are summarized in

Figure 3.2 as organizer, lecturer, instructor, tutor, and counselor. The range of intervention techniques Kuhlthau has devised are based on the "physician/patient interaction" model frequently used by doctors in choosing appropriate treatment levels (Kuhlthau, 1993b, p. 156). The appropriate role for the library media specialist in any given situation is to support students as they engage in activities that might be beyond their present levels of expertise, until such time as they can perform the tasks independently. Importantly, it also creates a diagnostic tool that librarians can use in planning the kinds of assistance a seeker would find most beneficial at any given place in his or her ISP and provides a description of best practices appropriate for librarians in helping students to learn from information. In short, the zone idea provides a point of access so that the student's needs for content of the information skills instruction drive the lesson. Since the assistance provided by the information professional enables

Figure 3.2
Professional Assistance and Instruction Available for Students Involved in the ISP (Kuhlthau, 1993b)

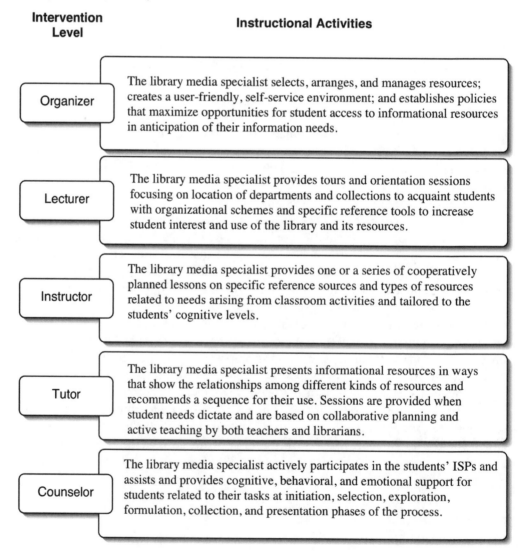

Intervention Level	Instructional Activities
Organizer	The library media specialist selects, arranges, and manages resources; creates a user-friendly, self-service environment; and establishes policies that maximize opportunities for student access to informational resources in anticipation of their information needs.
Lecturer	The library media specialist provides tours and orientation sessions focusing on location of departments and collections to acquaint students with organizational schemes and specific reference tools to increase student interest and use of the library and its resources.
Instructor	The library media specialist provides one or a series of cooperatively planned lessons on specific reference sources and types of resources related to needs arising from classroom activities and tailored to the students' cognitive levels.
Tutor	The library media specialist presents informational resources in ways that show the relationships among different kinds of resources and recommends a sequence for their use. Sessions are provided when student needs dictate and are based on collaborative planning and active teaching by both teachers and librarians.
Counselor	The library media specialist actively participates in the students' ISPs and assists and provides cognitive, behavioral, and emotional support for students related to their tasks at initiation, selection, exploration, formulation, collection, and presentation phases of the process.

the students to experience progress in carrying out an assigned task, the model reflects Dervin's (1983) initial view that gaps in understanding can impede an individual's forward progress in meeting personal goals. Finally, although primarily a diagnostic tool for librarians to use in planning instruction, the taxonomy may be particularly useful to librarians in explaining to administrators the range of instructional alternatives available for students in the library media center. In addition, library media specialists can use it as an interactional barometer in evaluating their own activities across students, classes, and grade levels.

Organizer Level

Acting at an organizer level, the library media specialist prepares the context for learning by selecting, arranging, organizing, and managing resources so that information is available in a wide variety of topics, formats, and media. Essentially, the librarian creates a self-service facility, perhaps providing maps, diagrams, and appropriate library signage. He or she also creates policies that maximize student access to library materials. At this level, the expertise of the librarian is apparent in the creation of collections that support the curriculum and of environments and opportunities that enable students to search for information independently. In brief, the central tasks for the librarian at the organizer level are managerial and clerical rather than instructional.

Locator/Lecturer Level

When operating at the locater/lecturer level, school librarians provide students an overview of library resources, services, and policies, with a focus on the location of particular items. Group tours of the library, orientation sessions, scavenger hunts, and locational games are typical of "lecturer level" support. As such, they serve to call the students' attention to the organizational schemes used in classifying and accessing library materials and the varieties of materials that are available in the library, in the community, and online. In many respects, such activities may increase student interest in the library and its resources, but they fall short of helping students seek information to meet their own information needs or solve particular problems.

Identifier/Instructor Level

At the identifier/instructor level, the library media specialist provides lessons on specific sources and types of sources and their usefulness to students involved in specific kinds of information tasks. In as far as the key to success in planning and conducting activities at the identifier level is to make information about the library's resources relevant to the individual user, librarians must plan one or a series of sessions in direct response to student needs. These sessions should be planned in advance in cooperation with the classroom instructor, so that the requirements of the lessons and the individual needs of the students can be directly addressed. Ideally this kind of source-oriented instruction occurs at the point when students are ready to use the resources to fulfill information tasks. To a certain extent, the locater and identifier levels correspond to Wyer's (1930) conservative level of library service, since the library media specialist plays a more or less reactive role in the educational process, responding to requests rather than initiating interaction or inquiry.

Adviser/Tutor Level

Providing instruction at the adviser/tutor level requires that the library media specialist plan a series of sessions to demonstrate the sequential use of a variety of informational resources. Basically, this level of intervention is reminiscent of the pathfinder model, in which the librarian helps students to understand the relationships between and among various types of resources in the library. To be effective, instruction based on a tutorial model requires that teachers provide the context for the lessons and plans with the library media specialist the objectives and outcomes for the lessons taught. Kuhlthau (1993b) recommends a team-teaching approach as the most useful way to conduct these kinds of instructional interventions even though the primary emphasis is still on "location and use" kinds of activities.

Counselor Level

Instruction provided at the counselor level is truly process instruction and is most often conducted over time; instruction in identifying and interpreting information to address an evolving problem requires instructors to "be there" for students, providing active assistance whenever the student feels uncertain as to how to proceed. The librarian, acting in the counselor role, structures sessions to support students in *learning the processes* involved in making information inquiries, and in learning *from the process* as well. Creating a research plan, getting necessary background information, narrowing or expanding topics to create a focus, identifying and evaluating appropriate resource alternatives, and interpreting the information found are the kinds of activities instructional counselors support. Assessing the students "moods," reading their emotional reactions, and providing encouragement to students engaged in the complexities of a research task are also appropriate and important.

The motivation of students involved in a complex research project is gaining increasing attention in the research literature. For example, Ruth V. Small's (1998, 1999) work at Syracuse University is looking at particular strategies that successful school librarians use to motivate students as they provide information skills instruction. Callison (2000) notes that "motivation helps to increase the chances that students will learn what is needed even when they may initially classify the activity as being overly demanding or of no interest." Although encouraging students seems like a straightforward and obvious part of being a good teacher, the truth is that it is "often left out or given little attention as teachers concentrate on academic" (cognitive) outcomes.

At the counselor level, the primary focus is to help students to become independent library users and problem solvers. It is when the library media specialist acts as a "counselor" that he or she collaborates on the project and can model the necessary skills, provide feedback, and support students as they learn the skills and the processes necessary to achieve a measure of competence and independence. These types of activities implicitly resemble Wyer's (1930) "liberal" service orientation. According to Scheidecker and Freeman (1999, cited in Callison, 2003), great teachers "take the we approach," partnering with students to assess what is wrong when they fail and celebrating with them when they succeed. Callison reminds us that "our own enthusiasm and values have much to do with our students' interest."

As noted, Vygotsky's (1980) zones of proximal development model can also be useful in describing the levels of assistance students might require at particular points in their ISPs. Figure 3.3 summarizes Kuhlthau's (1993b) suggestions for intervention zones and levels of assistance. Each higher level assumes the provision of services at

Figure 3.3
Instructional Activities Based on Students' Needs for Assistance (Kuhlthau, 1993b)

Intervention Zone	Student Need	Instructional Activity
Zone 1	No assistance	Organizer
Zone 2	Introduction to the library; reference assistance	Lecturer
Zone 3	Assistance in locating and using a variety of relevant resources	Instructor
Zone 4	Identification and use of relevant resources in a sequence	Tutor
Zone 5	Assistance in understanding the process, in the development of search strategies, in the formulation of a focus, and determining relevance of retrieved items, etc.	Counselor

all preceding levels. For example, students operating in Zone 1 require no direct intervention, although their ability to conduct research independently assumes access to a library that is well organized and managed to maximize physical and intellectual access to information. Organizer-level assistance might include comprehensible signs, information sheets, pathfinders, and computer-based "virtual" library tours. When operating in Zone 2, a student will require the help of the librarian in locating information to solve a fact-based or ready reference question. Students with Zone 3 information needs will require assistance and instruction in finding and using a number of library resources. At Zone 4, the student's information problems will call for the presentation of sources in a specific sequence and instruction in their use. At Zone 5, students' information needs may require a conference with the librarian to discuss the processes involved in the ISP and in learning from the information collected.

Understanding the level of assistance a particular student needs and wants at any given time requires sensitivity and keen observational skills. While Maslow's (1970) research indicates that students have high affiliation needs, "motivation may be complicated by conflicting needs for independence and dependence" (Callison, 2003). Acknowledging what the student does know and is able to do on his or her own, at the same time that guidance is being provided, is one way that librarians can respond to both of these needs.

Research Based on Kuhlthau's ISP Model

A number of research studies have drawn on Kuhlthau's (1993b, 1997) pioneering work and enriched and extended our understandings of the ISP she originally described. The insights from these studies can be applied by librarians "in the field" to improve both instruction and service. For example, Kuhlthau's model served as a guide to the research process for students in a high school science course team-taught by a library media specialist and their science teacher (McNally & Kuhlthau, 1994). Science topics also served as the focus of student research conducted by junior high students in an action research study² conducted by Loerke (1994), while Swain (1996) sought to verify Kuhlthau's model in a study of college freshmen.

In McNally and Kuhlthau (1994), Kuhlthau's ISP was presented to students as an instructional model and guide to information-seeking activities. Students were required to keep a log of their activities and their reactions to their readings, and instructors also used individual conferences to monitor student progress. Instructors found that student journals were especially helpful to students as they attempted to find an individual focus at the formulation stage. In implementing the ISP, the teaching team actively encouraged students to be "invitational" in their approach to the research assignment and "to be open to ideas" (p. 57). At the selection stage, when students were expected to find a topic for their projects, the instructors encouraged students to browse current periodicals and newspapers to gain background information. Researchers found that students experienced confusion as their exploration activities led them to identify scientists, gather factual information, and encounter the vocabulary that would assist them in online searching. Providing an opportunity for students to share their searches with one another also helped students build their confidence and "clarify the direction of their work." Strategies that students found particularly useful involved "expressing their thoughts aloud" (p. 58) as well as hearing that others in the class were experiencing similar difficulties. The collection phase of the ISP provided an opportunity for the library media specialist and the teacher to "suggest, introduce, and explain sources as needed" (pp. 58–59) in the library and beyond; in the presentation stage, the teacher facilitated the process by helping "students organize their notes" in anticipation of creating a final project. Reflection on the process followed, with students asked to consider their own study skills and thinking and their use of time.

In her study, Loerke (1994) applied Kuhlthau's theoretical frameworks and methods in an "action" study of 120 junior high school students involved in a research project that required the use of library resources. Of particular interest to Loerke were the steps taken by student information seekers, their feelings, and the processes they used to focus their topics. Loerke was also interested in identifying or creating intervention strategies that would help students engaged in the process of focusing. In general, Loerke found that, from the beginning, students experienced feelings that mirrored those of the high schoolers in studies conducted by Kuhlthau (1993b) and McNally and Kuhlthau (1994); initial uncertainty, which gave way to optimism at the point of topic selection, was followed by a period of confusion during prefocus exploration. Confidence increased as the creation of a focus proceeded and students had a "greater sense of where they were going . . . and felt more confident about what they were doing" (pp. 24–25).

Even though, as Loerke (1994) noted, students tended to choose topics with which they had some personal experience, focusing topics represented the most challenging aspect of the process. Seventh graders in the study experienced more problems with focus formulation than eighth graders, particularly those who "lacked background knowledge" (p. 25) of the subject domain of the topic or the topic itself or lacked cognitive competence to deal with topics on an abstract level. "Most of the grade 7 students," according to Loerke, "appeared to be reasoning at the concrete operational stage in their science thinking" (p. 25). However, Loerke also found that "providing background knowledge and teacher guidance allow[ed students] to work at more abstract levels" (p. 25). This supports the theory that students can operate at a higher level with assistance than they can if left on their own. Loerke concluded that even though "grade 8 students researched their topics in greater depth, these students also needed the structure of built-in checkpoints to ensure that they were not having difficulties" (p. 25). Based on her research, Loerke recommended a number of strategies that librarians can use in assisting junior high information seekers who are working on a research task. For one thing, Loerke suggests that research projects be assigned as the "culminating activity" for a unit of study so that students have some content knowledge upon which to build. In addition, teachers should allow enough time for the project to enable students to forge links between their topics and their prior knowledge. She also suggests the keeping of response journals throughout the instruction phases of the unit as an aid to topic selection and investigational focus.

Swain's (1996) study of college freshmen enrolled in an English class also sheds some light on information seeking and the information search processes of student researchers. Swain tracked students to compare their information-seeking processes with the one Kuhlthau described (1993b). Although students' activities in Swain's research mirrored those Kuhlthau's described in the stages of the ISP, they did so recursively and frequently in a different order. In addition, they combined steps. In addition, Swain's informants noted that interpersonal interaction and communication were important to success in developing and focusing their topics.

While Swain (1996) found that students' thoughts (increasing specificity and clarity and decreasing ambiguity) and feelings (from uncertainty to confidence) followed Kuhlthau's (1993b) model as their projects developed, their speed in moving through the phases varied. In addition, students were seen to change topics several times, which meant that initiation and topic selection stages had to be repeated. In addition, some students moved from initiation to focus formulation immediately. Interestingly, interactions with parents and peers had a direct impact on students' selection of both topics and library resources. These discussions frequently produced ideas for students to pursue and also helped them to create a focus. This finding is consistent with the implementation of the ISP model in McNally and Kuhlthau (1994), who also noted the importance of interaction with others at a number of points in the search process.

Suggestions from the research studies based on Kuhlthau's model are summarized in Table 3.2. It is compelling to note that, across these studies, the feelings expressed by novice searchers in approaching their assignments consistently reflect those in Kuhlthau's (1993b) studies. In addition, the importance of conferencing and interaction as strategies students used in selecting topics and finding foci, as well as to obtain emotional support, suggest that Kuhlthau's model might be expanded to consider communication as another dimension along with thoughts, feelings, and actions—a recommendation Swain (1996) suggested. In addition, it also appears that instructional

Table 3.2
Suggestions for Implementing the ISP (Kuhlthau, 1993b) with Junior High and High School Students

- Exploration of the topic should be built into the research process, and, for younger students, the research project should probably come after students have knowledge of subject-specific content or after the teacher has provided background information on the topic or topics students will be asked to research.

- Teachers should discuss the uses of journals, so that students can record their responses and their thoughts throughout the unit; in this way, students can use their recorded thoughts when the time comes to select a topic and create a focus for their research.

- The structuring of research assignments should include regular checkpoints or opportunities when teachers monitor student progress in thinking about the topic as well as the progress of the research project.

- The structure should also build in opportunities for students to share their thinking, their ideas for a focus, and their feelings about the process and their progress with peers, teachers, and parents and facilitate these conversations to make them focused and productive.

- The structure should provide times for reading and reflection at various points of the ISP.

- Students should be encouraged to find personal links to research topics; where their thinking may be concrete rather than abstract, students might find engaging topics with which they already have some personal experience.

- The development of a focus is essential before students move on to the collection phase of the ISP, but the focus may change during the process.

intervention should be planned with the developmental (cognitive) as well as the reading levels of the students in mind.

Notes

1. Kuhlthau's research has had enormous impact on practice as well as research in LIS. Kuhlthau (1999) writes that

> reference librarians who have become aware of the stages of the ISP describe important changes in the way they view students and faculty who approach the reference desk. They now listen for an indication of the stage in the process of the user and particularly note when someone is "in the dip" and needs some extra help to explore for learning in order to formulate a research focus. They are especially careful not to give too much too soon and to assist in pacing the use of resources by suggesting strategies for exploring information to form a focus for research.

2. Action studies represent an approach to research that is intended specifically to explore some aspect of professional practice. As Lindlof (1995) explains, action research in education is frequently employed when teachers wish to study new pedagogical techniques, such as "the introduction of new technology," in order to "diagnose problems, engage in collaborative analysis of data, and engender problem-solving skills" (p. 110) so that instructional techniques can be modified or improved. Action research studies have certain limitations; they often, although not always, lack a theory base, and they are site-specific, meaning that research findings are not transferable or generalizable to other situations or populations. However, such studies are extremely useful in that they often suggest new issues, topics, and avenues for other researchers to explore.

4 Process Models for Information Skills Instruction

Since the mid-1980s, a number of library media specialists and library and information scholars have developed process models for use in teaching information literacy skills. These models are based on the experience of practicing librarians and designed to improve the educational value of the research activities assigned in the classroom. Taken together, these models have become the nucleus of effective alternatives to stand-alone library "lessons," especially when they are aligned directly with classroom curriculum and delivered in response to students' research needs.

As discussed in Chapter 3, Kuhlthau's (1993b, 2003) information search process model is a seminal work and the only model that has been tested empirically. It is also the only model that acknowledges the "holistic" nature of information seeking, dealing directly with thoughts, feelings, and actions (Kuhlthau, 1999). However, the research model specifically describes the search process itself, that is, that portion of research activity that begins at the initiation of the assignment and ends at the point when students are ready to organize their information and begin writing. A number of other process models have been created to provide more comprehensive guidance. All of these process models are instructional in nature (Bates, 1979a); they suggest a "best practice" for students as they engage in information seeking and research projects, and all emphasize the development of cognitive "higher-order" or critical thinking skills. For this reason, library media specialists, teachers, and students may find any or all of them useful at different times and under different conditions, depending on the context, the task or problem, and the student or students involved. Among the best known of these are the term paper and REACTS models created by Stripling and Pitts (1988); Joyce and Tallman's (1997) I-Search model; the Pathways model, created by Pappas and Tepe (1997); and Flip It!—a model developed by Yucht. As noted, each of these models provides a framework for the research process in its entirety, covering the writing of the paper as well as the information-seeking processes that precede it. Although the process approaches proposed by Irving (1985) and Eisenberg and Berkowitz (1990) can also be applied to research paper projects, these authors believe that their models have applications beyond student research. For example, Irving suggests that her model can be successfully used by students in conducting a wide variety of tasks related to their schoolwork. In her view, information skills are, in fact, "life skills" (p. 115). Eisenberg and Berkowitz (1990), authors of *Information*

44

Problem-Solving: The Big Six Skills Approach to Library and Information Skills Instruction, regard their Big6 Skills as flexible enough to use in all kinds of everyday decision making. The Handy 5 model (Kansas Association of School Librarians Research Committee, 2001) was created as a framework for projects across the curriculum. Based on the Big6, the Handy 5 model sought to use Kansas state guidelines as they applied to all school subjects to create a common approach to problem solving in all curricular areas. The Handy 5 is typical of many regional and state initiatives that seek to reduce confusion and create links among and across curricular areas.

The description of the models provided here is meant as an introduction and as a framework for further reading. The texts created for each model can provide library media specialists and teachers with valuable strategies, and several also include lesson plans to extend understanding and suggest appropriate applications. Those planning to apply these models to practice should read: Irving's (1985) *Study and Information Skills across the Curriculum* (1985); Eisenberg and Berkowitz's (1990) *Information Problem-Solving: The Big Six Skills Approach to Library and Information Skills Instruction* (1990); Stripling and Pitts's (1988) *Brainstorms and Blueprints: Teaching Library Research as a Thinking Process* (1988); Joyce and Tallman's (1997) *Making the Writing and Research Connection with the I-Search Process*; Pappas and Tepe's (1997) *Pathways to Knowledge*; Alice Yucht's *Flip It! An Information Skills Strategy for Student Researchers* (1997); and Kansas Association of School Librarians Research Committee's *The Handy 5: Planning and Assessing Integrated Information Skills Instruction* (2001).

Irving's Study and Information Skills across the Curriculum

Ann Irving, an English librarian with many years of experience, developed a nine-step model for elementary school students to use in the completion of a range of school-related assignments, from relatively simple ones to those of considerable complexity. Although Irving's (1985) intent was to link information skills directly to the kinds of curricular activities "which form a substantial part of a pupil's school life" (p. 25), she was quick to realize that information skills are "inherently present in all learning tasks" (p. 23) and immensely important. In her view, information handling is key to enabling all students "to participate in the control of [their] future" (p. 157).

The nine steps in Irving's (1985) model (see Figure 4.1) create a cycle of learning that takes the student from the beginning of an assignment or project through to its completion and evaluation. As described by Irving, each of the steps serves as "a signpost to a wider range of skills" (p. 31) and creates a framework for appropriate questions and activities. Step 1 of the model, "Defining Tasks," is "primarily a thinking stage" (p. 42), which acknowledges the importance of understanding the nature of the assignment and the criteria that will be used to evaluate it. Irving states firmly that it is the responsibility of the instructor to provide "a clear and understandable statement of the task," the task outcomes, and the assessment techniques and rubrics. Instructors must also check with students to be sure that "everyone understands exactly what is required" (p. 33). At this first step, students should also be furnished a rationale for the assignment so that they can understand its significance. In Irving's view, "[A] knowledge of purpose . . . helps to structure the information-seeking, reading, note-taking and presenting" (p. 35) activities to come. In addition, the explanation of the assignment should contain information on the intended audience for the finished product, the amount of time the students have for task completion, and the level of detail

Figure 4.1
Steps, Activities, and Questions in Irving's (1985) Model for Completing Assignments

Step	Activity	Central Question
Step 1: Defining Tasks	"Formulation and analysis of the information need"	"What do I need to do?"
Step 2: Considering Sources	"Identification and appraisal of likely sources of information"	"Where do I go?"
Step 3: Finding Resources	"Tracing and locating individual sources"	"How do I get to the information?"
Step 4: Making Selections	"Examining, selecting, and rejecting individual sources"	"Which resources shall I use?"
Step 5: Effective Use	"Interrogating, or using, individual sources"	"How shall I use the resources?"
Step 6: Making Records	"Recording and storing information"	"What shall I make a record of?"
Step 7: Making Sense	"Interpretation, analysis, synthesis, and evaluation of information"	"Have I got the information I need?"
Step 8: Presenting Work	"Shape, presentation, and communication of information"	"How should I present it?"
Step 9: Assessing Progress	"Evaluation of the assignment"	"What have I achieved?"

(e.g., general overview or in-depth coverage) acceptable or expected in the finished work.

Topic selection is also a part of Step 1 in Irving's model. Irving believes that instructors must ascertain the state of the students' existing knowledge at the outset of the project and provide guidance and support for students as they undertake this important activity. In her view, "[C]hoosing a topic, or narrowing down one which has been chosen by a teacher" (p. 41), demands considerable cognitive effort, and its significance lies in that it is the basis of subsequent work. Essential as well is the identification of appropriate vocabulary terms related to the topic so that students will have some starting points and initiate the task of searching.

The importance of mutual understanding between instructor and student regarding the task and the topic has been highlighted in a recent study by Gross (1995), who also suggests that librarians working with students who are researching "imposed" questions will need to be sure that student expressions of the need reflect what was intended in the original assignment. A student's ability to execute information tasks that are incompletely understood may be undermined still further when the student articulates this "version" of the information need to a third party, such as the librarian. Including the librarian in planning assignments is one way a teacher can ensure that the library media specialist fully comprehends the intent and expectations of the research task and can assist students in an effective manner even when the teacher is not present.

The central issue addressed in Step 2 of Irving's (1985) model, "Considering Sources," involves finding the best resources appropriate for the task and putting them to the best use. At this stage, an important consideration for students is the physical (e.g., location, time constraints) and the intellectual (e.g., reading level, complexity) accessibility of potential resources. In fact, Irving suggests that mapping the possible alternatives (e.g., local agencies, museums, public libraries, community resources, types of print and electronic media) is a useful activity for students to undertake before actually beginning their investigations.

At Step 3, "Finding Resources," Irving suggests that students use their knowledge of classification schemes to find appropriate information sources. In Irving's view, the key to successful completion of this step is an understanding of how libraries are arranged. However, Irving points out that instruction should be directed at teaching the *concept* of "systems" and the "concept" of classification rather than the idiosyncrasies of a single system (e.g., Dewey Decimal System).[1] In addition, students need to understand how they can use signs, labels, and guidewords to navigate their ways through the library, its catalogs, and the subject indexes that describe aspects of each field of knowledge.

Irving's Step 4, "Making Selections," requires students to select appropriate resources by taking into account their "scope, suitability, reliability and level" (p. 68) and by considering information in a variety of appropriate formats, from realia to encyclopedias. "The crucial skill," Irving writes, "is not that of finding a book, but rather that of being able to reject a book which is unsuitable" (p. 76). In this regard, students may find indexes, book jackets, media labels, and introductory sections of sources helpful in estimating the relevance, currency, and bias of the resources they encounter. "Reading, viewing, listening, and understanding" (p. 76) are the essential skills Irving identifies as constituting Step 5, that is, making effective use of the resources located at Step 4. Strategies and activities necessary for successful completion of this step include skimming, scanning, viewing, and listening.

Irving's sixth step, "Making Records," refers to thinking, understanding, and identifying those elements in selected resources that are important and to the physical activity of taking notes. This notion of selection is essential since, as Irving tells us, a student's "desire to include everything often prevents the retention of anything meaningful" (p. 88). Irving also believes that "knowing when to quote is a skill in itself, and should be developed rather than ignored." Finally, note taking can take any number of different forms, from mind maps and webs to tables and diagrams, and may range from student-devised shorthand techniques to "near-verbatim" (p. 89) accounts.

Step 7, "Making Sense," in Irving's model is "the most intellectually demanding"

(p. 93), since it asks students to organize their notes in some way that aids learning, usually by interpreting it, reflecting upon it, analyzing it, and synthesizing it. These cognitive activities require students to link new information from their reading, viewing, and/or listening to what they already know. Irving contends that "synthesis can only occur when new information is matched with existing information or perceptions, and when students are confident enough to generate personal opinions on their learning" (p. 97). For this reason, reflection and discussion may help students draw together the strands of their thinking. Additionally, students performing Step 7 activities must decide if the information they have obtained is sufficient to address the requirements of their assignments. Finally, each student must determine if her or his information has been synthesized in a useful way and if the end result matches the intent of the assignment as originally described.

Students present their projects at Step 8 of Irving's model as written reports or essays or in some other format that meets task requirements. Although essays and written reports are traditional ways of presenting research "results," many creative alternatives exist appropriate for the expression and sharing of student ideas and learning. In any event, the choice of presentation should be consistent with learning outcomes and should also be, in this sense at least, "authentic."

Step 9 of Irving's model, "Assessing Progress," provides for an assessment of each project or performance, by the teacher, by the student, and by other students. In addition, the evaluation should include the student's own estimate of his or her learning related to the topic chosen. Irving believes that the students' self-assessments are "absolutely vital if they are to develop as learners" (p. 105) and must include reflection on all steps in the process in addition to assessment of content learned.

Irving acknowledges that not all curricular assignments will require the completion of the entire nine-step cycle. Furthermore, in instances where the attainment of particular skills may actually be masked when these activities are embedded in comprehensive assignments, librarians and teachers may wish to focus instructional attention on only one step. For example, it may sometimes be useful for students to practice analysis and synthesis tasks on information furnished by the instructor. Irving also emphasizes that the research process is most frequently a nonlinear one, and for that reason, some students may find that they repeat individual steps. Thus, application of the model and its steps will depend on the exigencies of the situation and the educational needs and experience of the students involved.

Although not formalized into a separate step, Irving suggests that an "evaluation feedback—a 'how am I doing?' intermediary stage" would help students track their own progress as their research activities proceed. At the same time, such a step would remind students of "the continuing possibility of improvement" and give teachers an opportunity to intervene in the process and adjust its direction when necessary "to avoid disasters" (p. 31).

Information Problem Solving: Eisenberg and Berkowitz's Big6 Skills[2]

Eisenberg and Berkowitz's (1990) Big6 Skills is an instructional model currently being used by thousands of library media specialists in school districts across North America and around the world. Although the Big6 model draws on the theoretical frameworks, structures, and applications suggested in Irving's (1985) model, it is far less cumbersome and for this reason has been adopted with enthusiasm by students and teachers alike. Since it provides a straightforward summary of activities related to information seeking and project completion, the Big6 serves as an extremely user-friendly approach to what are often extremely complex tasks. Big6 creators emphasize the model's utility for teaching technology skills, as well.

According to Eisenberg and Berkowitz (1990, 1996), student assignments that require the use of multiple informational resources are essentially information "problems," which can be resolved through a systematic process of thinking about the task at hand, the activities and resources required for task completion, and the nature of and expectations about the project or product involved. For this reason, the Big6 works well as a cross-situational model in that the same process can be used for homework assignments and real-world decision making as well as for school reports and projects.

Essentially, the Big6 Skills approach ties cognitive levels (Bloom, 1956) to various stages of the information process by identifying needs (knowledge level); relating resources to aspects of the problem (comprehension level); selecting channels and sources (application level); identifying salient elements within and across information sources (analysis level); restructuring and communicating information (synthesis level); and making judgments about the information obtained "in relation to specific needs" (Eisenberg & Berkowitz, 1990, p. 12) (evaluation level). In effect, the model calls for application of a six-step strategy that requires students to *define the task* that has been set for them and the expectations in terms of the quantity and quality of the product that they will produce; *select strategies* and resources for finding the information they are going to need; *locate and access* relevant and appropriate information resources; *use the information* by "engaging" or *extracting* it through reading, note taking, and highlighting and by determining its relevancy for the task; *synthesize* the information in making a decision or creating a project, writing a paper or producing a performance or exhibition; and *evaluate* the process and the project in terms of its effectiveness in meeting the criteria established by the teacher or library media specialist and the efficiency with which the project was carried out.

Although the Big6 appears to be a linear process with one step preceding the next, its creators argue that it can be used recursively as the student progresses through information seeking and learning; for example, students' evaluations of what they are doing are activities appropriate at all stages, and location and access tasks may have to be repeated any number of times. The particular value of assessment as an ongoing activity is that it calls students' attention to the thinking processes in which they are involved throughout the creation of their assignments or projects. The steps in the Big6 model are summarized in Figure 4.2.

The Big6 recognizes variability in student learning styles by acknowledging the reflexive and recursive nature of information seeking. It also emphasizes the importance of student-instructor interaction in brainstorming ideas and the desirability of using human as well as print and electronic information resources. The Big6 also supports a variety of search strategies, making this an appropriate choice for teachers and librarians who hope to address the needs of a variety of student learners. Further, when expanded to the "Little Twelve," or truncated to the "Super Three," the Big6 can be used successfully for and by students at all grade and developmental levels. According to Cottrell and Eisenberg (2001), the Big6 has also been used effectively in academic library settings as a strategy for helping college students understand reference skills and information-seeking strategies.

Ideally, Big6 Skills lessons are created through collaboration between librarians and teachers to make the most of library resources and student research time. Indeed, one of the model's major advantages is its apparent simplicity, which helps students

Figure 4.2
"Super 3," "Big6," and "Little 12" Models for Information Problem Solving (Eisenberg & Berkowitz (1990)

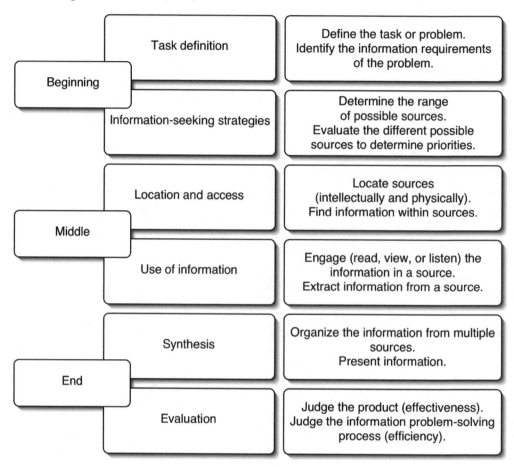

grasp the six steps quickly and in such a way that they can conceptualize the process as a whole as well as their own location within it at any given point in time.

First introduced in 1990, the Big6 Skills approach has proven so popular that it has spawned a variety of support structures, including a newsletter and an active Web site on the Internet (http://www.Big6.com), which is devoted to answering Big6-related questions, providing news and research updates, providing information on Big6 conferences and workshops, identifying and describing exemplary Big6 programs, and listing articles published on Big6 applications and success stories. A Web site for children, http://www.Big6/kids.com, has also been created.

Stripling and Pitts's REACTS Model for Term Paper Preparation

The REACTS model was originally devised by two high school library media specialists, Barbara K. Stripling and Judy M. Pitts, for use by students engaged in researching and writing term papers. As practicing librarians, these authors were primarily concerned with using the research project, a staple in many high school English and social studies courses, as a way to help students develop cognitive creativity and critical thinking and metacognitive skills. In their view, research assignments could be improved if they were structured and planned to promote cognitive skills along a continuum ranging from simple to complex. The result of their collaboration was a "taxonomy of thoughtful research" (Stripling & Pitts, 1988, p. 3), which arranges research activities from "fact-finding" assignments requiring thinking at the level of recall to "conceptualization" tasks in which students are called upon to synthesize their information in creating research projects. A summary of the REACTS model is provided in Figure 4.3.

At the level of "Fact-Finding" in the REACTS model, learners seek specific information on a topic in one or a variety of library sources and create reports on the basis of what they find out. At the level of "Asking and Searching," students create specific questions (e.g., Who? What? When? and Where?) about a topic and then seek information in the library to answer these questions. In this way, students are required to do something with the information, which shows that they understand it; frequently this takes the form of creating a summary or expressing the information in their own words.

At the "Examining and Organizing" level, students seek answers to more sophis-

Figure 4.3
Stripling and Pitts's (1988) Taxonomies of Thoughtful Research and Thoughtful Reactions (REACTS)

Levels	Research Tasks	Research Activities/ Outcomes	Cognitive Tasks
Level 1	Fact-Finding	Reporting on the information	Recalling
Level 2	Asking and Searching	Posing who, what, where, and when questions and finding answers	Explaining
Level 3	Examining and Organizing	Posing why and how problems and organizing information to fit the project	Analyzing
Level 4	Evaluating and Deliberating	Judging information on the basis of authority, significance, bias, etc.	Challenging
Level 5	Integrating and Concluding	Drawing conclusions and creating a personal perspective based on information obtained	Transforming
Level 6	Conceptualizing	Creating original solutions to problems posed	Synthesizing

Figure 4.4
Stripling and Pitts's (1988) 10-Step Model for Research Projects

Steps in the Process	Research Tasks	Questions for Student Reflection
Level 1	Select a broad topic	
Level 2	Obtain an overview of the topic	
Level 3	Narrow the topic	"Is my topic a good one?"
Level 4	Create a thesis statement	"Does my thesis statement of purpose represent any effective overall concept for my research?"
Level 5	Formulate research questions	"Do the questions provide a foundation for my research?"
Level 6	Develop a research plan	"Is the research/ production plan workable?"
Level 7	Locate and evaluate information sources	"Are my sources usable and adequate?"
Level 8	Evaluate sources, take notes, and create a bibliography	"Is my research complete?"
Level 9	Draw conclusions, create an outline	"Are my conclusions based on research evidence? Does my outline logically organize conclusions and evidence?"
Level 10	Create the project or product or write the paper	"Is my paper/project satisfactory?"

ticated "why and how" questions and then reorganize the information in a way that fits the requirements of the particular assignment. Thus students may be asked to explore cause and effect, to compare and contrast, to demonstrate problem solving, or to make predictions. Assignments that require research at the "Evaluating and Deliberating" level call on learners to evaluate the information on a set of criteria (e.g., accuracy, authority, significance, bias) they or others establish. "Integrating and Concluding" types of research tasks provide students an opportunity to "draw their own conclusions," form a personal opinion, or frame the results in a "personal context" (Stripling & Pitts 1988, p. 6).

The most sophisticated research projects occur at the level of "Conceptualizing," which calls for the creation of original solutions to the problems the learners pose for themselves. Research tasks at this level are similar to those undertaken by scholars and scientists. Working in a group and engaging in "practical, community minded problem solving" can challenge students to think at the "conceptualizing level" (p. 6). Although all levels of the taxonomy may prove of educational value under certain circumstances and at different times, it is only in response to questions posed at the higher levels (Levels 3–6) that students will be required to think critically.

Stripling and Pitts (1988) have also created a process model for the preparation of resource-based research: a 10-step guide that takes students from topic selection through project completion. The model is summarized in Figure 4.4. In general, it calls on students to do preliminary reading and information seeking in preparation for narrowing the topic, creating a thesis, and writing research questions (Levels 1–5). At Level 6, students themselves must develop action plans to structure their own searching activities. Level 7 finds students locating and selecting information resources. Note-taking activities take place during Level 8, culminating in the compilation of a bibliography of their information sources. Level 9 involves students in creating an outline based on conclusions drawn from the information, with final creation of the project or paper and project evaluation occurring at Level 10. One of the strongest features of the Stripling and Pitts model is the reflective aspect, which is provided in the questions students ask themselves at each step of the process. It is this sort of metacognitive device that educators have found so valuable in extending learning experiences and helping students deepen their understanding of information processes.

Pappas and Tepe's Pathways to Knowledge[3]

Pappas and Tepe (Pappas, 1997; Pappas & Tepe, 1997) have created a K–12 information skills model: Pathways to Knowledge. The Pathways approach provides resource guides, which are commercially available through Follett Educational Services, and the authors have presented the model at conferences, workshops, and in-service sessions. According to its creators, the Pathways model attempts to present the information search process in a holistic way, emphasizing the nonlinear path that most often characterizes the ways individuals meet their information needs or solve their information problems. In addition, the model reflects the information literacy standards adopted by AASL and AECT in 1998. Pathways to Knowledge is bimodal in that it includes both an outline and process to guide student research and a plan for teachers and librarians to use in creating integrated information skills lessons. Follett maintains a Web site, http://www.pathwaysmodel.com, which provides a complete explanation of the model as well as a graphic that aims to indicate the recursive nature of information-seeking tasks. A variety of other resources and services also are available through the site.

Pathways to Knowledge actually comprises a variety of strategies, that students can employ heuristically as the search proceeds. Pappas and Tepe agree with J.O. Carey (1997) that "literacy" in the use of information means the ability independently to enact a web of strategies that represent a best fit between those strategies that they have been taught and their own particular worldviews and cognitive styles. The strategies themselves are grouped as Presearch, Search, Interpretation, and Communication. The authors suggest that two other stages, Appreciation and Evaluation, are actually transcendent phases or steps, present in each of the other steps and extending throughout the student's search process.

According to Pappas and Tepe (1997), information seeking has its genesis in an appreciation of the arts, literature, and nature, which together foster "curiosity and imagination" (p. 1). At the *Presearch* stage, students must develop an overview of their topics or projects and explore the relationships among concepts that are related to it. The exploration of general sources, the formulation of initial questions, and the identification of key terms and words related to the topic are recommended. The creation of webs and outlines and the clustering of ideas and concepts are strategies that help students organize their thinking. During the *Search* stage, students are urged to plan their information-seeking activities ahead of time by identifying information providers available to students. These might include government and consumer agencies, museums and historic sites, as well as libraries and telecommunications providers. Selecting among available information resources and tools available through the providers is a next step, followed by the search process itself.

The *Interpretation* phase begins once the information has been gathered. Since "information requires interpretation to become knowledge" (Pappas, 1997), emphasis on "analyzing, synthesizing, and evaluating information" is essential if students are to select relevant resources and information and use them in meaningful ways. As Pappas asserts, "[I]f critical thinking is not a part of the learning plan, there is no need to interpret information and searchers are stuck at the knowledge level of learning" (p. 2). At the *Communication* stage of the Pathways model, students must apply what they now know to solve the problem, organize the information they have gathered, or answer the question, then share their new knowledge with others. Within the Pathways model, *Evaluation* by self and peers occurs as both formative and summative activities, such as assessing the project and evaluating the process so that students assess their own abilities in making information decisions regarding searching and problem solving.

Joyce and Tallman's I-Search Model

Joyce and Tallman (1997) have also created a model to guide student research, but their approach differs in a number of significant ways from the models proposed by Irving (1985), Stripling and Pitts (1988) Eisenberg and Berkowitz (1990), and Pappas and Tepe (1997). In all the others, there is an explicit or implicit assumption that the topics of research attention are either assigned by a teacher or chosen by students within the context of subject domains or curricular content and that the resulting reports and projects are formally and traditionally presented. In the case of the I-Search model, the research topic is chosen by the students on the basis of special personal interest or personal connection. In this respect, the topic can be seen to choose the student as well as the student choosing the topic. In addition, the resulting research report is presented not in the formalized style typical of academic writing but in the form of a first-person narrative or story, which not only presents information on the specific topic but chronicles students' information-seeking and data collection activities.

Initially intrigued by the connections they saw between writing process models and contemporary research models, and troubled by the student apathy that all too frequently accompanied the announcement of a research assignment, Joyce and Tallman (1997) set about finding an approach to the research process that would be personally meaningful for students. Like Stripling and Pitts (1988), Joyce and Tallman were particularly interested in sense making and making meaning from the information and in the intellectual benefits to be realized for students engaged in metacognitive activities. In the I-Search model, Joyce and Tallman saw a way to use writing and research "to foster critical thinking" (p. 16) and personal investment on the part of their students.

Although they reviewed a number of process models for writing and research in planning their research approach, the authors eventually chose Macrorie's (1988, cited in Joyce and Tallman, 1997) I-Search model, which asks students to select and research topics on a need-to-know basis and to write up the results in a narrative form. An important part of the narrative is the account of how the information students collected was "selected, evaluated and used" (p. 17). In creating their model, Joyce and Tallman also drew on theoretical frameworks suggested by Murray (1982, cited in Joyce and Tallman) and Kuhlthau (1993b). In defining writing as a special case of information processing, Murray's process writing model provided the conceptual link between writing and research. According to the authors, Kuhlthau's research on the ISP was also particularly helpful, especially as her methodology had originally been based on models employed in process writing research. In addition, Kuhlthau's emphasis on metacognitive activities, the importance she places on feelings as well as searching behaviors, and her use of interviews and conferencing techniques as a way of tracking individual student progress, also became parts of Joyce and Tallman's approach. In fact, the journals suggested in Kuhlthau's work were adapted by Joyce and Tallman, who asked students to maintain learning logs as records of their actions. Students used the logs to track their thoughts as their searches proceeded, and instructors used the logs in creating writing prompts and posing questions to stimulate student thinking and discussion.

Joyce and Tallman also employed the use of webbing as a conceptual frame and a process device at several key steps. An I-Search Process Web involves four central tasks: selecting a topic, researching the topic, using the information found, and completing a research project. Due to the personal nature of the research topics and the individual nature of student processes, library media specialists and teachers play key roles in the research process through conferencing activities. Information skills instruction fits into the model at times when students need particular skills or specific resources in conducting their research activities. The major elements of the I-Search Process Web are summarized in Figure 4.5.

At Step 1, *Topic Choice* or topic selection, students explore their own interests through webbing activities and discussions with parents, peers, and teachers. The skimming and scanning of resources in the media center to identify items of potential use follow these activities. It is at this stage in the process that information skills can best be taught, with instructional approaches based entirely on student needs and skill levels. At Step 2, *Finding Information*, students generate research questions, do background reading, create bibliographies of pertinent resources, and then enrich their knowledge through reading and interviewing. *Using Information* at Step 3 can be undertaken in a number of ways, including highlighting and note taking. Reflection is encouraged at this stage and facilitated through conferencing and the use of learning logs. The final project is prepared at Step 4 and includes the opportunity to share the experience and the project with peers.

Insofar as personal interest drives the selection of the research topic, and inter-

Figure 4.5
Steps and Activities in Joyce and Tallman's (1997) I-Search Process Model

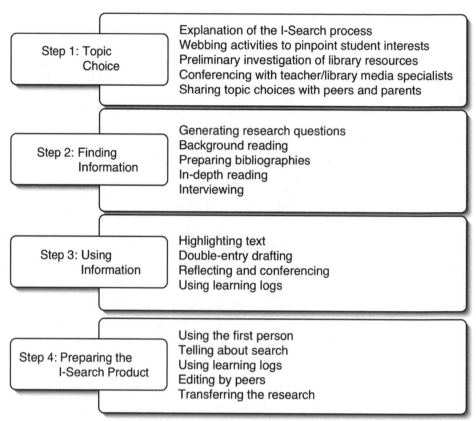

Step 1: Topic Choice
- Explanation of the I-Search process
- Webbing activities to pinpoint student interests
- Preliminary investigation of library resources
- Conferencing with teacher/library media specialists
- Sharing topic choices with peers and parents

Step 2: Finding Information
- Generating research questions
- Background reading
- Preparing bibliographies
- In-depth reading
- Interviewing

Step 3: Using Information
- Highlighting text
- Double-entry drafting
- Reflecting and conferencing
- Using learning logs

Step 4: Preparing the I-Search Product
- Using the first person
- Telling about search
- Using learning logs
- Editing by peers
- Transferring the research

viewing data as well as other informational resources are used by students in answering their research questions, Joyce and Tallman (1997) believe that the I-Search process creates the sort of authentic instructional environment that is most compatible with forms of assessment that are also considered authentic. In addition, the I-Search model stresses interaction and reflection with peers and parents as well as with teachers and the library media specialist. All of these strategies are consistent with the intent of authentic assessment and lend themselves readily to the creation of rubrics for evaluating the product and the process.[4]

Flip It!, The Handy 5, McKenzie's Research Cycle, and the Atlantic Model: Grassroots Models for Teaching the Research Process

Clearly the creation and use of models are the approach of choice in contemporary efforts to reframe the teaching of information literacy skills. Not only do we now have a number of wonderfully useful models from which to choose, but the emphasis on the process approach and the demand for curricular connections and collaboration between teachers and librarians have inspired practitioners to develop their own strategies for teaching and learning. In general, the proliferation of models reflects the local nature of education and the value placed on tailoring instruction to local children.

Some process models are local adaptations of major models described above that have been adopted by states or regions, by school districts, or by individual schools. Although some are relatively simple and straightforward iterations of research process steps, others are more elaborate and tied to library standards as well as standards for language arts, math, science, social studies, and so on. Assessment rubrics are also provided in many models.

Flip It!⁵

Yucht's (1997, 2002) Flip It! is a commonsense, problem-solving model for student research created in 1988 and based on the author's observations during her career as a practicing library media specialist. The title for the model is an acronym and mnemonic "to keep the thinker on task" and can be used as a guide and strategy for individual decision making as well as a variety of school activities and research projects. The four steps of the model can be summarized in four words: Focus, Links, Input, and Payoff. Students are to specify what they know about a topic or problem and what they need to find out or do; consider (strategize) the best research (connections) sources and locate them; investigate the topic by sorting and sifting the information found; and produce a solution to the problem and present the results. The "it" in the model stands for "intelligent thinking and the central question the model poses for students: If? . . . Then? What do I already know that will help me here?" As with other practice-based models, Yucht has made an effort to tie the stages and activities of the model to standards published in *Information Power: Building Partnerships for Learning* published by AASL and AECT in 1998.

Yucht describes her model as nonlinear "goal oriented," purposeful, and strategic (Yucht, 2002). Yucht writes:

> [T]he phrase Flip it! has been so successful as a mnemonic because:—it's easy to remember,—it sounds just silly enough to obviate any "serious thinking" fears, and—it reminds the problem-solvers that they *will* need to flip back and forth: evaluating, rethinking, and revising as they work through their information needs and activities.

The Handy 5

The Handy 5 model, published by the research committee of the Kansas Association of School Librarians in 2001, is an example of the effort of the state's professional organization to make sense of the information literacy standards published in *Information Power* within the context of state standards in math, reading, social studies, science, writing, and the arts. The authors also provide a rationale for changes in teaching and learning created when educators adopt constructivist theory as a basis for curriculum, especially the expectations and responsibilities for students within the context of a constructivist classroom.

Using Eisenberg and Berkowitz's (1990) Big6 Skills as a foundation, Grover, Fox, and Lakin (Kansas Association of School Librarians Research Committee, 2001) combined steps 3 and 4 (location and access; extraction and use) to create a 5-step model practitioners can use in planning curriculum-based integrated instructional units as well as guiding youngsters through the information-seeking and task completion processes. A key element in the Handy 5 is collaboration between librarians and classroom teachers and the sharing of responsibility for planning, teaching, and assessment tasks. As the authors suggest: "[T]he terms in the integrated teaching/learning model represent a common language for discussing and planning instruction with teachers from various subject areas" (p. 9). Special emphases of the Handy 5 as an instructional tool center on ensuring that students "have a clear, complete understanding of the assignment," create an action plan that represents consideration of the most appropriate strategies and resources, undertake the assignment based on the first two steps, and complete the task as understood.

One of the strengths of the model is the framework the authors have created for the systematic evaluation of student progress. To this end, a set of rubrics were created on a five-point scale and tailored to the specific standards and language used within the specific context or content of the assignment. A rating of NA indicates that "there is no evidence that the student has attempted to do the work" or that "there is no basis for evaluation" (p. 11). A rating of 1 indicates that "the student demonstrates an awareness of knowledge of the process or product" (p. 11) and signals significant misunderstandings or misconceptions. A rating of 2 indicates, through omissions or errors in the assignment, that the student's understanding of the problem or the process is "partial or incomplete" (p. 11). A rating of 3 is the benchmark or "expected level of achievement." The student at this level "has a substantial and acceptable measure of learning," with "evidence provided by behavior and/or example(s)" (p. 11). The highest rating on the scale is a 4, denoting a level of achievement beyond what is expected and demonstrated by the student's "thorough and complete understanding" of the task or assignment. In short, a level-4 student "has integrated knowledge and is able to apply it in a real-life situation" (p. 11).

Steps in the Handy 5 include the assignment, the plan of action, doing the job, product evaluation, and process evaluation. Under the supervision of a research scholar, the model was field tested with library media specialists and teachers in an elementary school, a middle school, and a high school. Results indicated that the model "effectively provides a step-by-step framework for planning, building, and delivering a unit that integrates information skills and curricular content" for children in grades K–12. The model was effective with low- as well as high-achieving students, had a positive impact on student attitudes to their tasks, promoted higher-order thinking skills, and provided a useful way to assess student progress. In terms of teaching and collaboration, the model facilitated collaboration, provided a structure for planning, saved time, and improved communication between and among teachers and library media specialists. However, as with other instructional strategies, the research indicated that the model requires both training and practice for effective use and a school culture receptive to collaboration.

McKenzie's Research Cycle

An example of a school-wide research model is the Research Cycle, created to take advantage of the information-rich environment made possible by the installation of a wide-area network. The Research Cycle depends on active collaboration between teachers and school library media specialists and was introduced to the school staff through a course called "Launching Student Investigations." The research tasks themselves are undertaken by students working together in research teams. The model specifically takes into account the possibilities and problems students encounter when searching online. For example, in order to avoid the sort of information glut that can result from indiscriminate downloading of information from the World Wide Web, research teams "only use the Internet when that is likely to provide the best information. In many cases, books and CD-ROMs will prove more efficient and useful" (McKenzie, 1997). Steps in the model include: Questioning (reframing research topics as problems to solve: "How might we restore the salmon harvest?"); Planning (consideration of the best and most reliable sources and how to store information retrieved); Gathering (making relevance judgments and structuring the information found as an ongoing activity); Sorting and Sifting (the "systematic scanning and organizing of data" to find "that which is most likely to contribute to 'insight' "); Synthesizing (arranging and rearranging information "until some kind of picture begin[s] to emerge"); Evaluating (deciding if more information is needed to answer the questions); and Reporting (creating the finished projects). McKenzie writes:

> As multimedia presentation software becomes readily available to our schools and our students, we are seeing movement toward persuasive presentations. The research team, charged with making a decision or creating a solution, reports its findings and its recommendations to an audience of decision-makers (simulated or real).

The Atlantic Model

The Atlantic model was created to include elements involved in the research process, including cognitive skills (critical thinking, creative thinking, problem solving), communication (reading, viewing, writing, representing, speaking, and listening), scientific method (proposing and testing hypotheses, experimenting), library and research skills, and technological skills. The model is unusual because it specifically includes the need for students to develop visual and media literacy skills within the framework of the research process. Stages in the model include: Planning, Gathering Information, Interacting with Information, Organizing Information, Creating New Information, Sharing and Presenting Information, Assessment, and Evaluation.

The basic Atlantic model has been "adapted for each of the 'keystage' levels in our public education in Atlantic Canada" (Prince Edward Island Department of Education, n.d.). The approach and sophistication level for instruction and resource-based activities provide for a range of ability and skill levels in response to developmental levels of students as they mature. Thus separate frameworks for instruction and assessment are created for grades 1–3, 5–6, 7–9, and 10–12, and are themselves tied to learning outcomes in the Atlantic Canadian Language Arts Curriculum. These outcomes are "descriptors of students' information literacy (their knowledge, skills, attitudes)." The complete program provides suggested strategies to help students organize, access, evaluate, use, and synthesize information as well as rubrics for assessing each skill and subskill. "It is important to remember that learning centres or stations that introduce skills and strategies only from the first two or three stages of the information process will not adequately or fully develop students' information literacy."

Gawith's (2002) extensive review of the literature across Western countries indicates that students worldwide experience the same difficulties. In brief, they encounter problems in investigating topics, creating research questions, determining relevance of information, interpreting information, and applying critical thinking skills. The result is that they tend to have little personal investment in the research assignments and approach research projects with little enthusiasm. The fact that these obtain across time (Gawith reviewed literature throughout the 20th century) and context is cold comfort to those for whom school research tasks are a primary mode of instruction.

Her conclusions and practitioner testimonials in the work of Kuhlthau, Irving, and others, posit teaching the process of information seeking as a remedy. The fact that both students and classroom teachers need assistance in framing research tasks as well as in engaging in information-seeking is also evident. Gawith makes the point, as has Kuhlthau, that teaching the skills inherent in the process is vital, and projects must be structured in ways that allow this instruction to take place and students to practice these skills. Planning between school librarians and classroom teachers is key. It is also evident that students must have a firm grounding in basic skills to be successful participants in projects that call for sophistication in using advanced technologies and evaluating complex media-based information products. The challenges to successful fulfillment of instructional goals and outcomes are well documented in the research. These are explored more fully in the chapters that follow.

Conclusion

J.O. Carey (1997) has argued that the most appropriate and valuable instructional role that teachers and librarians can have in creating students capable of lifelong learning is to offer students an array of models and strategies so that they may construct for themselves a personal approach to solving information problems. Indeed, Jacobson and Ignacio (1997) have asserted that especially in online environments "librarians and teachers cannot follow a prescribed theoretical model" if they are "to teach students to be effective searchers" (p. 793). Carey has suggested that, instead, teachers should pose for students problem scenarios that have intrinsic interest for learners, then model strategies, facilitate interaction among students as they consider together effective alternatives, and provide "scaffolding" and support as solutions are developed.

Taken together, the models reviewed in this chapter and in Chapter 3 offer a variety of attractive alternatives for librarians to suggest when they meet with teachers to collaborate on plans for research activities, and they provide a rich array of tools upon which librarians can draw in assisting students to become independent learners. It is evident from this review that the models vary in emphasis, scope, and complexity. However, each one "assumes learning as an active and creative process, and each promotes the development of critical thinking skills" (N.P. Thomas, 2000a, p. 1). Considering these models as alternatives to framing student research is one way teachers and librarians can avoid applying a "one-size-fits-all" approach to instruction. There may be generic models, but as Chelton (conversation with author, August 24, 1997) reminds us, there are no generic kids.

Notes

1. Originally, Dewey set out to classify all knowledge. In so doing, he created a system that would allow resources to be arranged on the library's shelves in ways that maintained what he considered to be the relationships among all elements of that knowledge system. In recent times, the notion of knowledge as a compilation of separate subject domains and the compartmentalization of subjects in this way have been challenged; in many instances, the distinctions between categories have become extremely fuzzy. To attempt to justify the relationships that Dewey established can be difficult given the number of resources that do not fit single categories. Under these circumstances, asking students to memorize Dewey's system seems problematic.

2. The Big6 is copyright © (1987) by Michael B. Eisenberg and Robert E. Berkowitz.

3. Pathways to Knowledge is copyright © 1997 by Follett Software Company.

4. The value of creating a meaningful (to students) product over the information search process is addressed by Oliver and Oliver (1997) in an experimental study involving 11- and 12-year-old schoolchildren. Specifically, the researchers studied the retention of information, "higher levels of knowledge acquisition" (p. 519), and the learning that resulted from a research task when the task itself involved the creation of a meaningful information product. Drawing on Brown et al.'s (1989, cited in Oliver & Oliver) model of situated cognition, the authors argue that "meaningful learning will only take place if it is embedded in the social and physical context within which it will be used" (p. 521), preferably when the contexts have "relevance to the ways the information might be used in later life" (p. 525). While the study results failed to find an increase in comprehension among students in the experimental group, they did note the "minimal cognitive processing" and retention of information when "the focus of research questions was not linked to any context or purpose" (p. 525). "It is evident," state Oliver and Oliver, "that the factor underpinning the achievement gains experienced by the students . . . was the level of engagement and cognitive processing the activity encouraged" (p. 525). Finally, "the context in which the activity was phrased was a significant factor in motivating the students to locate and retrieve information and to read and analyze that information for their own purpose" (p. 525). On the other hand, "the lack of need to use the retrieved information for any purpose other than display for assessment purposes appeared to limit the degree to which the students [in the control group] engaged in reflective and cognitive processing" (p. 525).

5. Flip It! is copyright © 1990 by Alice H. Yucht.

5 Diagnosing Informational and Instructional Needs

Strategies, Theories, and Issues

Teachers are being challenged as never before to tailor instruction to meet the educational needs of individual students and to make sense of their differences in cognitive development and ability, cognitive style, sociocultural context, and language.[1] Diagnosing instructional needs and customizing instructional approaches in this way assume the presence of "reflective practitioners" (Schön, 1983) able to apply educational theory to practice. As has been noted in previous chapters, school library media specialists have proven themselves to be both reflective and resourceful in reframing resource-based "library skills" to focus on information seeking, process learning, critical thinking, and problem solving (Bodi, 1992; Kuhlthau, 1993b).

Diagnosing Instructional Needs of Diverse Learners: Grover's Model

Robert Grover (1993, 1994) has proposed a useful approach to instructional customization that takes account of differences in thinking and learning. In essence, Grover's model reframes the standard reference interview as a "cycle of service" that shifts the focus of attention from the characteristics of the library's resources to a concern for the information seeker and his or her particular information needs. Originally aimed at recreating reference interactions as user-centered activities in public and academic libraries, the model can be used by school librarians in lesson planning because, as Grover suggests (1994), "information skills instruction is an educational service" (p. 176). When employed in this context, the model assumes that lessons proceed within the context of ongoing classroom activity and draws attention to the necessity of coordination and cooperative planning with the classroom teacher.

In creating his model, Grover (1993, 1994) invoked a clinical approach developed by doctors to diagnose, prescribe for, and treat their patients. In Grover's adaptation, the service cycle begins when a librarian and an information seeker first encounter each other and ends with the librarian's evaluation of the services provided. Two elements in the model specifically address accountability issues and deserve special notice. The first is that, from the outset, the librarian assumes responsibility for the successful outcome of the service interaction or information search process. The second is that it is the library user, not the librarian, who determines what constitutes "success" in terms of service or search outcomes.

The four steps in Grover's (1993, 1994) model are diagnosis, prescription, treatment, and evaluation (see Figure 5.1). At *diagnosis*, the information provider must inquire into the what?, where?, and when? of the user's information topic or need. However, the central question to be answered is "who?" According to Grover, factors to consider include the individual's literacy level, developmental level, cognitive style, worldview, format preference, culture, and technological skills. Age, gender, communication style, and English-language proficiency may also be germane at the diagnosis phase. This information is then used in the second or *prescription* stage of the model in determining the relevance and appropriateness of specific resources (available in the collection, online, or in another library) that will meet the user's need.

The information seeker and the resources identified by the librarian are brought together at the *treatment* stage of the cycle; at *evaluation*, the librarian assesses the service process in light of the user's satisfaction with the resources provided. The essential questions to be answered at evaluation, however, relate to the information need initially expressed: Has the user's need been met? Has the user's problem been resolved? If the answer to these questions is no, the process begins over again and is repeated until the user is satisfied.

When applied in a school context, diagnosis must involve initial assessments of a

Figure 5.1
Grover's (1993, 1994) Model for Diagnosing Information Needs

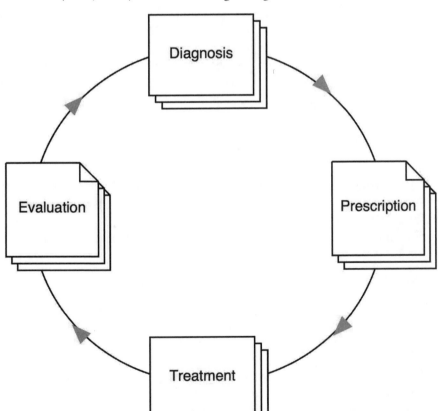

student's reading level, prior knowledge of the topic or subject, and preferred learning style, in addition to the other factors listed above (Grover, 1994). Based on this initial assessment, the library media specialist can create lessons that not only address specific curricular objectives and standards but will also meet the instructional needs and preferences of individual students. The implementation of the lesson corresponds with the treatment stage of Grover's model. Evaluating the outcomes of instruction concludes the cycle; at this stage, the library media specialist and teacher can assess student learning in relation to the objectives established earlier. This assessment can then serve as a basis upon which to plan further activities.

Student progress and learning can be assessed through observation; interviewing; student journals or learning diaries; portfolios; student projects; paper-and-pencil tests; and teacher, peer, and self-evaluations. In the event that assessment measures show that objectives have not been met nor skills learned, a new round or rounds of planning, instruction, and assessment can be carried out until such time as students achieve mastery. In sum, Grover (1994) proposes *diagnose, design, teach, assess, reteach*, and *reassess* as steps in an instructional adaptation of his service cycle.

Individual Differences: Approaches and Strategies

In addition to conceptualizing reference services and lesson planning in useful ways, Grover's (1993, 1994) model invites library media specialists to select and apply a variety of theoretical frameworks in creating "best fit" instructional strategies for their students. There are, of course, many ways to individualize instruction. In the LIS research literature, individual differences have frequently been viewed in terms of "user needs" and information-seeking behaviors. Within the educational literature, differences have been identified related to psychology, cognitive development, and learning styles. Research in sociology, communication, and other disciplines suggests worldview, culture, socioeconomic status, and gender as foundations of difference. Understanding each of these dimensions can help library media specialists design effective learning sessions. In a very real sense, they also reveal the layers of complexity embedded within activities that may appear, on the surface, to be straightforward and unproblematic.

Individual Differences: The Conceptualization of "Needs"

A useful place to begin an examination of approaches to library and information skills instruction is a discussion of the idea of information needs. Theorists in LIS and communication have made major contributions to our understanding of needs as an important aspect of information behavior. On the other hand, Abraham Maslow (1970) has framed the concept of "needs" in psychological and humanistic terms.

Taylor's Levels

In one of the foundational articles in the literature of LIS, Taylor (1968) explored the process through which information *needs* of users are transformed into the kinds of questions or *queries* that can be successfully addressed in a library setting. To this end, Taylor conceptualized information needs as a set of hierarchically arranged levels, based on the ability of the information seeker to express the need and the clarity of that expression. According to this taxonomy, Taylor identified as *visceral* those needs that are unexpressed and inexpressible; needs at this level may be experienced simply as a sense of uneasiness or dissatisfaction with a situation. In the event that the feelings persist, they will eventually come to the surface; needs at this level Taylor identified as *conscious*. Users with conscious needs can articulate or talk about them and relate them in a general way to specific subjects, topics, or situations (e.g., "I need information about . . ."). As the need becomes clearer in the user's mind, it becomes more focused and can be *formalized* as a rational statement or a specific question (e.g., "I need specific information on . . ."). Once the information need can be stated in this way, it can be reformulated or *compromised* into vocabulary (e.g., key words, LC subject headings) to which an information system can respond. Taylor's model is useful in that it raises awareness of the difficulties users may experience in expressing their needs in a library setting. At the same time, it suggests that librarians have a role to play and expertise to offer in helping users articulate their needs, especially at formalized and compromised levels. In a very real sense, the traditional reference interview was an acknowledgment of and framework for this role.

Belkin's Information Problems: Anomalous States of Knowledge (ASKs)

For Belkin and his colleagues (Belkin, 1980; Belkin, Oddy, & Brooks, 1982a, 1982b), the information problems that individuals experience are best described as *anomalous states of knowledge* (ASKs). An information science theorist interested in the design of electronic information retrieval systems, Belkin argues that information needs can more usefully be addressed if they are considered information "problems." These problems arise whenever a person realizes that "his or her state of knowledge" is not sufficient in quantity or quality to make a decision or reach a goal. The problem this poses for the information seeker is that the information necessary "to resolve the anomaly" (Belkin, 1978, quoted in Dervin & Nilan, 1986, p. 13) may not be known. As it is difficult for people to request assistance when they themselves are unsure what it is they are seeking, Belkin suggests asking users to describe what they do know about the topic or situation to determine what is "missing." In this way, it may be possible for the information provider to address the need behind the unarticulated question.

Dervin: Information Seeking as Sense-Making

One of the first theorists to introduce the idea of customized services as a goal for reference librarians was Brenda Dervin (1983, 1989). A communication scholar, Dervin sees information seeking as sense-making. Within this framework, information seeking is initiated when individuals encounter gaps in their knowledge sufficient to impede, prevent, or stop their progress through time and space (see Figure 5.2). These gaps may be perceived as dilemmas, confusions, or uncertainties of the sort that people face as a part of daily life. The "sense" or understandings that they ultimately construct from the information they obtain provide the "bridges" that enable them to proceed with their activities or decision making.[2]

In Dervin's view, what people require when they find themselves stuck in an information gap is personalized information based on their interests, their views of the problem, and whatever barriers they expect to encounter. As information problems do not arise in a vacuum but are tied to situations in which people find themselves, Dervin suggests that librarians create and pose one or a series of neutral questions (Dervin & Dewdney, 1986). Neutral questions are a subset of open-ended questions. The librarian's use of neutral questions can provide a framework, structure, and focus for the

Figure 5.2
Dervin's (1983) Situation-Gaps-Uses Model

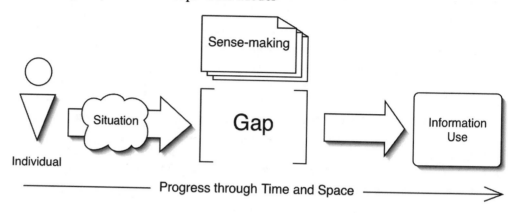

articulation of information needs while allowing information seekers to describe their situations, identify their knowledge gaps, and discuss their intended uses for the information sought in their own words. In this way, librarians come to understand the information need from the point of view of the information seeker.

Maslow's Hierarchy of Needs

Abraham Maslow (1908–1970) conceptualized individual needs as physiological and psychological or "human" rather than informational. In Maslow's (1970) model, needs are ranked hierarchically, with the physiological and physical needs at the base or bottom levels and self-actualization at the highest or top level. Originally, Maslow posited only five levels of needs; later he added two dimensions to self-actualization: the need to know and the need for beauty and order. Maslow holds that failure to have needs met at any of the first four (deficit) levels compromises an individual's successful achievement or fulfillment of needs at higher levels (see Figure 5.3).

The lowest or base level of needs comprises those *physiological* elements that support and sustain life: the need for food, water, rest, warmth, and shelter. Needs at the next higher level involve personal *safety* issues, including the needs for environmental and personal stability and physical and psychological *security*. At a third level are *love and belonging* needs, which are fulfilled in family relationships, friendships, and acceptance by one's peers. *Esteem* needs occupy a fourth level and are realized in acknowledgments of our personal competence by others and feelings of self-respect and self-worth. *Self-actualization* needs arise in feelings of self-acceptance and frequently are expressed in self-enhancement activities and activities that allow the exploration of personal values. The *need to know* and the *need for beauty and order* often translate into love of learning and the pursuit of personal interests, while the need for beauty is often realized in art appreciation, literature, and music. Maslow conceptualized this final state as episodic rather than static and characterized by peak experiences of creativity, spontaneity, happiness, and the fulfillment of potential that punctuate our existence. Maslow's hierarchy of needs makes acutely apparent the reasons why a hungry child may not demonstrate much intellectual curiosity, or why one who has been belittled at home, or is worrying about the acceptance of peers at school, may not take an interest in abstract notions of beauty or justice. Comer (2001) acknowledged the continuing value of understanding children's needs in school settings. "Despite

Figure 5.3
Maslow's (1970) Hierarchy of Human Needs

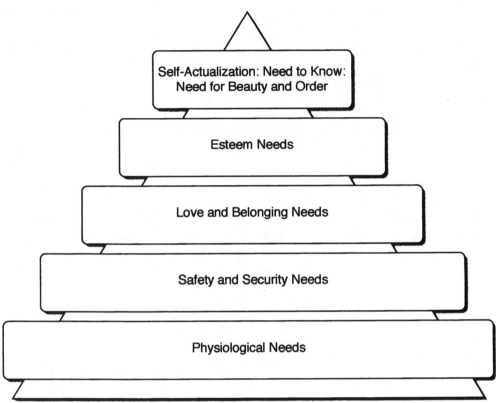

massive and rapid scientific, technological, and social change," Comer writes, "children have the same needs they always did: They must be protected and their development must be guided and supported by the people around them. They cannot rear themselves."

Individual Differences Related to Theories of Cognitive Development and Cognition

Although, as Kuhlthau (1993b) argues, information seeking and learning from information have behavioral and affective as well as cognitive dimensions, the primary concern of information models in LIS is on children's capacity to think critically. For this reason, Grover (1993) and others recommend that library media specialists consider theories of learning as they plan for library skills instruction to meet the educational needs of individual students and groups of students. Of particular value in this regard are the frameworks provided by theorists Jean Piaget (Inhelder & Piaget, 1958) and Benjamin Bloom (1956).[3]

Piaget's Theory of Cognitive Development

Piaget (Inhelder & Piaget, 1958) believed that cognitive development is dependent on physical maturation and interaction with the environment and proceeds for all children according to an orderly succession of learning states. Within Piaget's framework (see

Figure 5.4), learning structures or schemata develop in response to the child's concrete experience of his or her world and are extended with each new experience. The mechanisms of learning involve accommodation and assimilation. Accommodation involves modification of schemata in response to new information. Assimilation is the integration of new knowledge into what is already known. Although Piaget regarded the developmental stages as invariant, he acknowledged that children pass through them at different chronological ages and at different rates.

Piaget (Inhelder & Piaget, 1958) described the development of children's intellectual skills or "mental operations" as a progression of accomplishments related to perception (the ability to detect and organize information through the senses), memory (the storage and retrieval of information), reasoning (the ability to use knowledge to make inferences and draw conclusions), reflection (the ability to evaluate the quality of ideas), and insight (the ability to see patterns and to recognize and understand relationships among ideas). As they grow biologically, children move from a sensory stage, where learning is accomplished through direct experience and the physical manipulation of physical objects in an egocentric universe, to a state of formal thinking wherein a child is able to consider perspectives different from his or her own and to do mentally (or learn by thinking) what as a younger child he or she had to do physically (or by doing).

Figure 5.4
Piaget's (Inhelder & Piaget, 1958) Stages in Cognitive Development

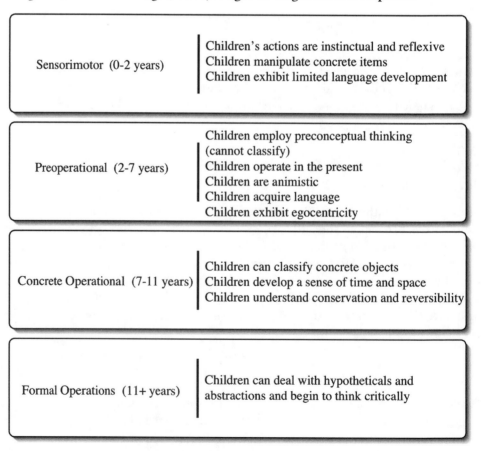

During the *sensorimotor* stage, the largely reflexive behavior of the newborn progresses to include responses to observed objects and the differentiation of self and other. Children at this stage become increasingly able to explore the world through their senses and begin to learn language. During the *pre-operational* stage, language development continues, and children grow in their ability to classify or group objects. Preoperational children are egocentric, however, seeing everything from their own points of view. They learn by imitating behavior they observe in others, and they are very busy exploring the environment. During the *concrete* operational stage, children continue to learn through the manipulation of tangible objects; but they also begin to develop a sense of time, and their thinking becomes increasingly logical. They begin to understand cause-and-effect relationships and can classify objects based on more than one characteristic. As their cognitive "operations" become increasingly "formal," children learn to take the point of view of others and to think abstractly and critically. It is at this stage that they begin to consider a number of solutions in solving a problem and develop the capacity to compare alternatives and consider hypotheses. As *formal* thinkers, children are able to consider their own lives from different perspectives and to think about and evaluate their own thinking.

Bloom's Taxonomy

Whereas Piaget considered the development of thinking skills as maturational, Benjamin Bloom (1956) proposed a taxonomy of mental activities, independent of physical development, which ranked thinking tasks on the basis of mental complexity or cognitive load. These levels are summarized in Figure 5.5. At the basic or beginning level, Bloom ranked *recognition*. As explained by Bloom, thinking at the level of recognition allows an individual to distinguish one entity from another and to give the entities names. Thinking at the level of *knowledge* constitutes the ability to recall information or report facts. At the next level, *comprehension*, thinking is described as an understanding of concepts. At the fourth level, *application*, thinkers are able to take what is known or has been learned in one situation and use it to solve problems in a variety of situations. *Analysis* is the ability to look at a whole by examining its constituent parts, while *synthesis* is the ability to construct new knowledge or new understandings out of disparate ideas or facts. At the highest level, *evaluation*, thinkers are able to make judgments regarding the value of an idea, an activity, or a project. "In this model," as Fitzgerald (1999) notes, "each skill potentially exercises all of the ones below it in the hierarchy."

Individual Differences: Exceptional Students

An important difference to be accounted for within the context of information-seeking and information skills instruction relates to cognitive, physical, or sensory ability levels of students in contemporary classrooms. It is estimated that 10 percent of American students receive some sort of "special education" support for conditions that include mental retardation, visual or hearing impairment, chronic illness, speech pathologies, and learning disabilities of various kinds. Since the mid-1970s when Congress passed the Education of All Handicapped Children Act (Public Law 94-142) (amended in 1986 by Public Law 99-457) and the Individuals with Disabilities Education Act (IDEA) (Public Law 101-476) in 1990, providing for children with special needs has been a mandate for public education. In effect, these laws required schools to create instruction for children with disabilities in the least restrictive environment possible

Figure 5.5
Bloom's (1956) Taxonomy

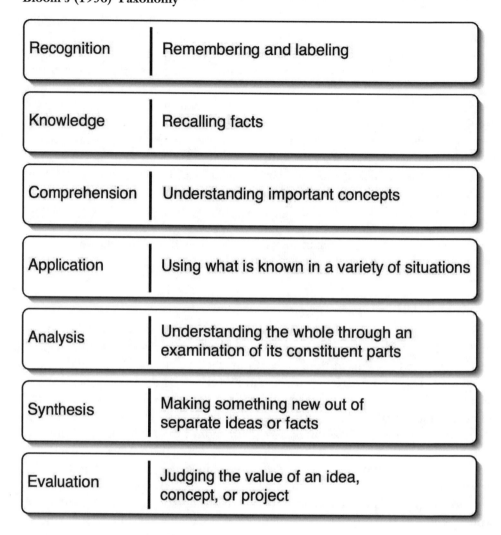

Recognition	Remembering and labeling
Knowledge	Recalling facts
Comprehension	Understanding important concepts
Application	Using what is known in a variety of situations
Analysis	Understanding the whole through an examination of its constituent parts
Synthesis	Making something new out of separate ideas or facts
Evaluation	Judging the value of an idea, concept, or project

in accordance with the IEP (Individualized Education Program) created for each exceptional learner. This practice assumes that each adult with whom the child interacts within the school setting has an opportunity to help structure the child's educational experience.

Two approaches used to structure education for children with disabling conditions are mainstreaming and inclusion. Mainstreamed youngsters spend a portion of the school day in a regular classroom. Inclusion provides all children an opportunity to have their instructional needs met within the regular classroom regardless of disabling conditions. Inclusion presupposes that special needs students may receive support within that setting. Research indicates that the mainstreaming/inclusion of exceptional students results in an improvement in student performance where instruction is tailored to the cognitive and social needs of these students and cooperative learning techniques (peer tutoring, learning buddies) and technology are part of the instructional repertoire (Slavin, 1990).

Callison's (1990) review of the research literature in school librarianship and special needs children in the early 1990s acknowledged a number of unpublished Ph.D.

dissertations that dealt with the collections for special needs students (Davie, 1978; Vinson, 1983), and practice and perceptions of school librarians with regard to exceptional students (Buckley, 1978). At that time, Callison called for increased attention in this area of school librarianship. While there have been a number of practice-based articles and books (e.g., Wesson & Keefe's *Serving Special Needs Students in the School Library Media Center*, 1995) that contribute to our ability to meet the special needs of exceptional students within the context of library and information literacy instruction, research studies have been rare. Much work needs to be done to support library media specialists and students in this important aspect of library service.

Individual Differences Related to Theories of Cognitive Processing

While it is useful to consider thinking in terms of developmental stages and complexity levels, approaches that focus on styles of learning and knowing can improve instruction by helping library media specialists tailor activities to take advantage of students' preferences, "potentials," and strengths. The inclusion of alternative ways of knowing and being in the world (McCarthy, 1996) within curricular assignments also raises awareness and appreciation of the many kinds of intellectual gifts that students possess, while honoring differences in ways that enhance both the learning and the learner. The following sections consider cognitive diversity in terms of learning styles (Kolb, 1983), problem-solving skills (Pask, 1972, 1975), hemisphericity (Bogen, 1969; Buzan, 1991); and multiple intelligences (Gardner, 1996, 1999b).

Kolb's Learning Modes

Kolb's (1983) theory of learning styles is based on the work of the Swiss psychologist and psychoanalyst Carl Jung (1875–1961), who theorized that people function in the world in four different ways: by thinking and reasoning; by feeling and relating; by perceiving and sensing; and by intuiting and imagining. As interpreted by Kolb, the ways in which people implement these "vantage points of human consciousness" (McCarthy, 1996, p. 47) create for them individual patterns or "modes" of thinking. There are no age levels attached to these different patterns of functioning, and there is no intimation that one way of thinking is better than another. For this reason, Kolb's theory is considered "experiential" rather than "developmental."

According to Kolb, every person has the capacity to function in all four ways. However, individuals develop preferences for one mode over the others and find operating in that mode entirely natural. Indeed, when individuals are asked to think outside their preferred style, Kolb believes they have to work harder to make sense of the learning task at hand. On the other hand, many individuals have the cognitive flexibility to use alternate modes depending on the subject, the situation, or the level of stress. Kolb labeled the four different ways of learning or "modes" as: concrete experience, reflective observation, abstract conceptualization, and active experimentation (Figure 5.6). Figure 5.7, which is based on Kolb's theory, shows the relationship of the modes to one another. Here, ways of thinking and learning are represented as two continua of experience. The horizontal axis extending from action (doing) to reflection (watching) represents how learners process information; the vertical axis, extending from concrete (sensing and feeling intuitively) to abstract (analyzing and reasoning conceptually), represents how learners perceive reality. Kolb maintains that

Figure 5.6
Kolb's (1983) Learning Modes

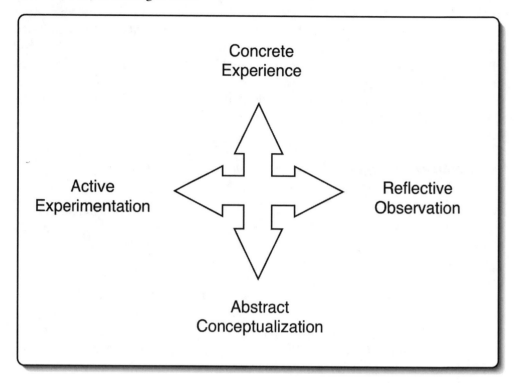

Figure 5.7
Kolb's (1983) Approaches to Learning

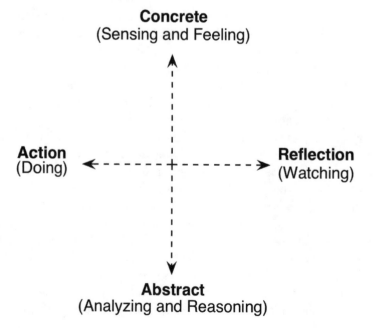

the intersection of the two continua not only defines four distinct learning abilities but also creates a four-step cycle of learning (see Figure 5.8). Kolb argues that learning can begin in any of the steps.

In Kolb's view, *concrete experiencers* enjoy problem solving in real-world situations, and they tend to personalize experience, emphasize feeling rather than thinking, rely on intuition, and enjoy creative approaches to decision making. People who prefer this approach tend to relate well to others and enjoy working under flexible as opposed to highly structured conditions. Kolb's *reflective observers* like to learn by watching others and observing situations and events. Individuals who take this approach to learning are thoughtful rather than pragmatic, frequently seeking understanding, meanings, and truth rather than "what works." Reflective observers prefer contemplation to action in problem solving, and they frequently excel at being able to see the implications of situations or actions. Reflective observers are self-reliant, preferring to work by themselves and depending on their own judgment rather than the opinions of others when making decisions. An *abstract conceptualizer's* mode of learning emphasizes logic and thinking rather than feeling, favors analysis and quantification types of activities, and approaches problem solving in scientific and systematic ways. These kinds of learners are often task oriented and highly productive. Finally, Kolb's *active experimenters* learn by doing and favor hands-on activities that allow them to use the ideas and theories they encounter for practical tasks and pragmatic problem solving. Active experimenters are often risk-takers and change agents, and since they are often results-oriented, they enjoy setting goals and completing projects. Kolb and Fry (1975) argue that effective learners possess all four learning modes to some degree.

Figure 5.8
Kolb's (1983) 4-Step Cycle of Learning

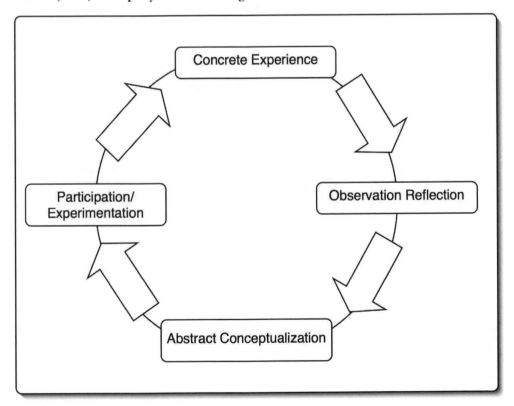

Few learners actually exhibit the "ideal" behaviors implied in Kolb's (1983) model, tending instead, "to develop [an] orientation to . . . one of the poles of each dimension" (E. Smith, 2001). To take this into account, Kolb and Fry (1975) acknowledge the existence of four learning styles (see Figure 5.9), which mark positions people can take between concrete and abstract thinking and between action and observation. In brief, these characterizations describe four ways in which people like to learn. *Convergers* are pragmatists who combine active experimentation with an ability to think abstractly. *Divergers* are watchers who enjoy learning through observing real-world activities. *Assimilators* are thinkers who learn best through reflecting on abstract concepts, while *accommodators* like to learn by doing.

While many educators acknowledge the value of Kolb's models to the creation of instructional strategies, critics have pointed to a lack of research verification for the theory itself. In addition, they argue that the model fails to account for individual motivation, cultural characteristics, aspects of the task, and contextual differences experienced by specific learners. Dunn, Beasley, and Buchanan (1994) have reviewed the educational literature on learning styles and achievement and assert that "most students can learn anything when . . . they are interested in the topic; begin learning with their preferred processing style"; receive reinforcement through their "secondary or tertiary modality"; and "apply new information" to the development of "a new instructional service" such as the creation of a game, play, poem, or "set of task cards" (p. 12). Still, Kolb has contributed a great deal to our understanding of the very real differences that exist in the ways people learn.

Figure 5.9
Kolb's (Kolb & Fry, 1975) Four Learning Styles

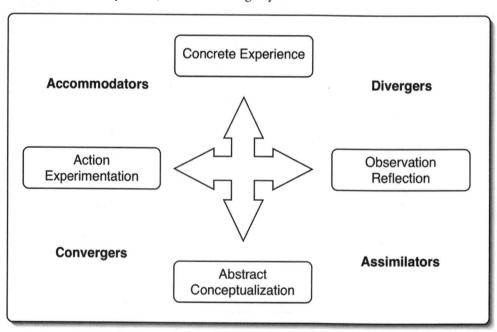

Pask's Holistic and Serialistic Problem Solvers

Pask (Pask & Scott, 1972) construes differences in thinking and learning in terms of problem-solving orientations. In brief, Pask suggests that people prefer to think holistically or serially when considering information to resolve an issue or dilemma. Holists take a global view of a problem, seeking to understand "the whole" and how a problem may be linked to other problems or topics. As information seekers, holists are top-down processors, who survey systematically all possible information resources and then examine each in turn (Eisenberg & Berkowitz, 1990). Holists tend to thrive on complexity and enjoy hypothesizing. Serialists, on the other hand, reach understanding through an orderly process of sequential steps, identifying constituent elements and focusing on specific details. These learners favor simple and straightforward solutions to problems they face. As information seekers, serialists may find and use resources in a linear fashion, viewing a succession of items and quitting when they perceive that they have found a sufficient number.

Individual Differences Related to Cerebral Laterality and Multiple Intelligences

A number of learning theorists consider structures in the brain the foundation of differences in thinking and learning. Major frameworks anchored in physiology include cerebral laterality theory and split-brain theory, left-brain/right-brain dominance theory (Bogen, 1969; Buzan, 1991), and multiple intelligences theory (Gardner, 1983, 1996, 1999a).

Theories of difference involving left-brain and right-brain orientation are anchored to scientific evidence that locates mental functions and patterns of cognitive activity within specific areas of the left and right hemispheres of the brain. The two sides of the brain work together to perform mental tasks, "shifting back and forth" (Gedeon, 2000, p. 260), depending on the skills required to complete the task at hand. Pathologists and neurologists who were treating patients who had sustained brain injuries first posited the theory of cerebral laterality in the 19th century. Twentieth-century advances in medicine and neurology allowed researchers to observe and study the brains of normal people as well as "split-brain" patients who, from injury or surgery, have lost function of the corpus callosum, a band of tissue that links the two hemispheres. Stated briefly, split-brain theory recognizes that for most right-handed people the left side of the brain is responsible for analytical tasks, separating a whole into its constituent parts. The left brain thinks logically, rationally, and sequentially. Verbal and computational skills are also considered left-brain functions in these individuals. By the same token, the right brain manifests abilities to integrate elements into a whole, to find patterns and relationships, and to perform spatial and visual tasks. Aesthetics and intuition are considered right-brain activities, as are the abilities to recognize faces and remember tunes.

Brain or cerebral dominance theory holds that the left side of the brain is the leading or dominant hemisphere because it controls language and speech (Springer & Deutsch, 1993). However, Gedeon (2000) explains the theory of brain dominance in this way: "As one grows intellectually, tendencies develop for hemisphere preference. These tendencies, influenced by an assortment of social and genetic considerations, generally become more entrenched with maturation" (p. 260). Although the preference of one hemisphere over the other can be very strong, Gedeon cites Johnson and Daumer (1993) in suggesting that "it is possible to cultivate use of the less dominant hemisphere." Psychopathologists have noted the relationship between hemisphere dominance and illnesses such as schizophrenia and manic depression.

Recent research in brain function recognizes hemisphericity as it is related to the task, to the individual, and to culture. Task hemisphericity recognizes the specialization of functions within areas of the brain. Individual hemisphericity relates to an individual's preference in performing a specific task. Cultural hemisphericity acknowledges cultural preferences in thinking styles that typify specific groups (H. Gordon, 1996). While it is safe to say that the complexities of brain functioning are masked in models that sort functions into a neat array of abilities and capacities, the simplicity of such models does assist in making them comprehensible to nonspecialists.

Another cognitive model identifies four learning "modalities": visual, auditory, kinesthetic, and tactile. Characteristics of visual learners include the ability to recognize words by their shape; an interest in visual display, graphics, and media; concentration on faces; the making of lists; and recall of information based on the location of information on a particular page. Auditory learners prefer verbal instructions, class discussions, and talking through problems and issues and can use music and rhythms as mnemonic aids. Storytelling and group work appeal to these learners. Learners who enjoy role-playing, dramatics, and games and find sitting for extended periods a hardship are exhibiting behaviors of kinesthetic learners, while tactile learners use the act of writing—as in note taking or outlining—as an aid to memory and enjoy hands-on kinds of activities.

Gardner's Multiple Intelligences

One of the most influential of the "cognitive theories" in contemporary psychology and education is the theory of multiple intelligences. In *Frames of Mind* (1983), Gardner challenged the contemporary wisdom shared by supporters of Binet's testing methodology that IQ is a genetically based and stable characteristic, retrievable and measurable through an examination of a person's verbal and analytical skills. On the contrary, Gardner defined intelligence as the *ability to solve problems* and *to create intellectual products* that closely reflect skills valued by families and communities that surround the learner. For Gardner (1996), frames of intelligence represent "biological and psychological potentialities"—"relatively autonomous intellectual capacities" that can be "realized to a greater or lesser extent as a consequence of the experiential, cultural, and motivational factors that affect a person" (p. 2).

While acknowledging the impact of social factors on the development of special abilities, Gardner (1999a) limits the designation of "intelligence" to those talents that can be shown to have a biological basis and to meet eight specific criteria. Gardner describes these criteria in this way:

1. Potential isolation by brain damage

2. Existence of savants, prodigies, and other exceptional individuals

3. An identifiable core set of operations—basic kind[s] of information-processing operations or mechanisms that deal with one specific kind of input

4. A distinctive developmental history, along with a definite set of "endstate" performances

5. An evolutionary history and evolutionary plausibility

6. Support from experimental and psychological tasks

7. Support from psychometric findings

8. Susceptibility to encoding from a symbol system.

Gardner originally identified seven intelligences (Lazear, 1991). However, in *Intelligence Reframed: Multiple Intelligences for the 21st Century* (1999a), he proposed the existence of two additional "intelligences": naturalist and existentialist[4] (see Figure 5.10). *Linguistic intelligence* is shared by writers, poets, and debaters, whose verbal gifts and interests in words and grammar make them good readers and articulate communicators. *Musical intelligence*, which emerges earlier in a child's development than other forms, includes the ability to sing, to detect perfect pitch, to discern rhythms, and/or to create original compositions. *Logical-mathematical intelligence* (which is traditionally tested and thought to measure "intelligence") includes the ability to reason and to think through problems in logical and sequential ways. Individuals with *visual-spatial intelligence* possess the ability to visualize patterns, to create maps and diagrams, and to use flow charts. This group would include architects, designers, and artists. According to Gardner's theory, dancers, athletes, actors, and others who can use their bodies in skilled ways, or who have highly developed fine and gross motor skills, exhibit *bodily-kinesthetic intelligence*.

Gardner also identifies self-awareness and sensitivity to others as forms of intelligence. Thus, those with *intrapersonal intelligence* are highly self-reflective and especially good at metacognitive tasks; while those in whom *interpersonal intelligence* is highly developed are especially sensitive to the moods of others and adept at both personal communication and group facilitation processes. *Naturalists* have a highly developed sense of the natural world, abilities that manifest themselves in affinity with the biological sciences as well as in activities such as hunting and farming (Hoerr, 1996); those with "*existential*" intelligence possess the ability to consider those questions that relate to the meaning of life and to the nature of human existence. Although individuals vary to the extent that they exhibit one or several of the intelligences to a high degree, Gardner (1996) asserts that everyone possesses some ability in each of the "intelligence" areas and that these are potentialities that can be strengthened in children if they are exposed to appropriate educational strategies and support.

While Gardner argues that multiple intelligences theory can be productively used to alter instructional approaches in ways that "reach more students, and give those students the opportunity to demonstrate what they have understood" (p. 3), he does not suggest them as a replacement for curriculum nor a short-cut to learning. The central task for teachers, as Gardner sees it, is to provide support for learners so that they can use their own unique sets of capacities in mastering the tasks and skills that will allow them to succeed as learners in contemporary society.

Individual Differences: Ways of Thinking as Cultural, Social, and Historical Constructs

Many researchers look to culture as a framework for considering individual differences. These scholars believe that ethnicity and culture shape "cognitive development, children's approach to academic tasks and their behavior in traditional academic settings (Hale-Benson, 1982)" (NW Regional Educational Laboratory, 2001). Others have pointed to the impact of social and economic contexts as keys to understanding the different ways that children learn. As will be seen later in this chapter, cultural, social,

Figure 5.10
Gardner's (1999a) Multiple Intelligences

Intelligence	Special Sensitivities and Capacities	Manifestations Applications Performance
Verbal-Linguistic	The sounds and meanings of words, grammatical structure	Writing, journaling spelling, reading poetry, debate, word games, puns, and jokes
Logical-Mathematical	Inductive and deductive reasoning, problem solving, sense of numerical order, discernment of patterns, abstract	Logic, mathematical fluency, scientific projects and activities
Visual-Spatial	Imaging and imagining, mapping and pattern making, visual-spatial relationships	Art, architecture and design, sculpture, wayfinding, photography, filmmaking
Bodily-Kinesthetic	Mimetics, coordination, motor skills, role-playing	Dance, athletics, dramatics
Musical-Rhythmic	Melody, structure and tone, pitch, and rhythm	Composing, music making, singing, humming
Interpersonal	Communication skills, awareness and concern for others	Teaching, parenting, counseling, politics, social engagement
Intrapersonal	Mindfulness, metacognitive awareness, self-awareness, personal understanding	Contemplation, self-reflection
Naturalist	Environmental awareness, biological aptitude, attunement to the natural world, classification of species	Farming, gardening, hunting, biological sciences, outdoor activity
(Existentialist)	Philosophical aptitudes, contemplation of questions related to life's meaning	Philosophical thinking, spirituality

and ethnic dimensions of learning have tremendous implications for teaching and learning in an information skills curriculum.

Differences Related to Worldview

J.A. Anderson (1988) understands differences in thinking and learning as differences in "worldview" and relates these differences to cultural traditions and values, which he characterizes as "Western" and "non-Western." It is well to note at the outset that any general statements made about groups is always tempered with the realization that no group is monolithic—that there are differences among members of any one cultural or ethnic group just as there are between disparate groups in our society.

Among groups Anderson classifies as Western thinkers in the United States are most American males of Anglo-European descent and members of minority groups who have become acculturated into the dominant Anglo-European culture to a high degree. In Anderson's analysis, populations considered non-Western include American Indians and Americans of Mexican, African, Vietnamese, Puerto Rican, Chinese, and Japanese descent, and many Anglo-European females. Anderson frames his comparison of the two groups on a variety of dimensions, involving values, social orientation, and cognitive style; these dimensions are summarized in Table 5.1.

According to Anderson, the differences in worldview he has identified are expressed in the classroom in a number of ways. For example, non-Western thinkers tend to perceive separate elements of a phenomenon as a part of a total picture; for this reason they prefer an overview of a topic or project so that they can see how the subsets or elements are related to each other and to the whole (field-dependent). In addition, they value "affiliation and conformity" over "individuality and competitiveness" (Clark & Halford, 1983, p. 281) and do best on verbal tasks. Hale-Benson (1982, cited in NW Regional Educational Laboratory, 2001) points to African traditions as the wellspring for the importance of personal connections and social interaction in the

Table 5.1
Anderson's (1988) Dimensions of Non-Western and Western Worldviews

Non-Western	Western
• Emphasis on cooperation/group achievement	• Emphasis on individual/competition
• Social orientation	• Task orientation
• Emotionally expressive	• Emotional expressions are limited
• Strong extended family relationships	• Strong nuclear family orientation
• Values harmony with nature	• Values mastery and control of nature
• Time is relative	• Time provides an invariant structure
• Religion permeates culture	• Religion is separate from culture
• Accepts worldviews of others	• Believes Western worldview is superior
• Holistic/relational thinking	• Analytical thinking
• Field-dependent thinking	• Field-independent thinking

learning preferences of many black children. Western thinking, on the other hand, is analytical, with elements perceived as separate from the background or "whole" and distinct from one another (field-independent). Learning that is personally situated and that involves a human aspect is preferred by many non-Western students to the more impersonal, objective, and detached view that typifies the Western approach to topics and subjects. Finally, for many non-Western students, performance in school is influenced by authority figures. This may make them especially sensitive to expressions of confidence and expressions of doubt from teachers, administrators, and other adults in the school environment. By the same token, students whose characteristics represent a Western worldview tend to be more independent and less likely to be affected by the opinions of others.

Claxton (1990) also recognizes the differences between Western and non-Western worldviews, which he characterizes as two distinct "ways of knowing" (p. 7) that have both sociocultural and cognitive dimensions. Echoing Anderson (1988), Claxton characterizes the Western way as intellectual, detached, and analytical; while the non-Western way is affective, relational, and attached. While Claxton believes that most people feel fairly comfortable with the idea of *learning styles* related to cognitive development, discussions of learning differences related to the social, cultural, and ethnic experience of learners tend to make many educators uneasy. In Claxton's view, these educators fear that calling attention to the learning styles of "minority students" will contribute to racial and ethnic stereotyping in ways that undermine demands for educational equity or justify educational "tracking." However, Claxton argues that a teacher's understanding of the instructional needs of individual children can be deepened through an appreciation of the differences created by culture and experience. Indeed, he maintains that as long as educators realize that individual differences within groups negate generalizations across groups, they can employ those approaches to learning "which are highly functional in the [students'] home environment" (Gorden & Allen, 1988, quoted in Claxton, 1990, p. 6) in ways that facilitate their performance at school. Understood in this way, knowledge of learning styles can validate minority students while helping teachers individualize teaching and learning.

Learning Styles Related to Gender

Claxton (1990) notes that the dichotomy between Western and non-Western worldviews also resonates with the work of feminist scholars such as Belenky, Clinchy, Goldberger, and Tarule (1986, cited in Claxton), who have argued, like Anderson (1988), that males and females in Western culture tend to view the world from two disparate perspectives. Belenky et al. characterize these differences as "Separate Knowing," which emphasizes impersonal, rational, and objective perspectives, and "Connected Knowing," which is seen as understanding, subjective, personal, and relational and "requires the learner to see the other person in his or her own context" (Claxton, p. 7).

One of the most outspoken and influential psychologists in the United States is Carol Gilligan, who was among the first to call attention to the fact that the major developmental theorists based their descriptions of human development exclusively on research from which females and female experience had been excluded. Since the appearance of Gilligan's book *In a Different Voice* (1982), many scholars have developed a research interest in the experience of women and girls.

Making Sense of Individual Differences: Implications for Student Research and Information Skills Instruction

While it is useful to consider a range of theories that explain individual difference as separate entities in formulating plans for information literacy skills instruction, it should be remembered that there is considerable overlap between and among the theories presented in this chapter. In order to frame instruction to make the most of what we know about differences, school library media specialists will want to use theories in combination with one another, choosing those that have special relevance depending on the context and the task at hand.

The Information Needs of Children and Youth

Studies by Gross (1995, 1997) and Walter (1994) have used the theoretical frameworks suggested in Taylor (1968), Dervin (1983, 1989), and Maslow (1970) to investigate the information needs of children and their information-seeking behavior. Although historically these topics have received little research attention, these studies offer valuable insights for library professionals in creating educational services for young people. They also draw attention to the problems that information tasks pose for many students.

In her studies on the expression of information needs by school-age children, Gross (1995, 1997) drew on the work of Taylor (1968) and his conceptualization of levels. Her findings suggest that although the ways in which information needs have been understood in the literature of LIS illuminate the evolutionary process through which self-generated questions pass as they move from visceral to compromised levels, the information questions teachers pose for students to answer present entirely different kinds of problems. If, for example, the question the student brings to the librarian is stated unclearly, it may be because the student lacks the background knowledge (possessed, presumably, by the teacher who created the question) to clarify the nature of his or her information need. Under these circumstances, the task of helping the student formalize the need (restate the need as a question) may be extremely difficult, no matter how well or compassionately the librarian conducts the interview. Indeed, the question the student poses when seeking assistance will reflect his or her *interpretation* of the teacher's intent, an interpretation that may or may not reflect the teacher's understanding of the task or question. Obviously, relevance judgments of resources and information provided to answer these kinds of requests are compromised as well. This is particularly true when the information to match the question cannot be found in student-appropriate resources.

Furthermore, as Gross notes, the student's request or question is also interpreted by the librarian, through layers of meaning based on the librarian's prior knowledge of the teacher, the subject, or the assignment. When both the teacher and the assignment are unknown to the library media specialist, and the student's understanding is incomplete, both the librarian and the student will be left to speculate on the teacher's intent.

Gross (1995, 1997) believes that understanding the ways in which a teacher-imposed question differs from a self-generated question will assist school librarians in providing guidance to students. For a start, it demonstrates how sensitive librarians must be to the *possibility* that the students themselves lack an understanding of the very questions they are asking. In her study with elementary school students, Gross found that determining the origins of their requests was not at all straightforward, because the children in the study interpreted even this question in a variety of ways.

The sorts of confusion that assigned questions can engender can be ameliorated to a great extent if the library media specialist and the classroom teacher work together in establishing the assignment objectives and creating the research questions. Another, perhaps better, solution would be to make the students part of decision making, so that the objectives of the assignment are understood by all parties before the library activity actually begins. But even in cases where the questions appear to adults to be clearly and unambiguously stated, the library media specialist must check for student understanding before acceding to requests for help. Indeed, Gross (1995) argues that librarians need to interview "all students who come to the reference desk regardless of whether they are the first, fifth or twentieth person to make that request in a given day" (p. 242).

Whereas Gross's (1995, 1997) research considered children's information seeking and needs related to instruction, Walter's (1994) study was concerned with identifying the information children need for daily living (e.g., personal safety and life choices). Citing the richness of the LIS literature on adults as information seekers and the lack of research on children's information needs, Walter set out to explore this issue. At the outset, she made two assumptions: first, that like adults, "children have information needs that, if met, would enable them to solve problems and resolve particular difficulties" and second, "that children are frequently unaware of their needs" (p. 115).

In the absence of field-tested strategies and guidelines as to how to implement such a study, Walter (1994) organized her research around interviews that she conducted with 25 adults (other than parents) who were involved in working directly with and/or planning services for children. In each case, the adults were asked to discuss what information they thought the children should have, how they thought the children were getting their information, and what information gaps existed for children.

Walter justified her decision to interview adults about children's needs rather than the children themselves because, in many instances, children themselves lack the experience necessary to know that an information need exists. Kuhlthau's (1993b) research confirms that children are often unable to express their needs in ways that will help them initiate the search process, while Moore and St. George's (1991) study demonstrated the problems children have in extracting and using information they find even when the research topics themselves are preselected. "Imagine the obstacles," as Walter directs, "when children must also" (p. 115) initiate information seeking and explain the original information need. It is for this reason that Walter asserts "adults must articulate those needs for them" (p. 113).

Walter's (1994) study revealed that, indeed, school-aged children do have information needs and that many of these needs are not being met. In reviewing the interview data, Walter determined that the articulation of needs closely resembled the hierarchy identified by Maslow (1970). Specifically, Walter found that children's physiological needs include health, hygiene, and disease (AIDS) prevention, substance abuse, and child abuse.

Children's safety needs included information on avoiding crime, safety procedures of various kinds, literacy skills, and traffic laws. Belonging needs identified in the study related to information on interpersonal relationships, multicultural issues, emotional awareness, and recreation. The esteem needs Walter reported included: "multicultural awareness, emotional awareness, social system knowledge (legal, economic, etc.)" (1994, p. 120), as well as information on values and ethics. Finally, at the level of self-actualization, Walter noted children's needs for education, recreation, values and ethics, and "cultural" opportunities related to reading, art, and music.

Sex education was mentioned by so many of the interviewees as being related to "so many different contexts" (p. 122) that Walter considered this an information need at every level except self-actualization.[5] Of interest as well was Walter's finding that adults in the study emphasized physiological and safety needs as being of primary importance for the development of skills necessary for basic survival. They also mentioned the *misinformation* supplied to children through the media and from uninformed or ineffectual caregivers, service providers, and peers as a central problem. Walter identified a number of barriers to children's information seeking; these included inadequate services, absence of adult-child interaction, and ineffective information programs and providers (especially noted were lack of rapport between service providers and children and failure to provide appropriate instructional approaches).

It is significant to note that some adults in Walter's study considered children's needs as relational rather than informational and did not see a role for the library to play in improving the situation. But if, as Walter asserts, all children are "information poor" (p. 126), isn't there a role for library professionals to play in helping children to meet these unmet information needs? Walter, of course, thinks there is.

Although Walter is mainly interested in public library services, school library media specialists, most of whom have direct access to children on a daily basis, are in an excellent position to address these needs. In addition, they can do so through the information skills curriculum. For example, creating "authentic" information tasks directed at addressing the information gaps children have could be easily incorporated into various content or subject areas assigned to meet classroom objectives. In addition, collecting pamphlets, periodicals, and magazines as well as nonprint resources that support such an information-rich and authentic curriculum, and making them easily available to children through the library, the classroom, and wherever children congregate, would serve as well. Although secondary school librarians often provide such pamphlets as a matter of course, the practice has been observed less frequently in elementary school libraries.

Harmon and Bradburn (1988) discuss information needs in terms of kinds of information that adolescents require in completing developmental tasks. Citing the work of Havinghurst (1953) and Abrahamson (1970), these researchers suggest that the needs unique to teenage youth pertain to social and gender identity tasks, the need to establish both emotional and economic independence, intellectual skills and ethical values, life skills, self-control skills, and coping skills. From these tasks, Harmon and Bradburn have identified three categories of needs: research needs (for academic and personal intellectual use), recreational needs (media resources in all formats), and information needs (life skills, coping skills). In their view, a problem with meeting all these information needs is the complexity of the adolescent tasks themselves.[6] It is interesting to note that the information needs Harmon and Bradburn identified in 1988 as needs of adolescents did not include the concerns for survival or personal safety identified by the informants in Walter's (1994) study.

Jonathan Kozol (2000) has written extensively about the needs of children in low-income neighborhoods where deficits in the availability of print resources and access to knowledgeable adults who can stimulate reading interests and guide information seeking is a continuing problem. In discussing the importance of school libraries, Kozol notes that without them the children "who ha[ve] the least to stimulate their reading appetites at home . . . find much less to stir their love of learning in their public schools." He speaks of this kind of deprivation as a form of "theft of stimulation, cognitive excitement, and aesthetic provocation" that is catastrophic. He writes:

> [S]chool libraries developed with the artfulness of skilled librarians—remain the clearest window to a world of noncommercial satisfactions and enticements that most children in poor neighborhoods will ever know. To shut those windows is to close down one more opening to democratic amplitude and one more opportunity for fully realized cultural existence.

(Such an eventuality clearly limits underprivileged children's access to the higher levels of Maslow's hierarchy.)

Neuman and Celano (2001) studied access to print resources in middle- and low-income neighborhoods. In particular, they looked at the nature of all kinds of texts available in each of these environments. Drawing on the work of Rogoff, Bronfenbrenner, McCloud, and others, Neuman and Celano believe such texts "shape children's first literacy experiences." As such, they constitute the very "architecture of every day life," which "embed opportunities for children to learn and develop through observation and apprenticeship" (p. 11). Their intent was to examine "access to literacy as a potential contributing factor for explaining differences in interaction, behaviors, and ultimately achievement for these children" (p. 11).

Particularly germane to some of the issues addressed in this book were Neuman and Celano's (2001) descriptions of the disparities between the school libraries in the neighborhoods included in their study. Chief among the differences were numbers of resources per capita, condition of print collections, availability of computers, presence of a certified library media specialist, and hours of operation. Statistical significance was observed in number and condition of books, number of days open, and availability of computers. School libraries in low-income neighborhoods lacked certified librarians; school librarians in middle-income neighborhoods held master's degrees. Their data suggest that "children who live in already print-rich environments tended to have school libraries that offered more books, more computers for research, better trained librarians with more experience, and more hours to visit during the day" (p. 22).

> **Unfortunately, those children likely to benefit most from school libraries were offered the poorest services, resources, and access on fewer days of the week.**
>
> —Neuman & Celano, 2001

Although clearly family interactions are immensely important to children's access to resources, the larger social setting within which families live exerts tremendous pressures as well.

Pervasive poverty, institutional settings like the workplace, and social welfare systems act as indirect environmental influences on children's interactions. They may affect the physical and emotional resources provided to the child (e.g., stress levels due to lack of work), adult responsiveness, and involvement in daily activities (Hart and Realey, 1995; McLoyd, 1990). (Neuman and Celano, 2001, p. 23)

When it comes to content on the Internet, a Report by the Children's Partnership (Lazarus & Mora, 2000) provides some insights into what children of "underserved Americans" (defined as low-income, rural, limited education, or racial or ethnic minorities) want the Internet to provide. Included on the list were participation and self-expression; high-impact packaging with interactivity; multimedia; and youth-friendly tutorials, easier searching and usability, encouragement, and involvement. The study's finding that "young people instinctively see the Internet as an entertainment source rather than an information source" (p. 21) also presents school librarians with additional considerations in framing an information literacy skills agenda for this new generation of information seekers. Finally, the study found that children as well as adults

> want coaches and mentors to guide them in finding what they want on the Web, suggesting sites or activities to get started, helping use a tutorial and the like. Moreover, they want an environment where they can get literacy support or help with English if they need it. They want to be in a place where others in their community are doing the same thing and where they can count on coaching and support to build their confidence, answer their questions, and guide them in new directions. (p. 21)

As McDonald (1988) noted, the inaccessibility of information is compounded in electronic environments; for this reason, the role of the school library in providing access, instruction, and guidance in information use is crucial to the searching success of today's youngsters.

Information Needs of Children: Access Issues and Media Literacy

In the economic and educational contexts of the 21st century, access to online resources and the expertise to negotiate Internet-based information are seen as basic to success. Although for many middle-class students access to the Internet is no longer problematic, the fact is that for many low-income students it remains a significant challenge. According to Carvin (2000), "[W]hen it comes to age, when it comes to color, when it comes to education and income levels, the Net's not even close to becoming a truly diverse place." Although clearly access to the Internet is not the only issue instructors must consider in helping kids understand the uses of technology and its importance as a tool in information seeking, for many children it remains an important issue.

Two initiatives outside education and LIS research domains contribute interesting and disturbing elements to a discussion of children's access to the Information Highway: The Kids Count (2002) program created by the Annie E. Casey Foundation and the Internet and American Life Project of the Pew Charitable Trusts. These studies support the earlier work of Walter (1994) and Kuhlthau (1993a) on children's needs for information-seeking support and instruction.

Researchers who are considering the digital divide in the United States and its impact on teaching and learning in and out of school have provided some disturbing facts: Ease of access to Internet information and resources depends in large part on race and income. For example, Wilhelm, Carmen, and Reynolds (2002) assert that as of 2002, 84 percent of children living in low-income neighborhoods did not have access to a computer, either at home or at school. What this means is that "children who are already disadvantaged are the least likely to have access to the new technology." The latest statistics appear to show that the digital divide is shrinking, thanks in large measure to the fact that more and more children have access to computers and to the Internet at school. However, "research has shown that the presence of educational resources in the home—including computers—is a strong predictor of academic success in mathematics and science" while home use of computers "is [also] associated with higher test scores in reading" (Wilhelm, Carmen, & Reynolds, 2002). As of 2001, children from upper-income families ($75,000+ per year) were still three times more likely to have computers at home than those in low-income families (less than $15,000). In addition, the use of computers varied, with "low-income children . . . less likely to use their home computers for word processing, school assignments, and other standard software applications and more likely to use them for games." Obviously, access to computers is only part of what is required if narrowing the gap in technology is to be educationally meaningful. It is also disturbing to note that government statistics on Internet access do not reflect Internet access among American Indians. Why has this group been excluded? Lujan (cited in Twist, 2003) asserts that it is because the data is not being collected, even though the government includes this population when it reports on "poverty, and disease, and social deviance." According to Lujan, leaving American Indians out of "the public discourse relating to the digital divide" is "an act of avoidance" that places them "at a further disadvantage in the emerging economy."

In the Pew study of Internet use by students, conducted from November 2001 to February 2002, researchers collected data by surveying 136 middle and high school students and conducting 14 focus groups in 36 schools (55 percent white, 26 percent black or African American, 13 percent Asian, and 6 percent Hispanic and Latino). Of the 200 narratives researchers collected through online solicitation, 85 percent were contributed by white respondents. Follow-up interviews during February and March 2002 were also conducted. Research questions targeted the use of the Internet by student interviewees and their contemporaries.

Many of the questions asked and answered by children in the study concerned questions of access and connectivity within the public schools. Of interest to school librarians within the context of student-articulated information needs were findings that indicated that students in the study themselves recognized a need for instruction on more effective use of the Internet. Among topics students specifically mentioned were computer skills, including keyboarding; instruction in effective strategies for Internet surfing, use of search engines, and maintaining security and privacy online; and information on the dynamics of computer viruses (how they are contracted and how they spread). Interestingly, students also expressed a desire for the development of more engaging assignments. Contemporary research indicates that technological training for teachers demanded in the high-tech environments available at least in some schools is not sufficient to meet the needs of today's Internet savvy youngsters. When one considers the research finding that two thirds of American educators do not feel competent to integrate technology into the curriculum, that an insufficient percentage of technology budgets are spent on teacher training (3 percent as opposed to the 30 percent recommended), and that 40 percent of all teachers lack technology training, a role for technologically savvy school librarians seems inevitable.

Understanding Cognitive Development: Implications for Instruction

The theories presented in the work of Piaget (Inhelder & Piaget, 1958) and Bloom (1956) have important implications for media specialists in crafting information skills programs and tasks. For example, many of the process models created to guide in seeking information and student research are highly sensitive to students' cognitive levels as described by Piaget. That is, most require students to examine information sources critically and to evaluate their own thinking as well as their own projects. In assigning research tasks, library media specialists need to be especially concerned that the complexities of their assignments do not exceed a child's present level of cognitive functioning to the extent that failure results. Furthermore, knowledge of developmental levels can assist school librarians in diagnosing instructional needs and in planning the kinds of scaffolding activities that will support the children in doing with assistance what cannot be managed by the child acting alone.[7]

By the same token, Bloom's (1956) taxonomy provides an extremely useful tool to use when considering the levels of thinking required to carry out instructional tasks and activities of any kind. Indeed, taking the taxonomy into account is especially important in implementing a successful information skills curriculum, as the processes involved in information searching and the creation of research projects are specifically intended to provide opportunities for students to develop and practice critical thinking skills. In fact, assignments that require students to explore a topic, construct research questions, narrow a topic, create a focus, and evaluate resources as well as the process and its outcomes demand that students operate at the highest levels of Bloom's taxonomy: analysis, synthesis, and evaluation.

Bloom, Englehart, Furst, Hill, and Krathwohl (1956, cited in Fitzgerald, 1999) describe evaluation as:

> the making of judgments about the value, for some purpose, of ideas, works, solutions, methods, material, etc. It involves the use of criteria as well as standards for appraising the extent to which particulars are accurate, effective, economical, or satisfying. The judgments may be either quantitative or qualitative, and the criteria may be either those determined by the student or those which are given to him [*sic*]. (p. 185)

Within the context of an information search task, the criteria relevant to evaluation of information "might include aspects of information quality such as objective content, sufficient depth, and clear articulation (Eisenberg and Small, 1993; Taylor, 1986)" (Fitzgerald, 1999).

Fitzgerald's (1999) study highlights the difficulty many students have in evaluating information. Her extensive literature review led her to view evaluation in terms of the many subtasks involved. These include goals of the task, a disposition to undertake the problem, some aspect of the information that "signals" a problem with the information (surprise, puzzlement, incomprehensibility, lack of clarity), and deliberation. The last involves a process of thinking through the information in a logical way and then making a decision as to its value or truth or some action to be taken as a result of the information found. Knowledge of the domain, knowledge of the processes of decision making, the context, culture, amount of time to devote, the nature of the problem, the willingness to expend effort, the level of support ("instruction, practice, and cues"), developmental level, and educational (or reading comprehension) level all have a bearing on a child's ability to evaluate information. For example, children have a tendency to trust adults or authority figures, believe " 'there is an absolute correspondence between what is seen or perceived and what is' (pp. 47–48)" (King & Kitchener, 1994, quoted in Fitzgerald 1999), and may lack the verbal skills essential in analyzing texts.

It is evident from the research that unless prompted to look for problems with an information source in advance, "elementary school-aged children are particularly unlikely to evaluate spontaneously (Markman, 1979, cited in Fitzgerald). Studies by McGregor (1994) and Pitts (1994, cited in Fitzgerald) noted the failure of older children to consider the quality of the information they encountered. Carey (1985, cited in Fitzgerald) ascribes this failure to a lack of domain knowledge "rather than an immature way of thinking." Fitzgerald believes that school librarians can play an important role in helping children with evaluation tasks. In addition to noting the fit between children's developmental levels and the cognitive demands of research tasks, school librarians can take account of the research on evaluation by challenging students to think more deeply about information and the information task and create structures to assist children as they learn the important subskills necessary for effective evaluation. School librarians can also call children's attention to the following: the influence that emotion may have on decision making or evaluation, the "flawed reasoning" that can result when they apply their subjective beliefs and biases in making judgments about new information, and the tendency to believe information they encounter first or last or that supports rather than challenges beliefs they already hold ("confirmatory bias").

Finally, Fitzgerald (1999) makes a case for teaching evaluation within the context of ongoing classroom activities. "Few topics could be more boring or incomprehensible to children than critical thinking or argumentation taught out of context," she writes. "The best approach is to choose a subject area of current controversial interest to the student in a given class and integrate the suggested strategies into a unit about that topic." Teaching strategies (see Table 5.2) Fitzgerald recommends include teaching evaluation strategies one or a few at a time over time, providing specific examples, teaching subskills involved in the evaluation of information, providing practice with well-defined and ill-defined problems, clarifying the biases that might be involved in information texts, providing practice in arguing both sides of controversial questions, assigning a variety of research tasks on a regular basis, and involving children in the production of a variety of media.

It is worth noting that when students are sent to the library to look up "facts" and report them back to the classroom, when they are required to participate in a scavenger hunt, or when they are given skills worksheets that essentially require them to "fill in the blanks" (e.g., questions that ask what, list, name, define, describe), they are seldom being asked to operate above the knowledge or recall level. Although this level of thinking may be entirely appropriate for the very youngest information seekers, it does little to extend the thinking and learning capacities of older children and youth, nor does it prepare students to engage in "authentic" and independent information-seeking

Table 5.2
Fitzgerald's (1999) Strategies for Teaching Evaluation Skills

- Teach a few strategies at a time
- Reinforce learning through repetition and practice over time
- Provide specific examples
- Teach the subskills involved in evaluation tasks
- Use well-defined and ill-defined problems
- Discuss the types of biases that might be encountered
- Practice arguing both sides of controversial topics
- Provide a variety of research opportunities
- Involve children directly in the production of media

activities upon which, as Walter's (1994) research indicates, their survival may well depend.

Learning Styles and Library Skills Instruction

Hensley (1991) has applied Kolb's (1983) model of the four learning modes in the library context, suggesting that reference assistance be provided in ways that reflect the learning style preferences of information seekers. For Kolb's concrete experiencers, librarians might want to provide affirmation for the user's request for assistance and respond to requests in empathetic and personalized ways. As reflective observers enjoy considering alternatives, librarians should be prepared to listen with patience to the students' explanations and thought processes as they work through assignments and projects. As Kolb's abstract conceptualizers often like to work independently, Hensley suggests preparing printed instructions that analyze searching techniques and presenting resource options. In providing personal assistance, Hensley suggests that librarians offer a rationale for suggestions they make and provide a number of alternatives. For active experimenters who enjoy learning by doing and prefer practical and simple explanations, librarians can offer instruction at the same time they demonstrate or present appropriate resources.

In planning instructional interventions and in choosing process models to help guide students in information-seeking activities and research projects, it is important to be sensitive to the different approaches students use in solving real-world problems and to consider allowing students a range of choices. In fact, it is interesting to consider the process models described in Chapters 3 and 4 in relation to preferences for teaching and learning. Indeed, Kuhlthau's (1993a, 1993b) ISP model, which emphasizes reflection and meaning making, Eisenberg and Berkowitz's (1990) Big6 model, which provides a conceptually neat, analytical and scientific emphasis, Stripling and Pitts's (1988) model, which features thinking and reflecting, Joyce and Tallman's (1997) I-Search model, which focuses on the personal experience of the student in determining topic and format for the project as well as in presenting the final project, can be seen to reflect differences in approach similar to the learning modes described by Kolb (1983).

Lesson Planning for Individual Differences

Research in cerebral laterality offers practitioners some suggestions for tailoring instruction to the needs of individual learners as well. As discussed above, left-brain learners tend to think analytically, rationally, logically, and critically; possess special facility in the use of language; prefer verbal and written instructions; like hands-on activities; enjoy learning facts and details; and excel at classifying, comparing, contrasting, and sequencing. They appreciate structure and understand processes best when they are presented in terms of a sequence of orderly steps. Those for whom right-brain functions are dominant tend to think holistically, creatively, and intuitively, rather than analytically, and are especially adept at creating visual images, recognizing patterns, making connections, and pulling ideas together. They enjoy inventing, predicting, and imagining alternatives. Such learners like to use metaphors and are talented at synthesizing activities.

While many people appear to favor one mode over another, some learners manage to integrate both modes when solving problems (Wilkerson & White, 1988). McCarthy (1996) believes that "every learner needs both for the fullest possible understanding of experience" (p. 31), and that training can alter or modify "the tendency to use a particular hemisphere during problem solving" (Wilkerson & White, 1988, p. 358). With this in mind, McCarthy created the 4MAT Learning System, which incorporates elements of cognitive learning style theory (Jung, 1923; Kolb, 1983), and brain research on cerebral laterality and hemispheric dominance (Bogen, 1969; Buzan, 1991). 4MAT calls for the inclusion of a variety of instructional approaches, so that the needs of all students are met in all instructional plans (Hagopian et al., 1996).

In creating a vehicle for the delivery of instruction, 4MAT explicitly tailors the presentation and implementation of the curriculum to the needs of diverse learners by asking teachers to use multiple instructional options and to provide for diversity in the assignments created for students as "proof" of their learning (McCarthy, 1987). Although interest in learning style preferences and hemispheric dominance theory has gained attention and proponents across the educational spectrum, McCarthy's 4MAT Learning System is apparently the only one that translates "the available research into instructional strategies" (Wilkerson & White, 1988, p. 358).

While noting the contribution to thinking that each "brain" makes, McCarthy argues that "every learner needs both for the fullest possible understanding of experience" (1990, p. 31). In addition, there is some research evidence to show that training can alter "the tendency to use a particular hemisphere during problem solving" (Wilkerson & White, 1988, p. 358). "According to Torrance (1981)," for example, "a child's preferred style of learning and thinking can be modified over 6 to 10 weeks (Reynolds & Torrance, 1978)" (p. 358). Within McCarthy's framework, Kolb's divergers are "Type One" or "imaginative" learners; "Type Two" or "analytical learners" are analogous to Kolb's assimilators; McCarthy describes Kolb's convergers as Type Three or "common sense" learners; while Kolb's accommodators are described by McCarthy as Type Four or "dynamic learners."

McCarthy (1987, 1990) has used the knowledge of Jung's (1923) learning modes to create an eight-stage cycle or "wheel" teachers can use to prepare instructional plans applicable to any curricular area or grade level (Wilkerson & White, 1988, p. 358). Briefly stated, lesson plans based on the 4MAT model provide a wheel of activities that are divided into four quadrants. Each quadrant is also divided, in order to provide for both left-brain and right-brain cognitive functioning. By providing activities in each quadrant that reflect right- and left-brain cognitive activity, the "cycle appeals to each learner's most comfortable style in turn, while stretching her or him to function in less comfortable modes" (McCarthy, 1990, p. 33). In this way each student is encouraged to develop "a broader repertoire of problem-solving skills" (Wilkerson & White, 1988, p. 358). In addition, the inclusionary nature of the 4MAT model makes diversity in the classroom an asset for learning rather than an impediment or a deficit.

Thanks in part to its capacity to accommodate diverse learners with a single instructional model and within a single instructional setting, McCarthy's (1990) 4MAT System for Teaching and Learning has been adopted in many school districts nationwide (information on 4MAT is available at http://www.excelcorp.com/). Although research into the efficacy of the model as an instructional strategy is in its formative stages, studies in several school districts have shown that 4MAT can have a positive effect on elementary student achievement in geometry (Lieberman, 1988), math (Hagopian et al., 1996), language arts and student attitudes (Wilkerson & White, 1988), and reading (Hagopian et al., 1996).

The relevance of the 4MAT Learning System for the teaching of library and information skills is that it involves children in their own learning. 4MAT also draws children's attention to the processes involved at various stages, and it creates awareness that learning is a constructive process. These elements, Kuhlthau (1996) suggests, "substantially increase" their "confidence and competence" as information seekers (p. 96). By creating a space for "brainstorming and preliminary discussion" of topics and concepts (perhaps alternative "search terms") among students, 4MAT supports thinking about the potential of topics. Callison (1995) argues that this sort of preliminary activity contextualizes the project and facilitates the information-seeking activities that follow. In addition, 4MAT's Quadrants 3 and 4 call for students to plan, complete, evaluate, and share a project—a project that arises naturally within the context of the unit being studied in the classroom and at a point where the potential for student learning is optimal. This makes a space for research and inquiry-based process models for teaching library and information skills.

The fit between 4MAT and the Big6 Skills (Eisenberg & Berkowitz, 1990) approach has been explored by N.P. Thomas (2001a). The Big6 adds an important component to 4MAT in that it provides a structure for steps students can follow in researching, synthesizing, and creating projects that is assumed but not described in the 4MAT model. Since the information-seeking and project completion are complex activities, successful management of the "task requires knowledge of the information retrieval process" and the "range of appropriate strategies" (Moore & St. George, 1991, p. 168) that can and should be taught to students as their projects unfold.

A useful way to accommodate the learning styles and capitalize on learning strengths individuals bring to learning tasks within the context of library-based information-seeking tasks is to reframe or have students reframe research questions based on their own preferences. Handling research assignments in this way ensures that students actually have to interact with and apply the information they find to resolve a specific issue and present a synthesis in their own words. Planning a variety of questions to guide student research is a useful way to accommodate learning style differences. Within the context of information skills instruction, alternative questions permit students to investigate a subject or engage a topic based on personal interests and perspectives (Thomas, Vroegindewey, & Wellins, 1997). Such an approach has the added advantage of promoting a type of inquiry-based learning that is "founded in gathering information for the purpose of seeking various perspectives, not just a single conclusion" (Callison, 1994, p. 55) and to do so in ways that reflect "the way we learn in 'real life' " (Donham et al., 2001). In addition, in creating research assignments that call on students to select questions from a list of predetermined alternatives or to develop their own research questions based on a personal perspective circumvents the tendency on the part of some students to download or copy information they find in print and online sources.

Generating research questions is often a very difficult task and requires practice (Irving, 1985). For younger students, learning style preferences can be accommodated by providing an array of alternatives in research approach from which students can choose. Changing the ways that questions are asked may provide students with practice in creating a focus for their topics (Irving, 1985). Kuhlthau (1993a, 1993b) considers the skill of focus formulation to be *the* crucial element in the successful implementation and completion of the information search process. When coming up with a thesis statement and the development of a personal focus are objectives within the overall assignment, teachers can assist students by providing models to serve as catalysts for student thinking. By assisting teachers in the development of alternative questions, librarians can use their expertise as instructional consultants to add value to the projects students create.

Accommodating Multiple Intelligences in Information Skills Instruction

Knowledge of Gardner's theory of multiple intelligences certainly argues for school librarians to move beyond the more traditional forms of instruction to provide multimodal approaches to teaching. In this way, students can build their competence in all areas and demonstrate those gifts not ordinarily valued in school or in school-related assignments. Recently, the move to permit students to present their learning through project options beyond the written report or term paper has made it possible for children and youth with special abilities to maximize their own interests and talents. Other strategies would include the use of games and role-playing, in addition to pencil-and-paper "seat-work"; graphics and visuals, manipulatives, and class discussion, in addition to lectures; journal writing and the use of graphic organizers, flowcharts, and timelines, in addition to formal, text-based outlines; and group activities and cooperative learning opportunities, in addition to individual activities. These strategies naturally take into account the visual, auditory, and kinesthetic preferences of students and create a context of support for all kinds of learners. It is well to note as well that accommodating children's differences in these ways is "culture-fair" (Ford, 1996, p. 19).

Gender and the Information Search Process

Burdick's (1996) study involved youth in grades 10 through 12 who were engaged in research activities in their English courses. Citing a report published in 1992 that raised concerns that models generally used to guide research projects and assignments "might favor males" (p. 19), Burdick elected to test this theory through Kuhlthau's (1993b) ISP. Kuhlthau's model essentially assumes a "generic" information searcher. Using an approach to data collection that Kuhlthau designed, Burdick explored gender issues particularly as they related to cognitive and affective information-seeking behaviors and to focus formulation. In short, Burdick found that the students in her study did demonstrate gender-related differences in their selection of topics, their searching behaviors, and in the feelings they experienced. A summary of Burdick's findings related to gender and information seeking appear in Table 5.3.

Burdick's data suggested that the girls she observed were "more likely to work together" and were more reflective on research-related activities than were boys, while boys were more active in their approach to research tasks and "less likely" to seek assistance or help. In addition, study results provided some evidence that "girls chose topics about either males or females," while "males chose topics only about males." While Burdick did not include the subject area of the topic as a research variable in the study, the tendency on the part of some girls to prefer affective approaches and some boys for logic suggests that "there might be gender associations with either the information seeking or the subject domain of the class in which the process takes place" (p. 21).

In terms of student perceptions of the information-seeking tasks, girls in Burdick's study emphasized the exploration and formulation stages of the ISP, while boys showed more interest in collecting materials and completing the assignment. However, both boys and girls considered the completion of the assignment to be more important than the creation of a focus. Burdick's research also revealed that boys were less tentative than girls about "expressing a personal perspective" (p. 22). While this quality may reflect gender differences related to self-confidence, Burdick suggests that there may

Table 5.3
Gender-Related Differences in the ISP (Burdick, 1996)

Girls were:	Boys were:
• more likely to seek assistance	• less likely to ask for help
• more likely to work together	• more likely to express confidence
• more likely to be optimistic at task initiation and doubtful and uncertain at completion	• more active
	• more emphatic in collecting data and completing assignments
• more reflective	• more comfortable in expressing personal opinions
• more interested in exploring and focusing topics	
• less confident overall in their abilities	

Both girls and boys:

• showed higher degrees of involvement for tasks in which their interest was high

• placed more emphasis on project completion than on focus formulation

• expressed feelings of confidence not necessarily related to the formulation of a personal perspective

• exhibited choice behaviors for topics related to gender

also be developmental characteristics that have a bearing on students' abilities to formulate personal points of view, as in, for instance, whether students consider knowledge as something that is "given" or something that is "constructed."

Burdick identified two approaches to information seeking employed by students she observed, which she characterized as "navigators" and "tourists." Whereas navigators tended to follow the phases of Kuhlthau's (1993b) model quite closely, tourists were much more likely to look for answers to their questions through the exploration and collection stages of the ISP and seemed both unconcerned and confident about their activities, even though they did not create a focus for their projects. In terms of feelings, Burdick's female informants were less likely than boys to express confidence in their projects, regardless of outcome, although in general, girls were more likely to discuss their affective responses related to the overall process than were boys. This led Burdick to conclude that Kuhlthau's theory of "decreasing uncertainty" may "be less applicable to these females" (p. 23). Finally, Burdick noted that interest and personal investment in the topics chosen proved motivating for students in her study and increased their overall involvement and enjoyment of the ISP. For this reason, she considers involvement an important, if previously unrecognized, aspect of the ISP and suggests that the ISP model be extended to include "enjoyment, satisfaction, confidence, and competence" as positive outcomes of the process. While it is important to remember that Burdick's findings are based on a single study, they raise interesting issues that should be pursued further.

In a recent study, Large (2002) documented gender differences in children's Web-searching behavior. Using videotapes as the principal data collection method, groups of same-sex sixth graders in a Canadian elementary school were observed using the World Wide Web to gather information for a school project. In fact, students were allowed to choose 1 of 14 Winter Olympic sports and to explore one of a dozen topics related to the sport chosen (e.g., training, personalities, diet, etc.). Each student was to present information obtained on the Web, in CD-ROMs, or in standard printed resources in a poster and an oral presentation.

Some interesting differences between the groups were reported: For example, girls in the study used multiword search terms, while the boys limited their use of key words to one or a very few. In addition, girls spent more time perusing each Web page retrieved; on the other hand, the boys moved more quickly between links and buttons than the girls. Overall, neither group spent much time in evaluating Web pages, and neither group chose to use options provided by *Alta Vista* and *Infoseek* to refine their searches.

Volman's (1997) study focused on the attitudes of girls and boys toward computers and their confidence in computer use, their knowledge of computers, and their interests in pursuing computer-related careers and on confidence levels. In addition to charting gender-related differences, Volman was concerned about the development of gender-inclusive instruction, understood as "content, context, teaching methods and hidden curriculum" "that contributes equally to boys' and girls' knowledge, insight and skills" in the creation of meaningful learning experiences that result in feelings of competence on the parts of the learners. Gender-fair computer instruction combines "computer-handling" skills with "the formation of information processing concepts" and the "social aspects of information technology" (p. 316). Of particular relevance were explanations of key concepts "geared to the everyday lives of pupils, including those of girls" (p. 317) and the sensitivity to stereotypes, gender roles, and interactional patterns that reinforce the idea of information technology, science, and math as primarily masculine interests.

The differences in behavior Volman detected led her to conclude that the boys she observed exhibited more confidence in their computer skills than did the girls and were less likely to take responsibility for mistakes when computer problems were encountered. Volman reported that the boys "talked more and with more enthusiasm and imagination" and employed "computer jargon" when discussing the technological and functional aspects of computers. Girls, on the other hand, evinced less confidence in their technological skills and tended to display a degree of helplessness during class lessons. They also tended to "attribute problems with the computer to their own failure" (p. 323). Even though the knowledge levels of girls and boys improved as a result of information and computer literacy instruction, gender-related differences in attitudes actually increased when instruction was not conducted in a "gender-inclusive" manner. Gender bias in teaching included such behavior as "taking over the computer more often with girls, giving girls fewer turns in class, and addressing boys as experts more often than girls (Sanders and Stone, 1980)" (p. 321).

Volman's research provides some very useful insights for library media specialists in terms of gendered approaches to teaching and awareness of the importance of creating gender-neutral context for instruction. As Volman argues, "Teachers should try to prevent an unintentional contribution to processes which exclude girls, or make girls exclude themselves, from certain areas of knowledge and skills. This demands an awareness of the importance of gender identity for pupils, as well as an alertness to the repertoires concerning computers and information technology that prevails in the classroom" (p. 327)—repertoires in particular that create boys as experts and girls as "outsiders" in terms of computers and computer use. The significance of attitudes to technology is that "the ideas [students] develop about the subject and about themselves in relation to it will contribute to their decision either to pursue computer activities further in their school careers or to drop out of this field" (p. 315).

Learning Styles, Ethnicity, and Information Skills Instruction

The importance of providing "culturally responsive instructional techniques" has been addressed by a number of scholars who have studied the instructional needs of African American, Hispanic American, and Asian American youth. Irvine and Irvine (1995) have outlined the difficulties that exist for African American and other minority youngsters when schools fail to take their differences in worldview and culture into account. As "black children's ways of doing and knowing often conflict with and are antithetical to the ways in which schools do and know" (p. 133), the kinds of cultural discontinuities that can occur in the classroom can lead these children to experience both "psychological discomfort and low achievement" (p. 134). In particular, Irvine and Irvine argue that where cultural "otherness" in learning and knowing is "not recognized" or is "rejected," educational contexts can prove alienating and diminishing to minority youngsters. On the other hand, research indicates that where teachers personalize the educational experience, encourage active participation, contextualize instruction, and link curriculum concepts to the "social, cultural, historical and political reality" (p. 138) of "students' everyday experiences" (p. 137), minority youngsters thrive.

> **We can continue to view diversity as a problem or we can recognize that diversity of thought, language, and worldview . . . can not only provide an exciting educational setting, but can also prepare our children for the richness of living in an increasingly diverse national community.**
>
> —Delpit, 1996

Specifically, Irvine and Irvine argue that minority youngsters who are "predisposed to learning" through "movement, variation, creativity, divergent thinking approaches, inductive reasoning, and a focus on people" are especially at risk where classroom activities and assignments promote only an "analytical style" and emphasize "rules and restriction of movement, standardization, conformity, convergent thinking approaches, deductive reasoning, and a focus on things" (p. 135). In explaining the sorts of misunderstandings that can arise when teachers are unaccepting of stylistic differences, the authors offer as an example the elaborate "stage setting behaviors" (e.g., "looking over the assignment in its entirety; rearranging posture; elaborately checking pencils, paper, and writing space; asking teachers to repeat directions that have just been given; and checking perceptions of neighboring students") (p. 135) that often attend initial task engagement for field-dependent students. Such activities are often misconstrued as "avoidance tactics, inattentiveness, disruptions, or evidence of not being prepared to do the assigned task (Gilbert and Gay, 1989, p. 277)" (p. 136).

Understanding behavior and being sensitive to cultural patterns and preferences will make school libraries a safe place for differences. Group projects, class discussion, and allowing time for student stories and the relating of personal experiences as well as positive feedback and interaction with instructors are strategies that will support African American students. Collaborating with teachers in creating research projects for students that permit student choice in terms of topics and approaches is a way of ensuring culture-fair practice in information skills instruction. Providing an overview of the search process and a rationale for its use are strategies that will be appropriate for many minority youngsters whose thinking is consistent with non-Western cognitive patterns. Finally, making sure that minorities and minority history and traditions are fully represented in the topics chosen as vehicles for student learning as a standard part of the curriculum (not just the focus of "black history month") and in the organization and patterns of classroom activity will help subvert institutional racism, which many educators see as subverting the achievement of minority youngsters. In stressing the need for culture-appropriate teaching strategies, Hale-Benson (1982) noted classrooms that depend primarily on technology, texts, learning centers, drill and practice sessions, television, and programmed instruction at the expense of socially interactive learning activities and people-oriented learning places many children of African heritage at educational risk (Kuykendall, 2001).

Lastly,

> Teacher expectations are particularly important in the development of positive self images in Black students. Positive racial attitudes by teachers are associated with greater minority achievement (Forehand, Regosta, and Rock, 1976). Low teacher expectations have been shown to reduce the motivation of students to learn. Perhaps the most damaging consequence of low teacher expectations is the erosion of academic self-image in students.

Indeed, "Black youth are more influenced by teacher perceptions than by their *own* perceptions (Garrett-holiday, 1985)" (Kuykendall, 2001).

In dissertation research that sought to test a variety of instructional approaches to the teaching of library skills, Bobotis (1978) compared the effectiveness of oral (lecture), visual (overhead transparencies), and performance approaches to instruction with 21 classes of Mexican American and Anglo-American seventh graders. Her findings revealed that Mexican American students in her study learned more when information was presented using performance-based methods that more clearly reflected "real-world" types of activities. For this reason, she concluded that there might be a relationship between ethnicity and learning style preferences in the acquisition of library skills. Lin (1994), who studied cultural differences in an academic library, reached a similar conclusion. Lin's research suggested that Chinese and other non-Western, holistic thinkers might benefit from an overview of the library as a system before being introduced to library routines, library resources, and searching skills.

Citing studies that indicated that there are gender differences (Canada & Brusca, 1991; Diem, 1986; Freedman, 1989) and ethnic differences (DeVillar & Faltis, 1991) related to attitudes and use of computers, Freedman and Liu (1996) found that there were "cultural differences in learning with computers" (p. 57) when they studied a group of middle school Hmong youngsters. In observing the exchange of email messages between their informants and minority students in other cities involving their ethnic traditions, family life, and school experiences, the researchers found that cultural values of the Hmong students created difficulties related to course content, the role of the instructor, and inquiry learning strategies. Content issues related to the assignment surfaced because the students in the study had been raised according to "a strictly patriarchal system," within which males are regarded as "keepers of cultural knowledge" (p. 48), of the sort that students were supposed to investigate. Since the possession of this kind of information is exclusively a male prerogative, "both boys and girls were concerned about the girls learning things about Hmong culture traditionally outside of their accepted range of knowledge" (p. 54). In addition, restrictions on access to cultural traditions meant that in many cases many Hmong students lacked knowledge of their own culture to share in response to questions that their "key pals" asked of them. Negotiation with students and parents was necessary to overcome these impediments to information seeking and learning.

The role of the teacher in the learning process also proved problematic for this group of youngsters. For example, even though learning the use of the computer was the intent of the course, many students were reluctant to ask for assistance because to do so would have been to admit that they "lacked computer knowledge"(Freedman & Liu, 1996, p. 52). Rather than lose "face" in this way, students tended to ask one another for help. Similarly, the Hmong students did not like others to watch "over their shoulders" while they were working, lest they be observed making errors. Finally, whereas Anglo students tended to jump into assignments and use a trial-and-error method when using computers, Asian students were reluctant to undertake an assignment without specific direction.

Experiential learning and an expectation of the participation of all students in learning tasks were also problematic. For example, since the values of this particular group included strong group identity, family loyalty, and respect for authority, male students whose fathers were community leaders acted as group leaders, and this influenced the ways that the girls "treated these boys." In addition, their "interest in supporting the common good" (p. 52) led the more expert students to take over and do the work of their less knowledgeable peers, rather than tutoring the novices or demonstrating for them appropriate searching techniques. Asian American students in the study also were inexperienced in asking questions of their respondents, even though they were quite candid at answering questions addressed to them. "The cultural background of the Asian American students, particularly on the part of the girls, tended to limit verbal investigation" (p. 52). And although some did become adept at asking questions once they understood the importance of posing questions to elicit information, "none of the Asian American students were really comfortable with this part of the project" (p. 52).

These kinds of differences pose problems for teachers and librarians in planning instruction for groups of students unless they have knowledge of approaches to learning that are part of the cultural experience of minority students. Where there are differences between the content and processes of instruction and the ways of knowing and learning of minority students, the differences will have to be discussed so that students and parents see the value of the assignments and develop a level of comfort with what may be for them entirely novel instructional situations. By the same token, changes in practice to ensure the personal and cultural confirmation of minority students are also appropriate; these might include the use of same-sex grouping; turn-taking with regard to leadership roles in group activities; and the explanation, modeling, and implementation of peer tutoring activities.

Creating Supportive Library Environments

Support for the use of individual differences in planning libraries for library instruction appears in a study by Dunn and Smith (1990). In their study, these researchers employed a 23-element construct of learning styles developed by Dunn, Dunn, and Price. The elements, which can "affect a person's ability to absorb, process, and retain information" (p. 33), can be grouped along five dimensions: environmental (sound, light, temperature, design); emotional (motivation, persistence, responsibility, and structure); sociological (sociability, in terms of self, pairs, peers, teams adults, variety); physical (perceptual, nutritional, temporal, mobility); and psychological (hemisphericity, impulsivity and reflexivity, analytical and global). According to Dunn and Smith, "[T]he most important aspect is the potent contribution to individualizing instruction" (p. 36) made possible through applications of this construct. This seems entirely consistent with the goal of customization promoted in most contemporary media centers and many schools.

The work of the many theorists and research scholars reviewed in this chapter offers library media specialists a variety of approaches and strategies to use in tailoring instruction to the needs of individuals and groups they serve. Some practical suggestions gleaned from this review are presented in Figure 5.11.

Figure 5.11
Strategies for Tailoring Instruction to Student Needs

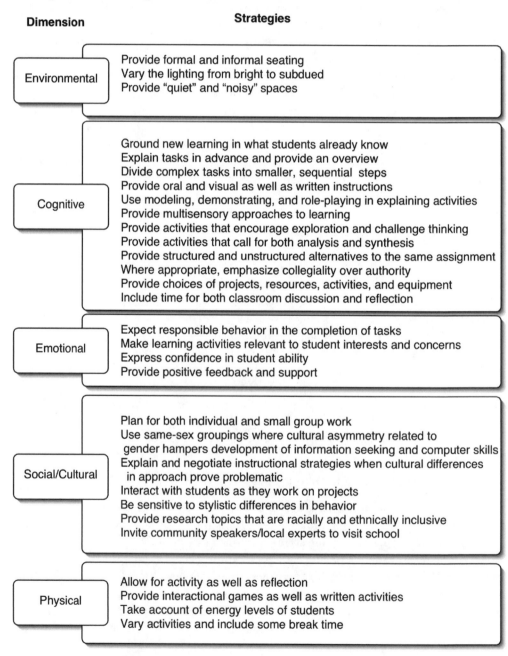

Media Literacy: An Essential Information Literacy Skill Agenda

Although media literacy is a recognized staple of the curriculum in many other countries, "there are no national standards in the United States" (Scharrer, 2002, p. 354), and American schools have been slow to create their own. This situation is changing, however. Surprisingly, impetus for the teaching of media literacy has come from within departments of communication[8] rather than from the LIS community. When one considers the fact that evaluating Internet resources is one of the benchmarks of information literacy instruction, the lack of emphasis on media literacy within an information skills curriculum is perplexing. Why aren't library media specialists in the vanguard of promoting the incorporation of media literacy standards?

Many states have created media literacy standards or outcomes within the curricula of language arts, health education, and social studies. This makes sense when one thinks of the texts or scripts created for media, the importance of media in creating messages for adolescents on health issues, and the political nature of media that has been of concern in social studies citizenship education in the United States for decades. Recently, there have been increasing calls for integrating media literacy outcomes across the curriculum, in much the same ways as information literacy skills instruction. School librarians have become increasingly proficient at teaming with educators; and their knowledge of media production, pedagogy, and collaboration makes including the media literacy agenda within information literacy instruction appear to be both logical and important.

Media literacy education is consistent with and extends the notion and use of constructivism, broadening it to make evident the social origins of what we believe is true and the importance of culture to an understanding or "reading" of the messages regarded as "information." Research approaches in the media literacy field have looked at the impact of TV on students, the use of TV in the classroom, and the strategies that media producers use to create images, raising student awareness of advertising techniques. The advantage of this last approach is that the techniques that are used in selling products in online environments are the same ones that are used to construct all kinds of media products including news. It is for this reason that these techniques should be taught within the overall framework of information seeking and use in the school library. In addition, there is some research evidence that whereas students who are taught media literacy skills become savvy media consumers when they are analyzing ads, they are unlikely to apply these same skills to online resources that they judge to be either entertainment or informational. The implications of this are profound and speak directly to the ability of students to recognize bias, identify stereotypes, or understand the social and intellectual implications of uncritical acceptance of media messages. Germane to this discussion is a research finding by Small and Ferreira (1994a) that middle school students were more confident in the trustworthiness and credibility of multimedia resources than they were of printed text.[9]

While media literacy has not been expressly considered within the information skills curriculum, there have been efforts to address media literacy issues within the LIS research community. For example, Vandergrift et al. (2000) have adapted readers' response theory in helping children to hone visual literacy skills as they explore book illustrations. These theorists propose visual interpretive analysis (VIA) as "a tool that helps students begin to look closely and deeply at the way an illustration from a picture book creates meanings that enhance and extend story" (Platzner & Vandergrift, n.d.). VIA assumes that the meaning of a text or an illustration is created "as the result of a transaction between an individual reader and a text at a specific moment in time"; visual interpretive analysis "creates a guide to some of [the] many possibilities" and alternative meanings that might exist for a variety of readers/viewers when they encounter a particular illustration in a children's book. "By guiding others to see what we see, we offer them new possibilities, new ways of looking (ways of knowing) not only at one illustration but at the world around them" (Platzner & Vandergrift, n.d.).

Conclusion

Clearly, the challenge of individualizing information skills instruction is multidimensional, and much more research on information-seeking behavior will have to be done before there will be definitive answers about how differences in learning styles can be best accommodated in instruction and supported in action. However, the research reviewed above provides a foundation and a rationale for the development of user-centered instruction. It is evident that students need to be made aware of the processes that underlie information seeking and to have opportunities to discuss with others the projects in which they are involved (Irving, 1985; Kuhlthau, Goodin, & McNally, 1996). Indeed, many scholars believe that the reflection on the process is essential for the retention and application of learning across situations and settings. Others would argue, with Delpit (1996), that attention be paid the products created by students in demonstrating their learning as well, since in many cases it is by those products that adults are evaluated in the larger world outside the school. Library media specialists who can take individual differences into account will be able to make a genuine contribution to the success of all students and model a type of inclusivity that honors "the many different ways students learn and process information" (Teele, 1996, p. 65). Indeed, the library should be a safe place for the expression of these differences.

Insights from the research in education and LIS can be summarized as including the following themes: that learning involves personal construction; that learning builds on prior experience or knowledge; that learning is inherently social as well as psychological; that children can understand at a number of levels; that they can perform at higher levels if they are assisted by knowledgeable others; that they learn differently; that intelligence can take multiple forms; that differences in learning styles are related to biology, culture, motivation, and experience. To create assignments supportive of only one style of information behavior is a discriminatory practice that works to disadvantage students whose cognitive styles and strengths reflect other orientations and interests. This fact challenges librarians to consider multiculturalism and its complexities in ways that truly support and extend learning, rather than merely to engage in cultural "tourism" of the type represented by sporadic, once-a-year tributes to ethnic heroes, multicultural food festivals, and multiethnic literature fairs. Although these gestures no doubt make multiculturalism objectives visible, their use addresses only the artifacts of culture. They seldom reflect cultural values and alternative ways of knowing.[10] As such, these practices are superficial and constitute a nod in the general direction of minority students rather than an invitation to dine at an educational table prepared with their instructional needs in mind. "We can continue to view diversity as a problem," Delpit (1996) writes, or "we can recognize that diversity of thought, language, and worldview . . . can not only provide an exciting educational setting, but can also prepare our children for the richness of living in an increasingly diverse national community" (p. 66).

Notes

1. The contemporary term for individualizing instruction is "curriculum differentiation," a strategy that calls on teachers to alter course content and processes, instructional environment, learning products, and assessment measures in response to the interests and abilities of individual students. Interdisciplinary approaches to content, independent activities, critical thinking, active exploration, and challenging assignments are current priorities in curriculum differentiation.

2. In recent thinking and writing on the topic of sense-making, Dervin has moved from conceptualizing gaps as obstacles in everyday life to an emphasis on the "hows" of sense-making as a "methodological tool" (Savolainen, 2003, p. 697). For a complete explanation of Dervin's current use of sense-making, see Dervin, B. (1999).

3. The theoretical frameworks related to moral and social development in the writings of Lawrence Kolhberg, Erik Eriksen, and others are also relevant to issues of individualization of instruction. Readers are encouraged to explore these theories in Kohlberg's Stages in the *Development of Moral Thought and Action* (1969) and Eriksen's *Identity, Youth and Crisis* (1968).

4. At this time, Gardner (1999b) reports that designation of this last intelligence is "in limbo" as it has not as yet met all the criteria demanded for its permanent inclusion as an independent intelligence.

5. Of interest in this regard is a recent (2002) Kaiser Family Foundation study presented ("See No Evil: How Internet Filters Affect the Search for Online Health Information") reporting that a health-related Web site, Generation Rx.com, reported that 75 percent of young adults (ages 15–24) relied on information obtained online to fulfill their health-related information needs with fully 44 percent seeking information on birth control and sexually transmitted diseases. The Kaiser report also studied three levels of Internet filters (least restrictive [blocking pornography] intermediate [blocking pornography, nudity, and discrimination] and most restrictive [blocking these categories in addition to profanity, drugs, and alcohol]. Filters assessed to be most restrictive incorrectly blocked 50 percent of sites dealing with safe sex and sexual health issues (as opposed to 9 percent for least restrictive filters) and 60 percent of gay health sites. Significantly, the kinds of information most often blocked related to sexually transmitted disease, pregnancy and birth control, and safe sex.

6. Julien's (1999) study of adolescent career decision making supports this view. In addition, career decisions require youth to make sense of information from an often bewildering array of sources: "parents, siblings, other family members, family friends, peers, guidance counselors, teachers, school and public library resources, the mass media, and government career centers" (p. 38). Add to this the social pressures, socialization patterns, and lack of confidence that accompany children into adolescence and one begins to understand the complexities of decision making—only some of which are, strictly speaking, *informational* in nature.

7. A recent study by Cooper (2002) takes into account frameworks created by Piaget, Vygotsky, and Kuhlthau in a study exploring the information-seeking behavior of second graders. Specifically, Cooper was interested in observing how students, operating cognitively between preoperational and concrete operational levels, find information in a school library. The research tasks chosen for the study included searching for books on general and specific topics on the library shelves and for information on the same topics in a CD-ROM encyclopedia. Cooper found that scaffolding techniques of encouragement and suggestions provided by the school librarian as the electronic searches proceeded enabled pre-abstract thinkers to operate more successfully and confidently in the "metaphysical world" of electronic searching. In addition, computerized searches, which channeled the seekers directly to relevant information, reduced the cognitive load for new readers required when these searchers negotiate finding aids such as titles, indexes, and tables of contents before actually locating information. Cooper's work also provided evidence for

Kuhlthau's (1993b) assertion that feelings are an important aspect of the ISP for "novice information seekers." Her observations led Cooper to conclude that "children tend to favor browsing types of strategies in their information seeking"; that they "rely on visual information if it is available to them rather than using textual information"; and that they can use "meta-information in textual format to find information if it is presented in a very directed manner."

8. Scharrer (2002) describes media literacy issues in terms of contemporary perspectives that ground contemporary approaches in terms of learning outcomes for a media literacy curriculum. The cultural studies approach "places great emphasis on students' own, often pleasurable, experiences with media." Learning outcomes within the framework of this perspective might address topics related to "media agencies, categories, technologies, languages, audiences, and representations (Bazalgette, 1989; Bowker, 1991)." The "impact mediation (Anderson, 1983), inoculation (Kubey, 1998), or interventionism" approach, on the other hand, directs attention to the "negative issues pertaining to the media (e.g., violence, sex-role stereotyping, or manipulation in advertising) and interprets media literacy as a strategy to help protect young people from harmful effects (Hobbs, 1998)."

9. Todd (1998) discusses the many ambiguities that characterize the Internet, especially for students used to working in school libraries where "resources are assumed to be 'good' by their mere presence in the collection" (p. 20). Among potential problems Todd identifies are the seductiveness of Internet searching as an easy-to-use information store, the complexities inherent in the ways information sites are organized and linked; the multimedia blitz in the application of text, audio, video, and animated graphics that can hinder comprehension of content; the "invisibility of web authors" p. 19 and the authentic and official appearance of Web sites that can both erase context and blur the boundaries between facts and falsehood. Todd also offers a list of questions that students might employ in "interrogating" Internet information sites. These include: "What is this site trying to do? What is this site trying to do to me? Whose interests are being served here? What is the text trying to say? What are the possible meanings? What do I already know and how does this relate to it? How does this relate to other sites? Other sources? What are the alternative/opposing views? Where can I find out about alternatives? How does this site help me construct an alternative position? What do I do with this site now? Who can I talk to about this site? Which voices are silent here? What actions can/should/will I take?" (p. 18).

10. Ford (1996) presents Boykin's (1994) list of cultural values and styles as follows: spirituality ("the conviction that nonmaterial religious forces influence people's everyday lives"), harmony ("the notion that one's fate is interrelated with other elements in the scheme of things so that humankind and nature are harmonically conjoined"), movement ("a premium placed on the amalgamation of movement, [poly]rhythm, dance, and percussion embodied in the musical beat"), verve ("a propensity for relatively high levels of stimulation and for action that is energetic and lively"), affect ("the centrality of affective information and emotional expressiveness and the equal and integrated importance of thoughts and feelings"), communalism ("a commitment to the fundamental interdependence of people and the importance of social bonds"), oral tradition ("the centrality of oral and aural modes of communication for conveying full meaning and the cultivation of speaking as performance"), expressive individualism ("the cultivation of a distinctive personality and a proclivity for spontaneity and genuine personal expression"), social time perspective ("a commitment to a social construction of time as personified by an event orientation") (pp. 85–86).

6 Current Trends in Research on Information Skills Instruction

Although the instructional nature of the school librarian's job description emerged at a relatively early stage in the development of school librarianship, it did not achieve priority status until the publication of *Information Power* by the American Association of School Librarians and the Association for Educational Communications and Technology in 1988. At that time, the statement that the librarian's essential role is "to ensure that students and staff are effective users of ideas and information" (p. 1) created an emphasis that continues to characterize "best practice" in school librarianship. Stripling (1995) and others have argued that "library programs must be based around learning, not around libraries" (Pitts, 1994, cited in Stripling, p. 163). This assertion is a succinct acknowledgment that, in assisting students to achieve curricular goals, teacher-librarians provide essential and fundamental support for the learning process.

If there is a theme that runs through the research literature on contemporary practice in library and information studies, it is the centrality of concern for the library user (F.F. Jacobson, 1997). In school settings, where the library's mission is by definition responsive to the school's curricular goals, this concern has been shaped by theoretical frameworks that guide contemporary educational practice, particularly those defined as "constructivist." Indeed, library and information science researchers who have come to consider information seeking as a cognitive process through which students create meaning and achieve understanding (Kuhlthau 1993b; J.B. Smith, 1987) have found in constructivism a way to redefine student research and to reframe instruction in the information skills that support it.

This chapter will look at constructivism as a theoretical framework for information skills instruction and consider other trends in school librarianship, including the contextualization of library skills lessons, the value of process models for research and reference skills instruction, new roles for teachers and students, and the contemporary emphasis on critical thinking. In one way or another, each of these topics reflects the influence of the constructivist view on teaching and learning. In addition, the chapter will identify those particular subskills students must acquire to become knowledgeable and independent "researchers." Finally, the chapter will discuss the components of effective "research" assignments as a guide for teachers and librarians as they together plan student learning activities and projects.

Basic to any discussion of library skills instruction in its many and various contexts and approaches is the assumption that the teaching of reference or information skills has educational value (Eisenberg & Brown, 1992). As K. Haycock (1992) has been able to point out, such evidence exists now, although more is clearly needed and would surely be welcome. For example, studies have shown a positive relationship between academic achievement and the level of library service (Greve, 1974), between library expenditures and student achievement (Lance, Welborn, & Hamilton-Pennell, 1992; Lance et al., 2000), between library services and reading (Lowe, 1984, cited in K. Haycock, 1992), between "knowledge and use of reference materials" (McMillen, 1966, quoted in Haycock, p. 168), and between the acquisition of library and study skills and the expression of learning (Yarling, 1968). Moreover, in studies (Hardesty & Wright, 1982; Kuhlthau, 1995; Todd, Lamb, & McNicholas, 1993) he reviewed, Todd (1995) found evidence that the information skills curriculum "can have a positive impact on" test scores, recall, concentration, focus and "reflective thinking" (p. 133). In addition, Todd suggested that "self-perception, self-esteem, control of learning, mastery of content, focus on tasks and reduced confusion and frustration seem to be linked to information skills instruction" (p. 133).

Constructivism

According to Von Glasersfeld (1995), constructivism is a theory of knowledge that has its roots in the domains of philosophy and cognitive psychology. Although in the literature constructivism has been variously defined, most scholars consider theoretical constructs in the work of John Dewey (1916, 1933), Jean Piaget (Inhelder & Piaget, 1958), George Kelly (1963), and Jerome Bruner (1975, 1977) as seminal and recognize a set of assumptions they share. For example, constructivists generally hold that learning is "something which the individual *does*" (J. Dewey, 1916, p. 390), that learning involves an act of personal construction, and that knowledge is the creation of meaning based on the experience of the learner. Thus constructivists assert that learners are active participants in their own learning rather than "passive receivers" (Kuhlthau, 1993b, p. 24) of knowledge imparted to them by teachers and others (Table 6.1). For this reason, constructivists emphasize the ability of the student to create a personal focus or "perspective" on a subject or topic as the hallmark of understanding and learning. In fact, the ability to de-

Table 6.1
Constructivist Assumptions about How Children Learn

- Learning is an active and constructive process
- Learning is the internalization and personalization of knowledge
- Learning is the meaning that is made from experience
- Learning involves understanding at a deep level
- Learning involves the ability to apply new knowledge
- Learning activities help students relate new information to past experience
- Learning involves cognitive (thinking), social (interactive), and affective (feelings) dimensions

velop a personal viewpoint is, according to Sauer (1995), "the ultimate goal" (p. 140) of education in general and library instruction in particular. When viewed in this light, learning becomes less a matter of acquiring a set of skills than the creation of a "deep understanding" (Von Glasersfeld, 1995, p. 10). According to Kuhlthau (1997), "[T]he constructivist approach seeks to foster deep learning that goes beyond the ability to respond to a text, to application in daily living" (pp. 710–711).

Moreover, constructivists argue that, to be effective, learning activities must connect to what students already know and have meaning for the learner at the time of the learning (Irving, 1985). Indeed, most constructivists would argue that learning cannot arise in a vacuum but is inherently interactive and built upon a knowledge base of previously learned concepts. Their emphasis also includes the social context and the role of learning communities (Bruner, 1986) in the creation of knowledge structures. Thus, an understanding of the social nature of teaching and learning not only provides important clues to how instruction may proceed within constructivist environments but also provides both a framework and context for the implementation of instruction. For this reason, constructivist educators call on teachers to redefine their instructional roles in the classroom and to change in fundamental ways the delivery of instruction to accommodate this new understanding of how learning occurs.

While they tend to focus primarily on the "cognitive" aspect of the learning, constructivists also recognize the importance of the "affective" (Kelly, 1963) nature of learning tasks and recognize the importance of providing support for the emotional as well as the cognitive needs of student learners. These approaches to instruction are sometimes advanced as something new in education; however, Von Glasersfeld (1995) reminds us that in point of fact "constructivism" creates a theoretical grounding for the kinds of activities and strategies that gifted teachers have long employed without fanfare.

Constructivist Contexts for Library Instruction and Learning

Although constructivism is certainly not the only theoretical framework upon which school librarianship draws, few would dispute the extent of its impact on practice or its value to the creation of learning experiences in the school library. In a very real sense, the acceptance of constructivism as "the fundamental theoretical foundation" (Kuhlthau, 2001) for library programming has led school media specialists to rethink their approach to teaching library "lessons" and to replace context-free "scope and sequence" approaches to "bibliographic instruction" with an emphasis on information literacy (Walter, 1994), critical thinking, information management, and information use. Stand-alone instructional sessions involving location and access "library" skills have been superseded by instructional practices that call for the "contextualization" of skills lessons presented as the need for their use arises within ongoing classroom instruction. This means, for example, that instruction on the use of a particular library resource is not introduced until its use is necessitated by curriculum-related tasks (Bowie, 1990, cited in Callison, 1994; Engeldinger, 1988). Perhaps more important, the "contextualization" means that library skills are considered as "information skills" and taught within the framework of an overall process model for information seeking (Irving, 1985; Kuhlthau, 1993b). An essential value of implementing a process approach to information tasks is that considering information in a variety of resources allows students to break free of the notion that knowledge can be "found" if only enough resources are gathered and to realize "that knowledge is something" that they themselves construct in "collaboration" with "the sources they find to inform their thesis" (Fister, 1990, quoted in Sauer, 1995, p. 142).

Major incentives to change the delivery of library and information skills instruction have come from research. In particular, studies have shown not only that integrated skills instruction results in higher achievement on library skills tests (Becker, 1970; Nolan, 1989) and an increase in student self-confidence (Nolan, 1989) but also that lessons provided within a skills-based library curriculum have not been learned sufficiently to allow their application to research projects undertaken in the same or different educational contexts (Goodin, 1987, 1991). In addition, a study by Todd, Lamb, and McNicholas (1993), cited in Todd (1995), suggests that "an integrated information skills approach to teaching and learning can have a positive impact on" such "learning outcomes" as test scores, recall, concentration, focus, and reflective thinking (p. 133). Perhaps even more significantly, Pitts's (1994, cited in Stripling, 1995) research shows that "instruction in information seeking and use must be integrated with content for subject matter learning to occur" (p. 164). This finding was corroborated in Todd's (1995) study where, "for the specific students involved, integrated information skills interaction appears to have had a significant positive impact on students' mastery of prescribed science content and their ability to use a range of information skills to resolve particular information problems" (p. 137). And in an experimental study of information seeking in research projects among primary school students, Brien (1995) found that teaching the complex skills of information seeking and use within the structure provided by class-related projects reduced "cognitive load" for students and resulted in significant gains in student learning.

New Roles for Teacher-Librarians in Constructivist Environments

The role for the teacher-librarian within a constructivist approach is to provide structures and opportunities for learning and support and guidance for learners. Although not denying the necessity or appropriateness of direct instruction in certain situations and for certain kinds of learners, constructivism emphasizes the coaching role of the instructor in planning appropriate activities and structures based on the level of the learner; creating supportive environments; demonstrating important skills; modeling successful performance behavior; providing opportunities for student performances and reflections; motivating students; and providing feedback for students as they attempt to perform their learning tasks (Kuhlthau, 1997; Means & Olson, 1994). This approach to instruction is largely based on the work of Russian psychologist Lev Vygotsky (1896–1934).

In essence, Vygotsky (1978) viewed the process of education as a joint enterprise that involves both the teacher and the learner acting together. "Every function in the child's cultural development," Vygotsky believed,

> appears twice: first, on the social level, and later, on the individual level; first, between people (interpsychological) and then inside the child (intrapsychological). This applies equally to voluntary attention, to logical memory, and to the formation of concepts. All the higher functions originate as actual relationships between individuals. (p. 57)

This emphasis on the constitutive nature of language, the importance of culture, and the primacy of social interaction in learning distinguishes the work of this theorist from many of the constructivists. However, his acknowledgment of the importance of emphasis on language and culture to thinking and learning and on the constructed nature of knowledge creation has made him an influential contributor to instructional reform in the fields of education and school librarianship.

Effective instruction within Vygotsky's (1978) model is tailored to each child's "zone of proximal development [ZPD]," defined as that "distance between the actual developmental level as determined by independent problem-solving and the level of potential development" that the learner may attain with assistance by a knowledgeable helper (p. 86). As a first stage of a lesson framed in this way, the learner receives assistance in completing a task and comes to understand what is involved in carrying it out. At a second stage, the learner completes the task independently, by following the directions and managing the process for herself or himself. In the third stage, the various aspects of the task are integrated, the learner having internalized the learning so that his or her responses and skills are automatic.

Within Vygotsky's approach, teachers prepare contexts for student learning by creating "scaffolds" or structures that take students beyond the limits of their own competence and experience. In effect, these structures provide the support necessary for the students to begin an activity or project; as each student's competencies and confidence grow, the teacher "withdraws" gradually, relinquishing control so that students can take over the responsibility for the project. Thus for Vygotsky, learning is an interactive, interpersonal activity that involves the " 'transfer of responsibility' " (Rogoff & Gardner, 1984, quoted in Belmont, 1989, p. 144) for "reaching the current goal" from teacher to student. This strategy creates opportunities for the teacher to learn how "the instructional activities are being interpreted" so that subsequent activities and practice are informed by what students are learning or failing to learn (Driver et al., 1994, p. 11).

When applied within a school library context, Vygotsky's (1978) framework provides strategies for planning and conducting instruction and a model for interventional support in information seeking and learning from information. The importance of student-instructor interaction has also been recognized by Kulleseid (1986), who describes as "dynamic learning situation[s]" those opportunities that involve instructors in modeling and "stimulating cognitive activity" (p. 43). These kinds of learning contexts allow students to see firsthand those strategies that either work or don't work and to talk through processes with others to "expose conceptual misunderstandings" (Jacobson & Jacobson, 1993, p. 128). Such opportunities resemble the kinds of group activities students are likely to encounter in real-world work environments.

Stripling (1994b) describes the facilitation role of the library media specialist in terms of a six-step process for "effective teaching." The steps Stripling advocates include conducting preinstructional activities, modeling the research process, and guiding student practice. In addition, Stripling suggests that teachers provide checklists for student evaluation and create additional projects that allow students to apply skills learned in new situations and different contexts.

Activities that provide "real-life" tasks and situations reflect instructional strategies sometimes referred to as "cognitive apprenticeships and collaborative learning" (Jacobson & Jacobson, 1993, p. 128). In these kinds of instructional approaches, teacher guidance is implemented through "situated modeling, coaching, scaffolding, and fading" in ways that support both interstudent discussion and cognitive reflexivity. As Jacobson and Jacobson observe, conceptualizations of the ISP that are "learned by students [only to be] repeated on tests" rather than to be applied in activities that necessitate their use are effectively "rendered inert [and] unavailable for application in new situations" (p. 125).

According to Bertland (1986, cited in Mancall, Aaron, & Walker, 1986), the zone of proximal development provides an ideal opportunity for the teacher-librarian to demonstrate and model metacognitive behavior and show strategies for tackling unfamiliar tasks. These strategies might include estimates of difficulty, goals, action steps, and elaborative plans. In addition, the coaching role gives the instructor the opportunity to provide feedback, stimulate student questions, and prompt students to summarize their readings and monitor their own understanding of the material. In a study by Palincsar and Brown (1984, cited in Belmont, 1989), the use of this sort of "reciprocal teaching" "resulted in improvements in children's daily independent reading comprehension" (p. 146).

Constructivist Strategies for Information Seeking in the School Library

As noted in the discussion of Kuhlthau's (1993b) ISP and intervention models reviewed in Chapter 3, Kuhlthau has invoked Vygotsky's (1978) ZPD model in creating a hierarchy of intervention strategies that provide direction for librarians operating in constructivist library environments. Specifically, Kuhlthau suggests five levels of assistance or mediation, any one of which may be appropriate at any given time, depending on the student, the context, and the task. These levels are organizer, lecturer; instructor; tutor; and counselor. Interventional activities Kuhlthau (1997, 2001) suggests as useful in framing support at the level of counseling include "collaborating, continuing, conversing, charting, and composing" (1997, p. 714). "Collaborating" acknowledges the value of social interaction in information seeking and critical thinking, as students brainstorm, mentor, coach, network, and learn together in working on joint projects. "Continuing" acknowledges the ongoing nature of information seeking within projects that extend over time and the series of cognitive events students experience as they move from "uncertainty" to "personal understanding" (p. 716). "Conversing" recognizes the importance of interpersonal communication to the process of information seeking. Student-teacher and student-student dialoguing helps teachers gauge student progress and encourages students to think aloud and to "think more deeply" (p. 717) as they focus their research topics. "Charting" provides learners with a model or mental "picture" of the entire information search process as well as the stages from initiation to evaluation. Charting can be accomplished in a number of forms. For example, a timeline can provide students ways to predict events and structure activities. Semantic webs, visual organizers, or Venn diagrams can assist students in categorizing ideas, understanding relationships among aspects of topics or steps in the process, and conceptualizing thinking. Finally, Kuhlthau (1993b) advocates "composing," or journaling, as a strategy that allows students to track their thoughts, reflections, decisions, conversations, and readings in a systematic way. Of course, the use of student journals also allows librarians to monitor student progress (McNally & Kuhlthau, 1994) and changes in students' feelings as well. Providing encouragement when students experience uncertainty or anxiety and providing feedback on what is being done correctly, what is being done incorrectly, and "how to do it correctly" (Carson & Curtis, 1991, p. 65) are also valuable strategies. By the same token, posing questions for students (Joyce & Tallman, 1997; Mark & Jacobson, 1995; Stripling, 1995) in their journals can demonstrate for students the strategy of self-questioning (Bondy, 1984), which, as Bondy concedes, is a skill that must be both activated and practiced if students are to think about their own thinking.

The rationale for supporting students as they engage in active learning tasks is established in the LIS research. For example, a number of studies indicate that the job of narrowing a topic called for within information process models such as Kuhlthau's ISP (1993b) may be very difficult for some students. This means that guidance, direction, and support for students engaged in this task are important services that teacher-librarians can provide (Loerke, 1994; Mark & Jacobson, 1995). Irving (1985) has argued that "selecting appropriate information sources is impossible without some knowledge of which are available, accessible and relevant" (p. 43). As this is the very knowledge that librarians are best equipped to provide, Irving suggests that librarians share the techniques they used in acquiring this knowledge with their students. Engeldinger (1988) believes that librarians also have a role to play in assisting students in making choices among information sources. In fact, this author asserts that "we do our students a disservice if we guide them to this mass of information and then desert them" (p. 196) without concomitantly providing them assistance in developing the skills needed to evaluate them.

Teacher-Librarians and Classroom Teachers: Collaborators in Teaching and Learning

New attention to the role of collaboration in learning has been an important outcome of the constructivist move in education. Within the constructivist project, collaboration is actually multidimensional. In fact, collaboration encompasses group activities for students, interactive relationships between students and teachers, and cooperative planning and team teaching between and among instructors. In short, collaboration in all its many and various iterations and configurations changes how education is done. Perhaps not surprisingly, the desire to make instruction more effective and learning more profound has led LIS researchers to advocate collaboration in planning and teaching of library and information skills (Kuhlthau, 1993a; Stripling 1995). Indeed, there is research to suggest that library skills instruction is more effective when it is implemented to meet curricular goals and delivered in sessions that are cooperatively planned and collaboratively taught (K. Haycock, 1992). Collaboration and cooperative teaching by teacher-librarian dyads also hold the promise of improving the nature of classroom assignments, particularly in terms of the kinds of questions/problems that students are asked to answer/solve. For this reason, school librarians must be "involved in the educational and developmental processes that begin and end outside the library door in the structure, use, and especially the creation of knowledge" (Sauer, 1995, p. 137).

Where collaboration has been successfully implemented (Kuhlthau 1993a), research indicates that a well-equipped library resource center, time for teacher-librarian planning, student motivation and time on task, administrative support, and an understanding and appreciation of a process approach to information seeking are all contributing factors. Elements that Kuhlthau (2001) identifies as enablers of collaborative projects include clarity in the roles teachers and librarians will play as they team teach, "a mutually held constructivist view of learning," "a commitment to inquiry-based learning," and "competence in designing and implementing inquiry activities." Hartzell (1994) and others discuss the importance of professional trust and the value of personal relationships in creating and maintaining a culture that supports successful collaboration, because in a very real sense it changes fundamentally the way education happens. For example, true collaboration between teachers and librarians assumes shared responsibility for assessing student performance on research projects as well as joint teaching. Understood in this way, collaboration may appear "threatening" to some teachers where subject-specific curricula and self-contained classrooms constitute the norm. In such cases, school media specialists must develop and use considerable interpersonal and social skills as well as professional expertise in enacting new models for teaching and learning.

An approach to engaging instructors in an academic library setting, as suggested in Engeldinger and Stevens (1984), may provide clues to the establishment of productive relationships in elementary and high schools. Engeldinger and Stevens found that instructors who were uncomfortable in teaching library reference skills actually welcomed assistance by academic librarians once they understood that their feelings were shared by other instructors. They also appreciated being given background information on library skills instruction and strategies to further cooperation between themselves and the members of the library staff. In addition, the researchers found that time for discussion allowed peers to create solutions to problems and that honest evaluation of cooperatively planned lessons resulted in "better projects" (p. 598). Providing teachers with the experience of finding information for themselves in an unfamiliar setting and in a subject about which they knew little was also an effective way to draw attention to the value to students represented by the librarian's assistance with information tasks.

New Roles for Active Learners

Within constructivist environments, tasks also change—from activities requiring students to "give back" to the teacher the information in the lessons taught to assignments posed as problems to be solved by active learners. In short, knowledge, within the constructivist view, is a process of construction rather than an act of reproduction (Jonassen, Myers, & McKillop, 1996). As noted above, this emphasis on the student's control of the learning tasks extends to include "metacognitive" activities in which students monitor the activities, reflect on their experiences, and evaluate their own progress in learning. Vygotsky's (1978) description of the transfer of responsibility as the student is led to take over the tasks at hand essentially posits a kind of cognitive apprenticeship, particularly where the information problems that students are asked to solve are in some sense "real" problems and require the collection of primary data. Peer tutoring, brainstorming, and the collaboration of class members call for students to contribute to their learning communities and play mentoring roles as well. This provides practice in monitoring the self and others and in giving feedback related to their experiences as required in the situations they will encounter as they enter the real world of work (Bruffee, 1984).

The Importance of Teaching the Research Process

The constructivist concern for "process" has created a shift in what is considered curricular content, that is, a concern for the processes involved in learning as well as—or in some cases, as opposed to—a concern for the final "product" or project. For this reason, the instructional design that educational "constructivists" tend to promote employs the use of multistage curricular units. Implementing instruction in this way provides opportunities for students to engage in "authentic" problem-solving activities, rather than in traditional and generic instructional sequences that proceed without reference to learners or context (Jonassen, Myers, & McKillop, 1996). (Loertscher [1985] and Eisenberg and Berkowitz [1990] have suggested the use of "collection mapping" as a way to target units and topics in all curricular areas and collect the resources to support them.) Research indicates that this approach to instructional design works in that it promotes comprehension, depth, and breadth in course content (Pappas, Kiefer, & Lewiston, 1990, cited in Winograd & Gaskins, 1992).

According to Eisenberg and Berkowitz (1990), "the first objective" of teaching process models "is to help students gain an understanding of the overall" process (p. 15) and, secondarily, to show students the relationship of specific subskills within the process that students need to develop and practice as "a series of instructional experiences" (p. 17). This approach permits students to consider the "means" (e.g., steps in the process), not as meaningless hurdles or portions of the task to be "rushed" through but as problem-solving skills they can apply to other complex tasks in other contexts and situations. It is, after all, this sort of "cognitive flexibility" (Jacobson & Jacobson, 1993, p. 126) that is the essence of active learning.

Teaching a research model creates a systematic approach to and structures for information seeking; by so doing, children develop a "vocabulary" to use in discussing the search process and their place within it. By the same token, an understanding of the process itself enables students to predict the activities that lie ahead and to visualize the goal of the research and the projects they will create. Research in LIS underscores the importance of this understanding to the meeting of curricular goals. For example, Pitts (1995) found that students' lack of a "mental model" of the steps involved in undertaking a curricular activity proved to be a serious obstacle to their success in completing their research projects. McNally's (2004) dissertation study of high school students engaged in online searching supports Pitts's conclusions. Given the complexity of the research task, and the fact that teachers making the assignments may themselves be operating on the basis of "flawed" models of informational resources (e.g., electronic databases) and/or inappropriate instructional strategies for teaching information searching (Tallman & Henderson, 1999), it is not hard to understand why children and adolescents experience so many difficulties in conceptualizing the information-seeking tasks in which they are asked to engage.

Effective "Research" Assignments

Research paper assignments or "source themes" have long been a staple in secondary school curricular programs in history/social studies or English/language arts. These projects seek to provide students experience in information seeking, problem solving, the use of primary and secondary sources, and the mechanics of writing. At least since the 1980s, these kinds of projects have been scaled down for use with ever-younger populations of schoolchildren. Indeed, it is not unusual to see Information Age kindergarten youngsters engaged in library activities requiring them to "research" sets of specific facts. While most assignments for primary school children are content with information in a single source from a "contained collection" (Kuhlthau, 2001), older youngsters are admonished to find information in a variety of print and networked sources. Citing Marland (1978), Moore (1993) describes this instructional strategy as "the project method," on which

> students are typically given a topic to research, generally a person, place or event, and are told to use resources from the library, take notes, make an outline, and produce a report. [Sheingold] makes the point that the kind of topic assigned in this context is often a category (Switzerland, music, the 18th century, spiders . . .) and the task can be completed by reviewing a limited number of resources writing about a few appropriate subcategories, and producing an attractive cover page. (p. 2)

In Moore's view, these kinds of activities "demand a fairly superficial interaction with information, not necessarily the critical information gathering and use essential to the research and inquiry skills supposedly developed through project assignments" (p. 2). A major flaw in information-seeking activities predicated on this model is that children develop an expectation that their hunt in the library will eventually uncover a source that provides "the exact answer to their questions in the exact format required" (p. 17). However, even where students understand the synthesis aspects of the task (C. Gordon, 1999), they expect to do little more than reflect, report, and make some conclusions for the teacher based on what they have read. Moore (1993) believed students in her study created simple rules for the research task: "[T]hink of a question, identify its keywords, look up the subject index for a Dewey number, go to the shelves and find the answer. . . . If any part of that sequence failed," Moore continued, her students "often seemed surprised and confused."

> In the real world, information seeking takes a long time. It is characterized by blind alleys and false scents and answers often need to be constructed following critical consideration of the available information. Few of the children [in the study] were prepared to do that. (p. 28)

Given such an understanding, it is perhaps not very surprising that students often bring little enthusiasm to the research task and that teachers and librarians often observe little evidence of "synthesis" and a good deal of plagiarism. In teaching information literacy skills through the creation of student-conducted information-seeking tasks, teachers and librarians may be making unwarranted assumptions about student learners. This has led Moore (1993) to conclude that "project assignments should be set with the purpose of promoting an understanding of thinking processes rather than the product alone" (p. 29).[1] She also suggests making "explicit the problem solving nature of the task and promote the notion that there are many ways of reaching a solution" (p. 28).

What does the research tell us about the framing of research assignments and its impact on search success and skill development? What kinds of research tasks will have the most educational punch? In planning research tasks, to what need we pay the most attention? In short, how can we design projects to ensure the achievement of information literacy standards so that our students become effective and efficient users of information? Research studies in the field of school media point to the framing of developmentally appropriate research tasks, the timing of the project within curricular activities or the unit, the relevance of the research task and topic to student experience and interests, the explanation of the project in terms of its educational value, clear exposition of project goals and expectations, the creation of research topics as questions that require students to think critically, structuring the project to allow time for presearch planning, attention to process learning and product creation, and the opportunity for student evaluation (Table 6.2).

Clearly, it makes sense to begin planning the research task with the students' developmental levels in mind. Hirsh (1997) noted particularly the appropriateness of the research assignment (a sports celebrity) for fifth-grade students operating at Piaget's (Inhelder & Piaget, 1958) concrete operational stages. "The assigned topic was concrete and relatively unambiguous," Hirsh opined, and "the topic was also one that generated high levels of interest and excitement" (p. 46). How the research activity fits into the overall plan for teaching content within a given curricular unit and activities planned prior to information seeking also have important implications for the

Table 6.2
Questions to Address in Planning Student Research Assignments

- What cognitive skills do students bring to the project?

- What will the research project contribute to student learning and skill development?

- At what point in the unit should the research project take place?

- What are the goals and objectives for this particular project?

- What research topics and questions will resonate with learners?

- How can the research questions or topics be designed to elicit the students' use of higher-order thinking skills?

- How can the project be structured so as to ensure time for student planning and reflection and minimize student stress?

- What are the outcomes for students in terms of the process and the product of the research task and how can these best be explained?

ability of students to carry out the research task. A number of scholars have drawn attention to the importance of content knowledge as essential background for information searching. In other words, research assignments should not be fact-finding expeditions that precede direct instruction and in-class reading on a topic; rather, they should be planned and timed to build on and deepen understanding after students have an overview and prior knowledge of the course content. Often, background readings are textbook based. However, Callison (1994) suggests moving beyond "textbook generalities and teacher-led discussion" to include the sharing of "books, newspaper articles, films, guest lectures" (p. 51), and the like as preresearch activities. In this way, students' knowledge of their topics will provide a basis for in-class discussion and a context for subsequent exploration and learning.

Research indicates that when students lack prior knowledge, their ability to conduct independent research in a meaningful way is compromised. For example, McGregor (1994) found that the student's prior knowledge of a topic "influence[d] the ability to narrow a topic" and to search effectively for "pertinent information"(p. 72). In addition, having students engage in front-end activities such as brainstorming and planning has been recommended by Kuhlthau (1985) and others as important preliminaries to information seeking. Significantly, Wesley's (1991) research indicates that student planning prior to searching helps to minimize student anxiety and frustration that can subvert or even derail research activities.

It is also clear that students are more successful when the goals and objectives are clearly stated (J.W. Thomas, 1993) and where assessment criteria and the reasoning behind research tasks are understood in advance. Irving's (1985) research indicates that children need to know upfront what is being required of them and what they are expected to learn or to gain from the research activity as well as to understand the criteria for success in terms of the completed project. Without this knowledge, they will lack the framework for "self-evaluation, which is essential to the development of good learners" (p. 35). Beyond this, the instructions created for each assignment should indicate the "level, depth, scope, and approach[es]" the students are to take, because this information will help them "structure [their] information-seeking, reading, note-taking and presenting" (p. 35). Students should understand the value and the reasons for the subskill tasks that are set before them as well. Indeed, "the admonishment 'use more than one book' carries little weight or value if it is not properly qualified; for example 'use more than one book in order to collect different views of the topic'" (pp. 26–27). To this end, instruction in the relative value of alternative sources should also be provided (Mark & Jacobson, 1995).

The ability to analyze and synthesize information in a variety of sources demands thinking at the high end of Bloom's (1956) taxonomy. Research projects that do not push students to engaged intellectually with course content have little educational value. Critical thinking is not an option, Norris (1985) asserts; it is "an indispensable part of education" (p. 40). For this reason, research assignments must be designed to ensure the use of higher-order thinking (Honebien, 1996; Jay, 1986) in completing the research task rather than permit students merely "to recite facts related to a topic" (Clark, Martell, & Willey, 1994, p. 70) obtained in a "search, print, and run" library activity (Jacobson & Mark, 1995, p. 116). Assignments that do not take this into account and are passed off as "doing research" serve to "reinforce" fact-oriented learning—a practice that can be antithetical to critical thinking. Perhaps the hardest lesson that students will learn "is that information is not the same as knowledge and that facts are not understanding" (Sauer, 1995, p. 142). But this is an important lesson and one that teachers and librarians must learn as well.

The importance of evaluation as a part of the process of learning is well established in the literature of school librarianship (Callison, 1994; Eisenberg & Berkowitz, 1990; Grover, 1993; Kuhlthau, 1994) and education (J.W. Thomas, 1993). Its purpose, Kuhlthau (1993b) writes, "is to identify what learning has taken place and where further instruction and practice are needed" (p. 59). Self-assessment by students is essential. As Irving (1985) notes above, the evaluation tasks for student researchers include not only a critical review of information sources relevant to their projects but assessment of their own learning as demonstrated in the completed project. Other LIS researchers and scholars (Craver, 1989; Eisenberg & Berkowitz, 1990; Kuhlthau, 2001; Pitts, 1995) agree. When evaluation of product and process is in place, there is a balance in emphasis among product, content, and skills that many educators feel is essential (Delpit, 1996). Without this feature, students lack the opportunity to learn from their mistakes (Irving, 1985) or to gain awareness of themselves as learners. Indeed, they may focus their time and energy on activities that, in the end, have little educational impact. For example, students in studies conducted by McGregor (1994) and Pitts (1995) were so focused on the product they were producing that what was being learned in terms of content and process was not considered. Students saw the research task as "a job." McGregor asserts, "[R]ather than as an opportunity for learning" (p. 74). A focus on learning and the learning process has another payoff: According to Kuhlthau (1997), students who are aware of the importance of process skill development are not as likely to copy the texts verbatim and tend to think more completely.

This begs the question, When should students assess their learning and to what issues and behaviors should students attend? Kuhlthau (1993b) suggests that "evaluation should take place immediately following the completion of the research assignment" (p. 59) and include consideration of their abilities to create a focus for their papers, their use of time in planning and carrying out the research activity, and their use of available resources, including the expertise of the library media specialist. Callison (1994) also suggests that students evaluate their information sources in terms of their usefulness, the effort expended in obtaining resources, the transfer of skills to other projects, and the value added to the educational experience (p. 54). To facilitate self-assessment, Kuhl-thau (1993b) recommends the use of timelines (to help students "visualize the stages in the process"), flowcharts (to help students track their progress), conferences with the library media specialist, and the creation of a "summary statement" (to assist students in evaluating their participation in the process and their creation of a final product).

According to Irving (1985), an effective lesson is one that has relevance and meaning for the learner and reflects the learner's "knowledge, ability, level [and] interests" (p. 112). Moreover, "motivation implies relevance, and relevance implies an understanding of both learner and learning material" (p. 112). Perhaps for this reason, Schack (1993), Giese, Cothron, and Rezha (1992), and Solomon (1994) suggest that assignments be structured to allow students to select topics based on their interests and that the introduction of the project might better serve both the students and the project if it began with a survey of student interests and hobbies rather than with background on the subject or topic. Finally, Hirsh (1999) attributed to student choice and topic of interest her informants' ability to personalize the search, their eagerness to undertake the research task, and their care in evaluating the search results. "Students were absorbed in the search process," Hirsh wrote, "and generally did not settle for the first piece of information they found" (p. 1278). Such an approach acknowledges in a tangible way the importance with which the teacher and librarian regard student preferences and feelings in planning research projects.

Jakobovits and Nahl-Jakobovits (1990) call attention to the salience of student affect (e.g., "how we feel about and value learning experiences") (Jacobson & Mark, 1995, p. 108) as a concomitant to success in information-seeking tasks. Kuhlthau's (1993b) work emphasizes the affective nature of the search task, specifically the feelings of uncertainty, confusion, and anxiety as common experiences for novice information seekers, and presents a schedule of intervention strategies for library media specialists to assume in providing targeted assistance. In planning student assignments, librarians should anticipate these feelings of insecurity and allow time and space for students to discuss them as the information-seeking task unfolds. The importance of this kind of guidance and feedback along the way cannot be overstated: They are absolutely essential if children are to understand the value the teacher and library media specialist attach to the student and the learning process over and above, and in addition to, the project that comes at the end (Pitts, 1995).

In her study, Burdick (1997) raised the issue of gender as it relates to information seeking and the character of student research assignments. Citing the work of Carol Gilligan (1982) and Mary Pipher (1994) related to the socialization of adolescent girls in the United States, Burdick particularly noted the need for library media specialists to support girls in creating and expressing their own personal perspectives in their research projects; to include women as well as men as researchable "topics"; and to legitimate connectedness and syntheses, which often characterize a feminine approach to learning, in addition to the informational approach and logical argument formats, which tend to reflect a male perspective. These themes resonate with the work of Ford (1996), who has noted the need to expand curriculum to include all races and ethnic groups. Ford reminds us that "students learn through acts of omission and commission; they learn from what is present in and left out of the curriculum" (p. 143). Where topic choices fail to acknowledge "the contributions [to history, literature, science, etc.] of various racial, cultural, and economic groups" (p. 143), the "invisible veil" (p. 193) of monoculturalism effectively masks the biases that such omissions portend.

When "research" projects are carefully planned and structured "as a planned series of intellectual challenges, rather than as a rote series of tasks" (Clarke, Martell, & Willey, 1994, p. 70), students have multiple opportunities to practice and use the information skills they are acquiring. This underscores the value to students of practicing skills within assignments that are meaningful to them rather than in make-work sorts of activities that were the warp and woof of the old "library skills," "scope and sequence" library curriculum.

"Effective" Assignments from the Student's Point of View

Garland's (1995) study of information seeking in school contexts sought to tap the information-seeking experience from the point of view of the students involved. Specifically, Garland was interested in finding out how 387 high school students in 18 classrooms studying a range of subjects from physiology to composition regarded the research task and those elements that related to student achievement and feelings of satisfaction. The tasks themselves were as "heterogeneous" as the students and subject matter and included formal papers and a variety of creative presentation formats. Table 6.3 summarizes the elements that Garland identified as important to students: choice of topics, which gave students "a sense of control" (p. 178); experience with the type of project assigned; background knowledge of the topic; access to assistance in choosing a topic and understanding the research process, particularly if the task "required a higher level of thinking" (p. 176); an explicit connection between course content and the topic; explicit goals and processes for task completion; specific evaluation criteria; and opportunities for social interaction and group work.

Taken together, research into research projects and models for information seeking conducted in the library provides some direction for school media specialists to use in assisting teachers in the creation of research assignments and in providing students with context and direction in undertaking an information search task.

Table 6.3
Effective Assignments from the Student's Perspective (Garland, 1995)

Students want:

- A choice of topic
- Opportunities to practice
- Assistance with choosing a topic
- Assistance with the research process
- Explicit ties between course content and particular research topics
- Explicit goals and evaluation criteria
- Opportunities for social interaction and group work

Authentic Research

"Reporting has masqueraded as researching for so long that the terms are used interchangeably," C. Gordon wrote in 1999, with the result that the ever popular research project has become a bromide, "analogous to '[t]ake two aspirins and call me in the morning.' . . . Educators adjust the dosage for older students: the length of the paper grows with the time allotted to the task but the prescription is the same." Gordon notes that students have come to view the research task as a writing assignment in which factual accuracy, grammar, and writing style are emphasized over individual thoughtfulness or creativity in problem solving. Alternatives to "secondary source" research papers have been explored by Gordon and by Schack (1993), both of whom advocate authentic research projects that involve students in gathering information from "primary sources" and address real-world problems "of personal interest for which there is no known answer" (Schack, p. 29). Within Schack's meaning, information seeking becomes data collection, and information-seeking skills become data collection skills. Within an authentic context, interviewing, surveying, observing, and analyzing documents, which are not usually included among information skills taught in elementary and secondary schools, are important additions to the more usual ones related to information handling. In addition, Schack recommends teaching of fundamentals of research design. The use of "authentic" research assignments is consistent with current trends in education that center on experiential learning (e.g., discovery learning; situated learning, Brown, Collins, & Duguid, 1989), cognitive flexibility, cognitive apprenticeship (Collins, Brown, & Newman, 1989), and anchored learning. There is a growing number of national and Web-Based centers that feature the papers of middle and high school students involved in researching real world problems and issues in health, community life, and the like. C. Gordon's (1999) study involved a group of tenth graders in an action research project as part of "a performance-based assessment task, including rubrics, student journals, and peer editing." Essentially, this researcher wanted to know:

> [C]an students successfully use primary research methods to collect their own data? What if teachers and librarians designed research assignments that distinguished between information and data—that is, between facts and ideas recorded in books and electronic sources—as evidence, or data, collected firsthand by the student researcher? What if teachers and librarians became reflective practitioners who saw the research assignments as an opportunity to . . . evaluate and revise the learning task?

The goal of Gordon's action research was to "elevate the quality of students' research papers" and "to heighten the awareness of teachers and librarians in their roles as reflective practitioners who use the same research methods they are teaching . . . to assess the design of" research assignments. In the process, students were also to learn the difference between report preparation and original research.

Before beginning their research projects, students in Gordon's study attended a 10-session "advisory" class to learn the fundamentals of action research: research design, proposal writing, research questions, research methods, data collection, and analysis. Results of Gordon's research indicated that students need time to write and reflect; they also require instruction in the correct form and use of citations, and practice in Internet searching and key word use. The study also provided additional evidence that student research is an iterative, idiosyncratic, and messy process that involves students in rereading background information at various points in the process and modifying research questions as the task unfolds. Importantly, "the authentic research assignment raised the level of appreciation of teachers for the complexity of independent student work." For this reason, Gordon asserts that presenting the research process as a simple and finite sequence of steps is not helpful for students or teachers. Gordon also advises that students build "prior knowledge of the topic" as preparation for authentic research tasks.

Gordon's study also revealed student preferences when undertaking research. Most often mentioned were: additional time to complete the task during the school day; timing the project earlier in the school year; in-school assistance; the use of forms, charts, and organizers in keeping track of sources; assistance with database and Internet searching strategies; and assistance with formulating research questions (see Table 6.4).

Table 6.4
Considerations in Designing Effective Student Research Assignments

Effective Assignments:

• Are developmentally appropriate for each student

• Do not arise in a knowledge vacuum

• Present clear objectives and evaluation criteria

• Make explicit the reasons for required components (e.g., numbers of sources, types of sources)

• Create a context for the development of process and project skills

• Explicate the importance of process skills

• Arise in a systematic program of research within the context of on-going classroom curriculum

• Are directly and explicitly connected to course content

• Offer gender-fair and culture-fair choices related to student interests

• Offer options that acknowledge learning style preferences

• Are meaningful for students and linked to student experience

• Involve students in critical thinking rather than recalling or reporting

• Take the affective needs of students into account

• Are broken down into manageable elements and supported by teachers and library media specialists

• Provide opportunities for group discussion and activity

• Are structured to allow time for searching and task completion based on a realistic appraisal of source and system availability

Skills and Competencies for Independent Research in the Library Media Center

Kuhlthau (2001) states that "teacher-librarians play a vital role in creating inquiry learning that prepares student for work, citizenship and daily living in the Information Age." For his part, Loertscher (1996) describes the "information literate student" as "an avid reader," a critical and creative thinker, and "an interested learner" who uses technology skillfully and investigates, organizes, and communicates what is learned in a responsible manner (p. 192). In many respects, this description provides a useful introduction to thinking about program development in school media centers, for it taps into the competencies identified by Doyle (1994) and Irving (1985) as frameworks for the "information skills curriculum." Among those identified by Doyle are the abilities to identify the information problem or need; formulate strategies to guide the search process; locate appropriate information sources: read, use, and evaluate the relevance of the information obtained; and apply the information created to new understandings of the topic in solving the problem or carrying out the task. According to Irving, student learners must also be critical thinkers, competent readers, perceptive questioners, resourceful information searchers, skilled information handlers, and accomplished presenters.

Taken together, Loertscher (1996), Doyle (1994), and Irving (1985) have identified a range of skills that not only inform information skills instruction but are also, as Irving argues, the same skills "inherently present in all learning tasks" (p. 23) and "decision-making activities" (p. 24). For this reason, their integration within curricular units, subject areas, and extracurricular problem solving is both natural and useful. Callison (1994) has challenged school librarians to take advantage of the important relationship between critical thinking and information skills instruction by moving beyond activities that "support, supplement, or enhance" (p. 47) critical thinking and to take the lead initiating programs and assignments that teach this important skill, by placing "critical-thinking activities at the forefront of lesson planning" (Bowie, 1990, cited in Callison, p. 46).

Critical Thinking: Skills

What is critical thinking? The skills identified by scholars and educators as dimensions of critical thinking include the ability to set goals, to adjust strategies, to carry out tasks, to distinguish fact from opinion, to establish the authority of sources, to assess the accuracy and relevance of information, and to detect bias and underlying assumptions. In a very real sense these are the sorts of skills that support information literacy and information literacy instruction. The positive relationship between critical and metacognitive thinking and student achievement and school success has been established in the research literature (Lavoie & Good, 1988). Indeed, as Norris (1985) suggests, critical thinking requires students "to assess their own view" as well as the views of others, "to seek alternatives [, and to] make inferences" (p. 44); and Mancall, Aaron, and Walker (1986) argue that critical thinking skills are essential to success in developing "insight and facility in structuring successful approaches to solving information needs" (p. 22).

How can these skills be taught? What strategies can library media specialists use to encourage their development? These are significant questions, and librarians intent on improving the educational value of their information skills programs must find practical answers. Many scholars agree that critical thinking can neither arise in nor exist separate from subject matter and experience and involves a complex of "considerations" including the "disposition to think critically" (Norris, 1985, p. 44). For example, Bodi (1992) has suggested that critical thinking is the thread that ties curricular concerns for course content and the process aspects of information seeking firmly together; Craver (1989) reminds us that "substantive knowledge of the particular subject" (p. 13) is not only the result of critical thinking but also its basis. What's more, this theorist asserts that "reading, writing, speaking, and group interaction play important roles in the development of higher order thinking" and "techniques such as questioning, tutoring, oral recitation, group discussion, and writing are successful in improving the ability of students to think critically" (p. 16).

Reading Skills

Research in the literature of LIS and education consistently acknowledge the importance of reading (Krashen, 1993) and reading comprehension skills as essential to developing competence in information seeking and learning (Kulleseid, 1986). The selection of reading materials that reflect the experience and reading levels of student learners has always been an important aspect of school librarianship. Another is the creation of library activities that enrich and extend that experience. However, research in reading suggests a number of activities that library media specialists can use in helping youngsters increase reading performance and comprehension. For example, Tierney and Cunningham (1984) recommend the use of prereading activities to stimulate student interest, to focus attention, and to activate student thinking. Tailoring the reading assignment "to the child's level of understanding," assisting the learner to focus on the main ideas in the passage, and promoting readers' awareness of their own comprehension by asking questions and activating their "schemata" in prereading exercises have been suggested by Baker and Brown (1984). These strategies help students maintain a focus, reflect on the new information, and relate this information to the "knowledge they already" possess (p. 375). In some instances, "advance organizers, structured overview, story preview, use of text adjuncts, pretesting, and setting objectives" (Kulleseid, 1986, pp. 43–44) have helped students improve reading comprehension. In addition, Kulleseid recommends asking questions about content, visualizing narratives through "diagrams and pictorial representation" (p. 44), reading aloud, using study guides, and group discussions as techniques that promote understanding.

Summarizing information is a difficult skill[2] for some students to learn, but it is also an information skill that can and should be taught in an "information curriculum." According to Brown and Day (1983, cited in Baker & Brown, 1984), useful strategies for instruction include teaching students how to delete information that is redundant or peripheral, how to create abstract or superordinate categories for objects, events, and activities, and how to look for topic sentences as clues to the main idea. Reading strategies that have proved especially useful for student learning in information contexts are skimming (Kulleseid, 1986) and note taking (Lavoie & Good, 1988).

Stimulating student interest and providing "interesting reading materials" are also essential prereading activities, since, as Wigfield and Asher (1984) suggest, they can help students both overcome their "insufficient knowledge base" (p. 375) and improve reading performance. Yet McGill-Frantzen, et al. (1999) assert that the availability of books in the classroom and library are "necessary but not sufficient" in promoting literacy. Training teachers to create inviting book displays, reading aloud, literacy activities, and encouragement create "a richer print environment" than merely providing print materials without these strategies. Perhaps ironically, these are just the kinds of strategies that school media specialists learn in library school!

Writing activities can also improve students' reading comprehension, especially when these activities help focus the students' attention and extend the time they spend on reading tasks. Among the most valuable writing exercises are summarizing, "abstract writing," "outlining, paraphrasing, notetaking and writing paragraph headings" (Stosky, 1983, cited in Craver, 1989, p. 15). Although no one strategy has been proven consistently superior for all students, Nagel (cited in Craver) found that "students showed greater comprehension when they summarized paragraphs in a single sentence" than when they "wrote nothing" (p. 15).

Although reading well is certainly an essential skill for information seeking, the ability to read critically is required if students are to make judgments about the relevance, point of view, authority, and bias of the sources they encounter. As Goodman (1976, cited in Baker & Brown, 1984) notes, critical reading is often inadequately taught and seldom practiced, and the lack of this important skill poses "a barrier to [student] development of an adequate repertoire of study skills" (p. 372). This fact begs the question, Why aren't media literacy skills, which are aimed particularly at the critical examination of media products, a standard part of the information literacy skills curriculum?

Searching Strategies: Bates's Idea Tactics

Information literacy is a complex cognitive task and must be taught if students are to develop this important life skill. Marcia Bates (1979b, 1989) has created a useful framework for information seeking by observing how successful searchers seek information. According to Bates, in real-world settings, information searchers may begin broadly and then narrow the focus of their inquiries, or they may change their focus entirely as they encounter information or the lack of it along the way. Bates (1989) has described as "berrypicking" these sorts of searches, which seem to evolve over time in response to information as each additional item is retrieved and reviewed. In fact, searchers who engage in this kind of process may not seek an overview of a research domain at all, nor desire a wide range of sources; instead, they employ a "serialist" (Pask, cited in Eisenberg & Berkowitz, 1990) approach, searching for "just enough" information to answer their specific information need or research question.

According to Bates (1979b), information providers can assist users in their searches by suggesting or teaching strategies to use when searchers get "stuck" or when their search strategies do not produce the desired results. Bates's "idea tactics" is a facilitation model, comprised of "heuristics" or "rules of thumb" for searching. These tactics can help learners think more clearly (e.g., think, brainstorm, meditate, consult, rescue, wander); alter the direction of the search (e.g., catch, break, breach and or reframe); or think more creatively (e.g., notice, jolt, change, focus, dilate, skip, and stop) (see Figure 6.1). This facilitation model provides library media specialists a wide range of specific strategies to suggest to students as they assist novice and expert searchers. "Thinking" refers to planning ahead in order to save time and energy later. "Brainstorming" helps students to generate new ideas, new search terms, new sources, and types of sources; these can prove very useful in the presearch phases as well as later, if the search stalls or if the beginning strategy is blocked. "Meditating" may help students use both sides of their brains, in adding imagination and hunches to logic in planning the search strategy. "Consulting" as a tactic accepts the validity and value of discussing the research task with others and is a forthright admission that no one

Figure 6.1
Bates's Idea Tactics

Thinking	Thinking about the search will generate new ideas
Brainstorming	Getting ideas and considering alternative ideas can enrich understanding and approaches
Mediating	Thinking logically/rationally and creatively/intuitively activates both sides of the brain
Consulting	Talking ideas over with others provides valuable information and feedback for ideas
Rescuing	Persistence can prevent the premature abandonment of a useful approach
Wandering	Browsing in a variety of resources can help stir the imagination and ignite thinking
Catching	Realizing that the current approach isn't working or that a mistake has been made in a citation
Breaking	Doing something different perhaps searching in a different way
Breaching	Considering a different subject area or domain, database, or discipline when a given search strategy is exhausted
Reframing	Reexamining the question to get rid of distortions or erroneous assumptions
Noticing	Attending to what is being learned about the topic as information is encountered
Jolting	Changing the point of view by looking at the question as it has been addressed for different age groups or in different formats or in different disciplines
Changing	Breaking whatever patterns are in use in terms of the types of sources, the disciplines, and the terms being used in searching
Focusing	Narrowing the search or the concept or looking at only one part of it
Dilating	Expanding the search to widen the focus or considering larger issues
Skipping	Looking at another aspect of the same topic or considering subtopics as a way to view the whole
Stopping	Doing something else while your mind continues to work on the problem

person, neither student nor teacher, can know everything. In light of Solomon's (1994) finding that youngsters may not think to ask for help, reminding students that consulting presents a viable option seems wise. "Rescuing" is an effort to make sure that the early frustration or failure a student experiences in the search doesn't result in the premature closure of an otherwise promising search.

"Wandering" recognizes that quite frequently ideas may be generated as one pursues various resources and materials if only we are open to the possibilities. Allowing for this sort of flexibility may spark interesting ideas and directions. "Catching" oneself is the awareness that an approach is no longer yielding the desired results. "Breaking" suggests that when one line of approach isn't working, it's time to risk going off in another direction or perhaps searching in a different way. "Breaching" requires the searcher to get out of one set of domain resources and into another—for example, to search a different online resource or a different database. "Reframing" asks a student to take another look at the question that is being posed and to ask it in a different way. "Noticing" indicates that students must appreciate what they learn about the topic or question as they move through the search and make use of the new information to enrich the scope or the depth of their approach to the search enterprise. By "jolting" students change their points of view, perhaps by considering how the question might be addressed by different groups, in different formats, or in other domain fields. "Changing" requires students to try new terms, new types of sources, and different disciplines when current ones fail to provide the needed information.

"Focusing" asks students to narrow the current search or the topic itself, perhaps by looking at or considering only one part of it. Limiting the scope of the topic by specific time, era, or epoch, by a specific group of people, or by a particular geographic location are all useful ways to reframe a topic in a more targeted way. "Dilating" calls on students to do the reverse: to expand the question or the search, perhaps by looking at the larger issues involved in the research question or taking a more general approach to the topic. "Skipping" asks students to move around in a topic and to look at different aspects or subtopics involved, in order to get a handle on the "big picture." "Stopping" acknowledges the fact that fatigue plays a role in any search situation and that in some instances stopping for now and coming back fresh on another day is the best strategy possible.

Ellis's Research Strategies

Ellis (1989) has identified "starting," "chaining," "browsing," "differentiating," "monitoring," and "extracting" as useful search strategies to assist searchers in presearch planning and in locating sources and finding information during the search process itself. "Starting" activities employed at the beginning of the search include identifying key articles and key authors in bibliographies, abstracts, indexes, and catalogs. "Chaining" refers to a strategy for using citations as clues to other information on the same topic. In "backward chaining," searchers follow up citations listed at the end of the documents they initially find; "forward chaining" involves the perusal of citation indexes to find articles or research based on the original study or publication. In these ways, relevant information on the same subject can be located in an efficient manner. "Browsing," within Ellis's meaning, is a sort of semidirected searching of resources and books in an area of potential interest. Using differences between sources as an indication of their nature and quality is a strategy that calls for searchers to "differentiate" among the alternatives to select those that are likely to be the most useful. Ellis suggests "monitoring," which requires that searchers check to see that the most recently published information in a field is not overlooked. Finally, "extracting" involves the systematic perusal of each source to locate information of interest. Any or all of these strategies can be of use to both novice and seasoned searchers and should become part of the instructional regimen of an information skills program.

A recent article by Meho and Tibbo (2003) describes a study following up on

Ellis's pre-Web research on information behavior and suggests some additions to Ellis's model: "accessing, networking, verifying, and information managing" (p. 583). Accessing acknowledges the many strategies information seekers employ in obtaining relevant resources identified through starting, chaining, browsing, monitoring, and extracting activities, as well as the problems searchers may encounter in their acquisition. Accessing specifically addresses activities, issues, and problems inherently a part of information seeking outside major research libraries. Networking activities, once the terrain reserved for invisible colleges of scholars, are now possible through access to the Internet. Verifying deals directly with problems related to the reliability, accuracy, and authenticity of information seekers locate on the Internet. Finally, information management involves the arrangement and storage of information located during a search. "Although," as the authors point out, information management "processes are the exact opposite of information searching or gathering activities, they are activities that have a significant role in enhancing information retrieval" (p. 584).

The elements involved in information seeking first identified by Ellis (1989) and expanded by Meho and Tibbo (2003) are not sequential; the latter have suggested a four-stage recursive model that groups the activities relative to various stages in the information-seeking process: searching, accessing, processing, and ending. Searching activities include starting, chaining, browsing, monitoring, differentiating, extracting, and networking. Accessing involves decision making with regard to direct and indirect resources. Processing activities might include chaining, extracting, differentiating, verifying, and information managing, as well as analyzing and synthesizing information and initial writing activity. Ending involves the completion of search tasks and projects.

Information-Handling Skills

Providing support to students in tasks involved in information use is an important aspect of the teacher-librarian's job. Some of the same strategies that assist learners in comprehending what they read are also useful in helping them become competent in handling the information they find. These include skimming, underlining, highlighting, paraphrasing, and note taking (Irving, 1985). Although outlining has been found useful in focusing attention, Bretzing, Kulhavy, and Caterino (1987, cited in J.W. Thomas, 1993) indicate that activities such as summarizing, "cognitive monitoring," and note taking are more often "associated with significant gains in achievement" (J.W. Thomas, 1993 p. 577).

Students frequently find narrowing a topic or finding a frame very difficult. In fact, Irving (1985) regards this step in the information-seeking process as "the most sophisticated skill" (41) and suggests that it is made even more problematic when one is compelled to do it in the absence of deep understanding of the topic or field. Irving suggests that breaking down the task and the topic is exceedingly important. "Unless we know clearly what we are looking for," she writes, "finding out" about a topic may be virtually "impossible" (p. 42) even when students have an opportunity to choose their own topics.

Knowing what to do with the information is also a critical task (Wesley, 1991). Until constructivist scholars called attention to the importance of information seeking as a process, a great deal of student time was devoted to the location and access of resources. With the shift in paradigm has come the acknowledgment that the use of the information gathered is the most critical aspect of information seeking (C.A. Haycock, 1991). In a very real sense, it is through the arrangement, organization, and presentation of information, first as an outline, sketch, or diagram, and then as a finished paper or project, that students create a synthesis and repackage the information in a meaningful and "learningful" way.

Irving (1985) has conceptualized steps in this important task as "presentation skills": organizing information, ordering and arranging it, outlining the project, writing it up, creating sentences, creating paragraphs and writing topic sentences, editing, and proofreading. Information handling also includes attention to the appropriate use of quotations and the proper form and use of citations and footnotes. In this way, students learn to give credit to their sources in an intellectually honest manner. All of these are skills that librarians are eminently qualified to help students acquire.

Akin's (1998) research considers the issue of information overload as a problem for youngsters engaged in information-seeking activities. In this context, information overload may occur when too many topics are offered as research alternatives, too many resources are suggested as relevant, or too much information is retrieved as a result from information seeking. Akin's study sought to learn through survey data how fourth and eighth graders in two Texas public schools felt about information overload and what they did about it. It was Akin's view that "knowing how the child feels can help the librarian be more empathetic. But knowing what the child does allows the school media specialist to respond with instruction" (p. 6). Particularly, Akin was looking for strategies students used and the relationship of gender to the overload experience. Results indicated that 80 percent of students surveyed reported the experience of information overload, with girls and younger students "more likely than boys" and older students "to have felt overloaded" (p. 4). Techniques reported by students of use in easing overload included selecting a few items from all those available, "filtering" and "chunking" the information, or linking "large amounts of information into some common shape" (e.g. "a teacher supplied outline"). Akin noted that

> the difference between filtering and omission is one of time economy. A pile of material may be filtered piece-by-piece (based on individual decisions regarding each piece of information), or by an initial global decision to disregard all material meeting specific criteria (such as all information contained on microfilm).

Feelings reported by fourth-grade students in Akin's study included confusion, frustration, depression, anger, and physical distress ("bulging," "bursting," "exploding," "headache," "fatigue"). As Akin notes: "These visceral responses speak to the degree of disillusionment or disappointment with the information at hand and the expectations of the child." Eighth graders experienced similar reactions to overload, although the expression of their reactions tended to the vulgar, in boys, and expressions of stress, tension, and panic in girls. "The eighth graders reported additional feelings of being stuffed and bored." Akin concluded that some kinds of inattention and acting out, swearing, or physical ailments necessitating trips to the school nurse observed in the library might be the result of overload.

Although limited in terms of the number of students and the self-report method involved in survey research, Akin's study is interesting in that it indicates that overload affects children as it does adults and that admitting and discussing the possibility of overload and strategies for coping with this syndrome are an important part of library and information skills sessions. Kuhlthau (1999) describes this feeling as "the dip" in confidence that searchers experience when encountering new and confusing information; "Advances in information systems that open access to a vast assortment of resources has . . . in many cases . . . intensified the sense of confusion and uncertainty." This is especially true when information retrieval systems overwhelm "the user with everything all at once, rather than offering a few well-chosen introductory pieces for initial exploration."

Taking the availability of information into account in structuring lessons and information tasks also seems reasonable. According to Akin, helping students reduce the number or types of materials to be considered, changing the topic, actively seeking assistance, and taking a break may also be useful to suggest as ways to cope when the demands of the task overwhelm learners. Brainstorming coping techniques in advance would also assist learners to "identify the overload reduction strategies on their own, learn more about manipulating information products, and adopt a pro-active response to information overload." C. Gordon (2000) has identified a presearch strategy for coping with information children are likely to encounter: concept mapping. In fact, Gordon's informants indicated less overload where concept maps were used. Gordon indicated that this technique is one way to provide an overview of both general and specific terms that describe the topic.

Motivating the Information Seeker

Teachers have long understood the importance of student motivation in achievement, although "motivation alone does not guarantee that children will achieve to their potential" (Ford, 1996, p. 46).[3] Even though, as Callison asserts, children are learning all the time, motivating students to learn is still an important part of the instructor's task. This is especially true in information seeking, as the task is complex and can be frustrating. Students who lack perseverance are at a distinct disadvantage when independent initiative is seen as vital to their success as information seekers. Burdick (1996) noted that a majority of youngsters she studied manifest a bored attitude and a lack of interest in the research task. Successful searching is surely compromised when students are not motivated to engage in the information-seeking tasks set before them. How can teachers and library media specialists motivate learners? A number of theories provide options. Based on operant conditioning models, behaviorists look to reinforcement as a tool for motivating learning. The mechanism in reinforcement is that its application increases the likelihood that a desired behavior will be repeated. Reinforcement is extrinsic in that it comes from "outside" the learner. Gold stars, rewards, even including good grades are examples of extrinsic reinforcers. This contrasts markedly with intrinsic motivation, which involves the personal satisfaction that an individual feels "from simply participating in a learning experience that stimulates curiosity and interest, promotes feelings of competence or control, and is inherently pleasurable" (Small, 1999, p. 3). According to Small, "[T]eachers who encourage an intrinsic orientation created challenging learning situations that allow students to have some control over their learning and that promote competence and mastery" (p. 3).

As we saw in Chapter 5, Maslow's (1970) hierarchy of needs is a theory of motivation in that unless children's deficiency needs (physiological, physical, safety, and social/belonging) at the lowest levels are satisfied, they will not be motivated to consider higher-order or "growth" (self-actualization, beauty, and order) needs. A third option is attribution theory, which is an effort to explain how people understand their own failures and successes in life. Within this framework, the locus of control is important. Internal locus of control seats the cause of success or failure in personality, personal attributes or abilities, and personal effort. An external locus of control places credit and blame on forces outside the individual in the situation, community, the context, the task, fate, or luck.

Achievement motivation recognizes the need for achievement (personal excellence), for affiliation, and for personal power. Research based on this model suggests that regulating the challenge inherent in a learning task to take into account these needs will enhance motivation and achievement. "Students with a high need for achievement prefer moderately challenging learning tasks"; "students high in 'need for affiliation' prefer" cooperative learning and group work, while "students with a high need for power prefer activities in which they can assume leadership roles and have an impact on others" (Small, 1998).

One explanation for the dynamics of intrinsic motivation is found in Flow theory in the work of Csikzentmihalyi (1990) and is also germane to a consideration of student motivation. According to this theorist, a flow state is achieved when a person is so involved in an activity that he or she finds both challenging and rewarding that he or she loses all sense of time and space as participation in the activity proceeds. Expectancy—value theory argues that motivation depends on the individual's valuing of a given activity, a valuing of "success," and his or her estimation of the likelihood of success as a result of a particular action or activity. Small suggests that school librarians can apply this theory to teaching and learning by making the content of the lesson "engaging and meaningful" and promoting "positive expectations" in terms of achievement through demonstration and examples of successful work done by others.

Motivational strategies based on these frameworks include gauging the difficulty of the task to a specific group, providing students an explanation of learning goals as personal accomplishments and competence, and having high expectations for all members of the group. Making judicious use of external incentives (rewards, positive feedback for effort and improvement and achievement as evidence of personal competence), in addition to enhancing intrinsic incentives (arousing student curiosity, maintaining student interest, choice) is also good practice.

Teacher behavior has also been recognized as an important element in motivation (McKeachie, cited in Callison, 2003). As Callison asserts: "[W]e should never forget that our own enthusiasm and values have much to do with students' interest in the subject matter. Nonverbal as well as verbal methods are used to communicate such attitudes. Smiles and vocal intensity may be as important as the words we choose." For their part, Scheidecker and Freeman (1999, cited in Callison) list some strategies used by "legendary" teachers in motivating student learning.[4] These include conveying to students how much the teacher enjoys teaching and the students they are teaching, partnering with students and sharing in failures, and finding strategies that will help students achieve success. Finally Scheidecker and Freeman advocate the use of what they call safety nets—opportunities for students to practice developing skills, to retake or redo tests and projects in which they are not successful, and to review essential skills without risk or embarrassment.

Many individuals who are drawn to the information professions find the kinds of problem-solving tasks represented in information seeking and the creation of multi-resource term papers and projects stimulating and fun. For many school media specialists, the "thrill of the hunt" for just the right resource or just the right information is motivating enough. What one must recall is that this sort of motivation is born in previous success with these kinds of activities. For those without such a background, the task of information seeking may be decidedly off-putting. It is toward motivation of these kinds of learners that Small has devoted her research attention in recent years. "Ideally," Small (1999) writes, "effective library and information skills instruction not only helps students acquire the skills they need to be able to solve their information problems, but also stimulates and encourages intellectual curiosity, information-seeking, and exploration behaviors."

What can librarians do to inspire and motivate students involved in information seeking? What interventions can they plan to improve student persistence and ameliorate the destructive elements of anxiety, uncertainty, and frustration? (See Table 6.5.) Using Keller's (1983, 1987, cited in Small, 1999) ARCS Model of Motivational Design (attention, relevance, confidence, satisfaction) as a framework, Small set out to explore motivation issues and strategies in the school library. Within Keller's lexicon, *attention* refers to the "curiosity and interest" in the activity a teacher can stimulate in students; *relevance* refers to a teacher's ability to show the value, utility, or importance of the activity for students and its ties to the learner's experience; *confidence* refers to "building learners' confidence in their abilities to succeed"; and *satisfaction* refers to "promoting the potential for learning" by "encouraging and supporting [students'] intrinsic enjoyment" of the task at hand.

Research into motivation in teaching and learning has established the importance of teacher behavior in the classroom and the use of intrinsic rewards in boosting "on-task behavior and higher motivation toward the task" (Small, 1999). Techniques linked to the development of an intrinsic reward orientation include support for student autonomy, "helping students set reasonable learning goals," and "having students reinforce and monitor themselves for accomplishing steps toward their goals (Hilker, 1993)." In reviewing the literature, Small found that there were some decidedly negative outcomes including a decrease in personal motivation when extrinsic motivators

Table 6.5
How School Library Media Specialists Can Motivate Students to Learn

- Stimulate interest in the activity at the outset in an engaging way based on individual differences in interests, learning styles, media/format preference, and the like

- Ensure relevance through the use of clearly articulated learning outcomes tied to search success and academic success and appropriate and reflective of student experience, culture, and values

- Increase student confidence by explaining what is expected, what the students will be doing, and the availability of assistance, expertise, and emotional support provided by teachers, librarian, and peers

- Ensure that expectations are achievable—challenging but not overwhelming—and that the achievement of goals lies within student ability levels

- Recognize students for effort and improvement

- Inspire intrinsic motivation by encouraging student enjoyment of the research experience and discussion of the value of the activity to other school- and life-related tasks

- Judge the outcomes of the task in gender- and culture-fair ways

- Provide opportunities for students to practice important skills and to revise unsuccessful projects

were employed, most especially when such rewards were "unrelated to the learning task."

Essentially, Small (1999) wanted to find out what kinds of motivational strategies were used by the librarians in her study (attention, relevance, satisfaction,) and whether or not such strategies were factors in terms of on-task student behavior (indicated by raised hands, student questions, note-taking activity). She chose to observe the use of motivational strategies (as formulated in the ARCS model) by library media specialists engaged in teaching fully integrated and exemplary library and information skills programs to upper elementary and middle school youngsters. In this study, Small found that school librarians employed motivational techniques as "an important part of their overall instructional style," that middle school librarians used them more often than elementary librarians, and that they used attention-focusing strategies "more than three times as often as relevance, confidence and satisfaction strategies." In addition, Small observed that middle school librarians tended to use more attention, relevance, and confidence strategies, while elementary librarians used more satisfaction strategies. Attention strategies observed included posing questions, "novelty, humor, enthusiasm" and "variations in media, grouping students," and the like. Overall, Small found "the relatively low number of relevance, confidence, and satisfaction strategies" employed by school librarians in the study "troubling," especially when one considers Kuhlthau's (1993b) observations that "students experience significant anxiety and low confidence" at various stages of the ISP. Small suggests that "negative feelings" may be reduced if library media specialists employ "confidence-building strategies" especially "during the information-gathering phase" of the ISP. "Furthermore," Small argues, "using strategies that reinforce the relevance of information skills to information-seeking tasks and promoting the relationship between successful information seeking and student effort is critical." It is also significant to note that extrinsic motivators (verbal praise) were used more than intrinsic ones. Small concludes that this kind of motivation is more "informational" than "controlling" and is therefore "less likely to decrease existing high intrinsic motivation and may sometimes even increase existing low intrinsic motivation."

Conclusion

As previously noted, Eadie (1990) has voiced his concern over the move by librarians to take on the responsibility for creating programs to teach "bibliographic instruction" in academic libraries. "I'm not sure," he has written, that "we should be 'educating' students but I am sure we should answer their questions. I think (to echo Radford) that we should dismantle barriers rather than train people to climb over them" (quoted in Sauer, 1995, pp. 137–138). While few would argue with the goal of simplifying systems to enhance student abilities to use the library as independently as possible, most media specialists would assert that today's students encounter far more difficulties in searching for information than those posed exclusively by the idiosyncrasies of information systems. In fact, research indicates that since students frequently lack an understanding of the research process (Kuhlthau, 1993b; Pitts, 1995) as a whole, they both need and would welcome assistance in understanding the process in carrying out their projects. Moreover, Eadie's comments appear to reflect a view that considers information as an objective entity and research as fact-finding, rather than as a set of learning activities that require students to seek evidence to support a personal perspective, as it is understood within a constructivist framework.

Mancall, Lodish, and Springer (1992) have asserted that "the task of the school is to be sure that students leave grade 12 ready for the information-rich environment in which they will live" (p. 527). If we accept this statement as a goal as well as a challenge, then as educators we must take the responsibility for instructing students in information seeking, information handling, and information use. Eadie's (1990) angst serves a useful purpose in that it draws attention to the tension between service and instructional models of professional intervention that is created when we assume that they are based on disparate views of the librarian's proper role. Indeed, some might argue that the "service-only model" is appropriate for "knowledge as fact," while "knowledge as process" (Buckland, 1983) requires more intensive levels of support and instruction. Certainly, where the "barriers" to system access have been removed, the student can concentrate on the attainment of content and process skills and learn to ask the right questions rather than to "find" the right answers (Keefer, 1993, cited in Sauer, 1995). However, in a very real sense, constructivist approaches to education, particularly in terms of modeling and coaching, demonstrating and scaffolding, represent the bridging or the blending of the service/instruction dichotomy, preserving the best intentions of both in ways that support the development of student competence, independence, and learning. When constructivist environments are well established, school libraries can become arenas where posing questions, discussing ideas, and pursuing understandings become the central activities, and where students can come to solve the sorts of ill-defined problems (J.O. Carey, 1998) that arise in the real world.

The realization that information skills are "survival skills" (Irving, 1985, p. 115) and essential for the development of lifelong learners has created a new sense of urgency among many school library media specialists and other librarians responsible for planning programs of instruction. Perhaps for this reason, LIS theorists have sought to change the terms we use to describe the skills students need to develop. Breivik (1989), for example, insists that using the terms "bibliographic instruction" and "library instruction" only perpetuates the notion that what goes on in the library is separate from what goes on in the classroom and in life, effectively rendering contributions the library can make to student learning peripheral or superfluous. For this reason, we might be well served and we might better serve the students who are our primary constituency if we settle upon *information skills* or some other broader term that more accurately describes what we actually want students to learn as a result of our intervention (Irving, 1985).

J.O. Carey (1998) claims that the differences inherent in the terms "library skills" and "information literacy" are philosophical and substantive, denoting two distinct wings of cognitive psychology: the objectivist wing and the constructivist wing. In Carey's view, the now defunct scope and sequence approach to instruction is objectivist, as is an approach that calls for the sorts of lesson planning frameworks that specify in advance the goals and outcomes of instruction, the skills required for the implementation of the activity, the ability levels and needs of student learners, and the tasks to be undertaken in implementing the lesson. Constructivist approaches, on the contrary, focus on problem solving and call on the students to struggle through the complexities of the problem and themselves to come up with the "tactics and strategies" (p. 7) they will need in resolving research questions for which no single answer exists. As is evident, the instructional design involved in the case of constructivist lesson planning is entirely different from the sort of preplanning to which one has become accustomed. Carey describes this planning in terms of "a learning environment" or "problem scenario" (p. 8), for which the instructor furnishes the guidelines. Because there is value in both approaches to instruction, Carey articulates a middle ground, which calls for the teaching and learning of a given model in constructing understandings from a variety of sources. "It appears that the approach to learning the problem-solving process is quite objectivist in its design, while the approach to learning from a variety of sources is quite constructivist" (p. 8).

Finally, contemporary understandings of teaching and learning rely on theories that recognize "the inescapably social nature of cognitive development and of cognition itself" (Belmont, 1989, p. 142). For this reason, library media specialists need to rethink the ways in which instruction has traditionally been delivered and adopt an instructional role that meets the exigencies of the task and reflects the needs of the specific group of learners for whom the instruction is planned. Balancing the roles of instructor and coach, of expert and peer, of partner and authority are tasks that require consideration. Knowing students and observing "their responses to instruction" (p. 143) will be especially important in assessing learning and planning for further instructional interventions.

Notes

1. Delpit (1995) has taken exception to a blanket approach that values the use of process-oriented models over, or at the expense of, emphasis on student-created products as evidence of learning. Arguing that diversity in the classroom demands diversity in instructional strategies, Delpit asserts that "teachers do students no service to suggest, even implicitly, that 'product' is not important" (p. 31). "[T]here is little research data supporting the major tenets of process approaches over other forms of literacy instruction," Delpit writes,

> and virtually no evidence that such approaches are more efficacious for children of color. . . . In this country, students will be judged on their products regardless of the process they utilized to achieve it. And that product, based as it is on the specific codes of a particular culture, is more readily produced when the directives of how to produce it are made explicit. (p. 31)

Although she is discussing the emphasis on process over product in contexts other than information seeking, Delpit's concerns have important implications for planning information literacy skills instruction for many African American youngsters.

2. According to Delpit (1995), some Native Americans may experience difficulties in summarizing tasks based on a community-based "prohibition against speaking for someone else" (p. 170). It was apparently for this reason that college students in a study by Basham (cited in Delpit) offered their opinions of "various works rather than the summaries of the authors' words" (p. 170) they were assigned to create.

3. Ford (1996) reminds us that "motivation is not synonymous with achievement, and . . . cannot be inferred by examining achievement test scores" (p. 68). In addition to learning style differences discussed in Chapter 5, Ford points to "study skills, work ethic, . . . attitudes toward school and the quality of the classroom climate or learning environment" (p. 46) as essential to student success.

4. Delpit (1995) asserts "it is impossible to create a model for the good teacher without taking issues of culture and community context into account" (p. 37). If, as is the case with many black youngsters, students "expect an authority figure to act with authority" (p. 35), it seems likely that library media specialists will have to enact a counseling or coaching role in a professional way and one that does not undermine his or her persona as an authoritative individual.

7 From Reference Skills to Technological Literacy

The Impact of Electronic and Internet Resources on Information Skills Instruction

The profound changes in education wrought by computer technology have created opportunities for students unparalleled in the history of education. In connecting students with an ever-expanding, increasingly "interactive informational universe" (Huston, 1989, p. 19), these changes have transformed the concept of "library" from a place to a "function" (Ely, 1992) and vastly increased the contributions library media centers can make to teaching and learning. At the same time, the ability to access electronic resources has brought into sharp relief the layers of complexity surrounding online searching and the challenges that confront school librarians in helping students find and use information to meet academic and personal needs. At the same time, late-20th-century preoccupation with automating library collections, obtaining Internet access, and expanding holdings to include new CD-ROM resources (Kafai & Bates, 1997) has given way to millennial efforts to integrate technology across the curriculum, keep pace with technological innovations, and thrive in a climate of school reform, competing interests, and budgetary shortfalls.

> [T]here is no longer any question that knowing how to seek information electronically will be an essential skill for all individuals.
>
> —*Aversa & Mancall, 1989*

Basic to research in the area of technology and information skills instruction is the assumption that a contemporary definition of information literacy must include the ability to locate, retrieve, and use *electronic* as well as print-based resources. While our commitment to helping children learn remains unchanged, the charge put forth in *Information Power* (AASL & AECT, 1998) has been amended; school library media specialists must now ensure that online and electronic resources be used to enrich instructional objectives and that students have the skills necessary to succeed in the workplace today and tomorrow (Kuhlthau, 2001).[1] Morton (1996) argues that "the value of a computer environment is not so much the improvement of students' achievement through computer use as it is the improvement of students' ability to achieve" (p. 419).

"Computers in themselves do not automatically change the nature of teaching and learning" (Woronov, 1994, p. 1) nor improve the quality of education (Broch, 2000) or learning (Oliver & Oliver, 1997), political rhetoric to the contrary notwithstanding. Rather, it is the ways in which their use is integrated into classroom activity that produce educational benefits (Todd, 1998). In Neuman's (1995a) view, the costs of technology in terms of energy, money, and time "can be supported only to the extent that the resources contribute to what schools are all about—learning" (p. 1). It is within this context that library media specialists have shifted their instructional focus from information access issues to information use.

Research interest related to technological issues in library and information studies has been very high, for there is still much to be learned that will help designers create more user-friendly retrieval systems for "the brave new world" of hi-tech school libraries. By the same token, many LIS researchers are conducting studies to further our understanding of children's information seeking in electronic environments and their experiences as they attempt to find information online. These studies are, and will continue to be, extremely useful to library media specialists in planning instruction related to online searching.

This chapter begins with a discussion of how children think about and use the Internet and then reviews major studies related to information skills instruction and online searching. Some of the educational opportunities that online resources provide are identified, some of the problems that students have encountered are described, and ideas suggested in the research to maximize the benefits and minimize the problems are provided. In fact, pinpointing specific skill areas where instructional intervention can be most effective is a major contribution research makes to practice. A significant finding in this regard is that "many of the search and retrieval skills are equally applicable to electronic, printed, and audiovisual resources" (Irving, 1990, p. 14). Perhaps ironically, research also indicates that many of the problems that students encounter in electronic environments reflect deficits related to their command of the basic literacy skills.

How Students Think About and Use the Internet

The research on children's information seeking online has progressed in recent decades to keep pace with the changes in technology and the expansion of its applications in an ever-widening information universe. Thus have studies of children's use of automated catalogs (OPACs) given way to research into their use of CD-ROM encyclopedias, electronic databases, search engines, and the World Wide Web. Many of the studies are exploratory in nature, with small and purposive "samples" of students. Some have strong theoretical frameworks; some are action projects designed to solve practical problems. This means that, in many instances, the findings lack generalizability to other populations and contexts. While these limitations argue for more and more robust studies, library media specialists can use the insights provided so far in designing instruction and support for children's online research tasks.

> **Overall, I really think that the Internet has a great impact on how much I learn at school and without it I don't think that I would have the opportunities to learn as much as I do.**
>
> —High school girl, quoted in Pew Research Center, 2001

What does the research tell us about the Internet use of children and youth? The Pew Internet & American Life Project (Pew Research Center, 2001) interviewed students from across the country and provides statistical evidence for what most educators suspected—students are using the Internet in ever-increasing numbers, and most of them are thoroughly enjoying the experience. For example, 94 percent of the teenagers who reported having access to the Internet indicated that they rely heavily on online information for research tasks;

71 percent of them used "the Internet as the major source for their most recent school project"; "58% have used a Web site set up by school or a class; 34% have downloaded a study guide; and 17% have created a Web page for a school project." As Bilal and Watson (1998) maintain, "[T]he Web's ease of access, speed of finding information, convenience of access from home and richness in graphics" so appeal to 21st-century youngsters that their continued participation online for school-related research, personal information seeking, and entertainment is virtually guaranteed.

Clearly, kids have had a love affair with computers from the start and were among the first to embrace their use in the school library. While some of their elders were mourning the passing of the "card catalog," youngsters were eager to search the library collection electronically (Armstrong & Costa, 1983) and could do so successfully (Borgman et al., 1995; Marchionini & Teague, 1987; Solomon, 1994). Completing research tasks using online sources continues to motivate and excite youngsters (Borgman et al., 1995; Irving, 1990, 1991; Lewis, 1989), particularly when they have the chance to select topics to explore in which they have a high personal interest (Bilal, 2001, 2002a; Hirsh, 1999).

Except perhaps in cases where computer inexperience caused some initial user anxiety (Oberman, 1995), the use of electronic resources such as those made available through "telecommunications projects, video-based technologies, and CD-ROM have documented positive effects of technology on student attitudes" (Bialo & Sivin-Kachala, 1996, p. 54). In fact, a study by Newbold (1993, cited in Bialo & Sivin-Kachala) reported not only that children preferred researching the electronic encyclopedias to their print counterparts but also that the use of these electronic sources was related to positive attitudes about the library and about writing. Students in Large and Beheshti (2000) found that their informants preferred using the Web as a research resource even though they reported that it was harder for them to use than print sources. In addition, Suton's research (1991, cited in Martinez, 1994) found "some evidence that . . . disadvantaged students find computer technology especially engaging" (p. 399). It is perhaps for this reason that students surveyed by Todd and Kulthau in *Student Learning Through Ohio School Libraries* (Whelan, 2004) emphasized technology support and instruction as such an important aspect of their school's library program.

The Meaning and Experience of the Internet for Children and Youth

Research indicates that children's search experience online is multidimensional, engaging them in cognitive, behavioral, affective, and social activities. The cognitive effort of thinking about a topic and coming up with search terms to describe it, as well as keeping track mentally of search options, engage children on a number of cognitive levels. Judging relevance of retrieved items is also a complex cognitive task. Behavioral demands of Internet use relate to eye-hand coordination, keyboarding and typing, mouse management, and operating peripherals (e.g., printers, zip drives). Children are also engaged on an emotional or affective level, particularly when screens freeze, printers jam, and searches result in an avalanche or a dearth of "hits." Perhaps because technological advances and/or media hype have conditioned them to expect near-instantaneous responses from information systems, speed seems to be an issue and an expectation for many students. Outdated equipment and insufficient bandwidth can combine to produce slowdowns in retrieval that exasperate students, especially when connection time in school is limited to one or a portion of a class period. Finally, children's use of the Internet has a social dimension. Research indicates that youngsters enjoy assisting one another and sharing ideas and Web sites. They also seek and appreciate Web site recommendations from teachers and library media specialists (Hirsh, 1997, 1999) when such assistance doesn't jeopardize self-image or "face."

Student participants in the Pew (Pew Research Center, 2001) study described the Internet variously as a "textbook and reference library," a "tutor," a "study group," a "guidance counselor," and a "locker." These metaphors and the images they evoke provide useful insights into how many contemporary youngsters think about and use the Internet in everyday life. In the first instance, the Internet represents access to a world of primary, secondary, up-to-date, and state-of-the-art sources students and teachers believe essential for engaging in school-related research tasks. A second benefit is the online availability of assistance, in the form of "how to" technology information, homework shortcuts, and online term papers! Indeed, Pew researchers reported that some students see in "the Internet . . . a way to complete their schoolwork as quickly and painlessly as possible, with minimal effort and minimal engagement . . . [and] as a mechanism to plagiarize material or otherwise cheat." On the other hand, students also find the Internet a resource for education, life, and career decision making and as a source for health-related information. For many students, the Internet functions as a kind of virtual study hall that provides an opportunity to communicate with peers online, collaborate on school projects, share notes, and study together for tests. Finally, students spoke of the Internet as a virtual "locker, backpack, notebook"—as a "place to store their important school-related materials" as well as to send papers to peers and teachers, keep track of their schedules, stash course syllabi, and check assignments. In short, students in the Pew study found that the Internet "help[ed] them navigate their way through school" and to balance school tasks and extracurricular activities.

Students in the Pew (Pew Research Center, 2001) study also identified a number of barriers to using the Internet in school. These included restricting access to specific times, places, and conditions; the proliferation of filters that "raise barriers to students legitimate educational use of the Internet"; and the lack of parity in terms of at-home access to computers that makes teachers reluctant to require Internet use for homework. For these reasons, many students in the Pew study considered Internet access an "at-home" activity. These students also considered surveillance and prohibition on email use as reducing the value of Internet access at school.

Online Searching Behavior in Children and Youth

Graphics and the interactive features of Internet searching are particularly popular among today's Web-surfing youngsters. The interactive qualities and animation reflect the active learning style of many children, while the graphics help them to make sense of the information, especially when interest levels exceed cognitive ability and reading proficiency. In fact, search efficiency is not necessarily a priority for many youngsters. For example, Hirsh's (1997) students failed to keep track of search paths or URLs (Uniform Resource Locators) they found useful and had to begin the searches from scratch when they wanted to revisit a Web site.

Research indicates that children are successful browsers, whether they are searching OPACs (Armstrong & Costa, 1983; Borgman et al., 1995), electronic encyclopedias (Cooper, 2002; Liebscher & Marchionini, 1988; Marchionini, 1987), in Borgman et al., 1995, p. 666; or the Internet (Bilal, 2001; Hirsh, 1998), perhaps because browsing "requires less well-defined search objectives than does directed keyboard searching"

(Armstrong & Costa, 1983). Children also use keywords as search terms rather than focused queries or controlled vocabulary (e.g., subject headings) and use of natural-language queries and keywords over subject lists, subject categories, Boolean operators, or other functions offered by search engines. Liebscher and Marchionini (1988) found that long lists of subjects on screen can present problems for children, and it may be that this makes browsing and keyword searching attractive alternatives.

It also appears that the ability to view information online as authoritative, true, or accurate does not come naturally to youngsters searching online (Watson, 1998). In fact, one of the most disturbing elements of children's online searching behavior evidenced in the research literature is their approach to evaluation of the information they find on the Internet. Indeed, most research indicates that children searching online are oblivious to concerns for truthfulness or authority. In their study, Wallace and Kupperman's (1997, cited in Hirsh, 1998) sixth graders accepted what they found on the Web at face value and judged the utility of sites based on whether or not the search terms they were using were repeated in the online text. Schacter, Chung, and Dorr (1998), Todd (1998), Kafai and Bates (1997), and Shenton and Dixon (2003) reported similar behavior on the part of their informants. "As with books," report Kafai and Bates, "the children were quick to assume everything they found about their topic on the Internet was correct just because it was there" (p. 101). However, with guidance and experience, many students were eventually able to "distinguish sales and marketing sites from more neutrally informational sites" (p. 109).

Hirsh suggests that children's acceptance of Web-based information can be partially explained by the fact that her fifth-grade informants "were in the concrete operational stage of development, which means it is difficult" for them to "question authority" (p. 59). However, this probably does not excuse Fidel et al.'s (1999) high school students, who showed a similar disinclination to challenge information retrieved online. Kuhlthau (1997) believes that the "abundance" of information on the Internet is a barrier to evaluation. In Kuhlthau's view, when information is available in such "abundance," it is "particularly challenging for a library media specialist (LMS) or teacher to convince an unmotivated student to distinguish between an adequate and a better than adequate source" (Broch, 2000).[2] It might be well to note that unless youngsters are taught and also expected to appraise critically the resources they find on the Internet and pursue research questions rather than fact-finding tasks, the potential for inspiring the development of higher-order thinking skills represented by the activity of Internet-based searching will remain largely unrealized.

In their study, Kafai and Bates (1997) found that children under 10 years also experienced difficulty with evaluation tasks including the ability to articulate evaluative criteria. However, once criteria (e.g., "easy to read") were suggested, these students could evaluate the sites they visited. Hirsh's study (1998) indicated that children can articulate criteria for relevance, although these may differ significantly from those that adult or expert searchers might apply.

Having said that, Hirsh's (1998) study showed that highly motivated fifth graders "were generally able to articulate their reasons for selecting relevant information in both text and graphic formats." These students made use of "metadata and other descriptive elements" in searching in "an online catalog, an electronic encyclopedia, an electronic magazine index, and the Internet" (p. 58), at home and at school. As concrete thinkers, Hirsh's fifth-grade informants judged topical relevance on the basis of "exact matches" between search terms they used and the vocabulary used by the teacher and the retrieved documents. Students also had difficulty in recognizing the larger categories within which their topics or subjects might fit. For example, "when the book titles [reviewed] did not include their athlete's name," they did not identify the book as relevant. This behavior mirrors that of students in Wallace and Kupperman's (1997) study (cited in Hirsh, 1998), and Hirsh (1996, cited in Hirsh, 1998), where children looked for matching terms in the subjects of retrieved bibliographic records.

The three most mentioned criteria identified by Hirsh's (1998) students included: topicality, novelty, and interest. Novelty as a relevance category translated as "new information" for Hirsh's informants. In other words, if a source provided some facts they needed to complete the research assignment that had not been encountered previously, the information was considered "new." By the same token, an assessment of "interesting" in terms of texts and (especially) for graphics was taken to mean that the information was of personal interest to the searcher. Some students also considered peer interest as a mark of relevance. Following Kuhlthau (1993a), Hirsh noted that relevance judgments changed as the research proceeded with "interesting" replacing topicality as the information search neared completion.

Agosto (2002) explored the searching behavior of 22 ninth- and tenth-grade girls involved in a leadership institute. Her study led this researcher to conclude that the theory of bounded rationality could be applied to information seeking with this group of students. In brief, the theory states that, due to constraints of time and patience, information seekers will rarely attempt to find every bit of information or even the best information when searching; instead, they tend to settle for information that is "good enough." Students in Agosto's study used two strategies to cope with the information retrieved: "reduction" and "termination." Students reduced the cognitive task of reviewing information by using familiar or recommended Web sites, reading site synopses and summaries, descriptions supplied by search engines, and skimming. They found the categorization of sites in terms of "personal websites, scientific websites," or "best for science, for math, for fun" as particularly useful. Termination strategies involved truncating searches as soon as an acceptable Web site was located. This behavior is consistent with the notion of "satisficing" first introduced by Herbert Simon (1955, 1956, cited in Agosto) and typical of approaches many adult users employ in online searching. Shenton and Dixon (2003) report that the English primary, middle, and high school—aged youngsters they observed "were generally intent on retrieving sufficient information to meet the need with the minimum of inconvenience" and tended to close down their searches once a single relevant source had been retrieved, "rather than forming a pool of information from various sources" (p. 1041).

A key issue in terms of the persistence, personal investment, motivation, and enthusiasm for searching online seems to be the interest that students have in the search task itself (Agosto, 2002; Hirsh, 1998). In other words, it seems to matter whether students feel personally connected to the topic or whether they look on the research task as an assignment to be "gotten through." Nor do students evidence much patience online. For example, high school searchers in Fidel et al.'s (1999) study made relevance judgments on the basis of a cursory look at a site, examining the images at the top of the page; this behavior reflects that of students in Bilal and Watson's (1998) research, who rarely bothered to scroll down through the entirety of an online text. Ninth and tenth graders in Agosto's study and Hirsh's fifth graders evinced similar behavior, relying "heavily on summaries describing links" or reading "the first paragraph of an Internet document." One of Hirsh's students summed up this approach in this way: "I don't like to take the time to read the whole thing."

Agosto's (2002) informants also considered goodness of fit with personal convictions, opinions, and beliefs as well as tone of the site (e.g., friendly, patronizing, humorous) in their choices of information resources on the Web. Agosto concluded that "[p]ersonal preferences are an aspect of the affective side of information seeking, as these preferences are based on personal feelings (such as personal dislikes for particular colors), rather than on cognitive or behavioral information seeking" (p. 18). For this reason, Agosto sees a role for "adult intermediaries who work with young people and information" (p. 25) in explaining evaluative criteria and providing search training.

How Technology Changes the Context of Learning

Thanks to the promotion of Internet use initiatives like the Technology Literacy Fund (1996), E-Rate discounts, and the Enhancing Education through Technology Act of 2001, a majority of public schools now have Internet access in the library and in the classroom. "With the notable exception of students attending schools in very poor districts, it is now the case that the Internet is as common a school fixture as lockers and library books" (Pew Research Center, 2001). This means that the context of learning in public education has changed in substantive ways.

Inquiry-Based Learning

During the 1990s, DeWitt Wallace launched the Library Power initiative in 19 cities across the country in school districts where school libraries had been allowed to languish or disappear. The grant funds were awarded to local education funds, which worked with school administrators, teachers, media specialists, and parents to reinvent school libraries on a contemporary model. "Each community developed its own plan for improving its school library program and determined the way in which the school library could improve student performance" (Donham et al., 2001, p. vi). Schools chosen to participate in the project were given money for the purchase of books, software, and furniture; school libraries were reopened and run by certified staff who launched instructional programs conducted on flexible schedules. Across contexts, Library Power librarians adopted inquiry learning as the framework for information-seeking skills instruction. Research conducted to evaluate the programs indicates that Library Power was effective in improving student learning (Donham et al.).

> The challenge for the information-age school is to educate children for living and learning in an information-rich technological world.
>
> —*Kuhlthau, 2001*

As described by its proponents, inquiry learning "centers on the research process" (Kuhlthau, 2001) and mimics "real-life" contexts where learners consider problems, develop strategies, and seek solutions. According to Donham (2001), "For children to own their own learning, they need to own their own questions" (p. vii). These questions include: "What do I already know? What questions do I have? How do I find out? And finally, what did I learn?" (Kuhlthau, 2001). Kuhlthau continues: "Inquiry takes students out of the predigested format of the textbook and rote memorization into the process of learning from a variety of sources to construct their own understandings." In short, "[I]nquiry learning enables students to meaningfully accomplish the objectives of the curriculum by preparing them for living and learning in the world outside of the school." The emphasis on sharing what children learn "with others in the community" (p. 9) sets inquiry-based learning apart from product-centered research projects.

The introduction of the Internet into school libraries creates access to a universe of information resources students can use in inquiry learning tasks and provides a channel through which they can share their knowledge. As Kuhlthau reminds us, "[t]he challenge of the information-rich school is to educate children for living and learning in an information-rich technological world" (Kuhlthau, 2001, p. 10).

Mancall, Lodish, and Springer (1992) believe that online resources create authentic contexts for learning because their use replicates real-world complexities and provides access to perspectives and viewpoints that stretch students and encourage them to think critically. The availability of online resources in school libraries has also created opportunities for independent learning and strategies for individualizing classroom instruction (Peck & Dorricott, 1994). For example, Woronov (1994)'s research indicates that computers have been useful in "supporting inquiry-based science teaching, inclusion of students with disabilities in regular classes, interdistrict collaboration, [and] distance learning" (p. 1). The potential that information skills and technological access provide for enabling students to engage in "active, self-directed learning" has also been noted by Kafai and Bates (1997, p. 104). Indeed in Morton's (1996) view, access to technological resources provides students with an unparalleled opportunity to exercise critical thinking, create their own perspectives, and take charge of their own learning, in ways that make computers "interactive learning extensions of the children themselves" (p. 417). Irving's (1990) study confirmed that online resources facilitated children's independent pursuit of academic topics of individual interest, observing that their use provided information for personal decision making for which the library's own collection offered little support. Since independently conducted activities allowed students a unique opportunity to control many aspects of their own learning, Bialo and Sivin-Kachala (1996) suggest that use of electronic resources will enhance both the self-confidence and the self-esteem of students. In addition, Mendrinos (1994) reported that where resource-based learning initiatives were combined with electronic resources, students felt themselves exerting a measure of control in meeting curricular objectives. In Irving's study, this sense of ownership seemed to arise from the children's ability to download information they themselves chose.

It is well to note here that the computer expertise that students bring to the classroom and library has the potential for changing the dynamics and direction of instruction in the classroom and the library media center. In his book *Growing Up Digital*, Tapscott (1998) reminds us that contemporary teenagers often know more about computer technology than their parents and teachers. Morton (1996) asserts that allowing students to take the lead in pursuing personal lines of research enables librarians and teachers an opportunity to participate as co-learners—those "who also did not know the answers" (Irving, 1990, p. 115) but who were willing to accompany students on their intellectual journeys.

Online Resources Expand "The Collection"

In the days when children's research tasks were based solely on resources available in the school library, information seeking was relatively straightforward. Children used standard "tools" to locate information in print and media formats on hand. The library was "a collection" in a very real sense, for in most instances the resources had been painstakingly, even lovingly, selected by informed adults with the developmental needs, domain knowledge, and language requirements of library users and the specifics of the curriculum in a particular school in mind. In such an environment, the authority, accuracy, and truthfulness of resources could be assumed. Online catalogs and electronic encyclopedias that signaled the library's entry into the Information Age were essentially extensions of this early, controlled, well-structured library environment (Hirsh, 1998). Searching on the Internet of today shares none of these characteristics (with the exception perhaps of Web sites created to offer a number of carefully selected links for children's use) and is an activity of an entirely different sort. The old saying that "on the Internet no one knows you're a dog" seems particularly apt in this regard. Today, anyone can create a Web site for any purpose. Many Web sites that present themselves as informational are, in fact, commercial. Even informational Web sites "sell" a point of view, a specific slice of the experiential pie, a preselected reality. While Mancall and others have pointed to the benefits of being able to access different points of view, such access also raises many concerns and calls for development of new skills. "Since the Internet has no built-in filters to publishing and children are making greater use of the Internet for their school assignments, children need to understand how information is placed on the Internet and how to verify" (Hirsh, 1998) its authenticity, accuracy, and timeliness. While there is some overlap, search engines tend to provide access to a unique and limited portion of the Web sites out there. For learners who expect to search exhaustively online, the information scatter that characterizes the Internet may be especially perplexing.

The School Setting

Online searching requires an environment that supports its use, including equipment that can be used in demonstrating search techniques for large and small groups; facilities that support interaction and group activities engendered by use of online resources; and funding support equal to the financial demands of online services and support (Irving, 1991). Policies that support staff development opportunities and permit flexible access scheduling of online searching activities, as well as technical support for equipment troubleshooting, are also essential in maintaining educationally valuable, information-rich environments (Chelton, 1997).

It goes without saying that a school climate that supports instructional innovation is also necessary if inquiry learning is to be implemented with any degree of success. In the Library Power experience, school districts, administrators and teachers, and parents and community supporters "bought into" the concept and goals, providing political, financial, and moral support for change (Bishop, 2001). Limberg's (1999) study of library-based school reform in Sweden underscores the importance of this kind of support. Limberg reported that even where model libraries had been redesigned in line with the expectations and needs of the school, the changes were perceived as threats rather than opportunities by teachers wedded to traditional pedagogy and instructional roles.

Technology and Learning: Promise and Possibilities

Many studies conducted since the 1980s have led educators to conclude that the use of technology offers many benefits to students. Chief among these are the promotion of critical thinking skills, the development of writing skills, enhanced opportunities for language development, and an increase in student motivation (see Table 7.1). Although it is useful conceptually to consider these benefits as separate entities, research shows that they are interrelated.

Research studies aimed at showing the relationship between use of computers and cognitive development emphasize the possibilities for critical thinking and problem solving that access to technology provides (Means & Olson, 1994). Researchers also

Table 7.1
Benefits for Students from Access to Internet and CD-ROM Resources

Internet access at home and school:

- Motivates students

- Improves attitudes toward reading and writing tasks

- Improves language skills (reading, writing, spelling, vocabulary)

- Provides an audience for student work outside the classroom

- Creates opportunities for inquiry learning, student independence, and individualized instruction

- Increases student choice and sense of control of his or her own learning

- Provides immediate access to resources not available locally

- Provides access to other points of view that create opportunities for critical thinking

- Promotes collaboration between students

point to growth of student learning in the area of oral and written language development as a result of computer use. For example, a study by Bialo and Sivin-Kachala (1996) found that the use of computers for word processing helps "students produce high quality writing" (p. 52). By the same token, Kafai and Bates (1997) observed that the opportunity to exist online as creators of information provides an incentive to students to improve their written work. Other research indicates the importance of social interaction among students working together on computer-based activities in the same classroom (Clements & Nastasi, 1988; Dwyer, 1994; Irving, 1990; Morton, 1996; Nastasi, Battista, & Clements, 1990; Turkle, 1984) as improving thinking skills, vocabulary development, and conversational competence (Bialo & Sivin-Kachala, 1996; Irving, 1991). For example, Irving (1990) found "the fact that on-line searching requires careful and logical query description in order to avoid difficulties led" many children to discuss together the alternatives and the language itself, which resulted in "a good deal of language development" (p. 31). Students also realized language benefits in a study conducted by Diaz (1984, cited in Kleifgen, 1989), which demonstrated that "strong gains in English" were made by students when their learning activities included "complex computer tasks." Finally, Bialo and Sivin-Kachala (1996) found that reading achievement as well as spelling improved as a result of computer use and that the "use of on-line telecommunications for collaboration across classrooms in different geographic locations has been shown to improve academic skills" (p. 52).

Challenges for Students and Library Media Specialists in Using Electronic Resources

While the potential for learning in the classroom and the library in tapping the information potential of the Internet and other online sources cannot be overstated, researchers have identified a litany of problems children encounter when they attempt to search electronic sources to carry out their research tasks. Even sophisticated computer skills do not automatically translate into skills in searching. That youngsters experience difficulties as novice searchers should not be surprising when one considers that we are now expecting them to negotiate complex online systems that not so long ago were the exclusive province of highly trained professional intermediaries (Huston & Oberman, 1989).

> **Unless we are vigilant about teaching our students to be effective searchers, "www" may end up as an abbreviation for "way worse on the Web."**
>
> —*Broch, 2000*

According to Sullivan and Seiden (1985, cited in Chen, 1993), problems that beset student searchers in online environments appear to involve three important information needs: knowledge of the library and its new role as an online information center; knowledge of information systems, databases, and their organization; and background knowledge of their research topics. In addition, Irving (1990), Neuman (1995a), Solomon (1992, 1993, 1994), Todd (1998), and others have also suggested lack of information-seeking skills, lack of basic language and literacy skills, lack of time for searching, and Web site design as potential stumbling blocks for students in online search environments. Finally, studies by Oberman (1995a), Irving (1990), and Neuman (1995a) suggest that there is frequently a mismatch between the cognitive demands of information available online and the developmental levels of many student searchers (see Table 7.2).

Table 7.2
Problems Students May Encounter When Seeking Information in Electronic Resources

- Difficulties in accessing materials are compounded in electronic settings
- Students lacked knowledge of database design
- Students had problems with mechanics of online searching
- Student difficulties with literacy skills transferred to electronic settings
- Students' lack of background knowledge made selection of search terms difficult
- Students' lack of background knowledge limited ability to select appropriate databases
- Students' lack of domain knowledge reduced relevance of some retrieved items
- Students' lack of knowledge of search process and search strategies hampered their searching
- Teachers' lack of understanding reduced the effectiveness and value of student assignments

Lack of Mental Models for Information Seeking

An important finding in the work of Irving (1990, 1991) and others is that just as searching online "bring[s] into a more prominent position the need for information-handling skills" (Irving, 1990, p. 5), it calls for an understanding of the overall search process. While such a model also provides instructors with the opportunity to monitor student progress and to assist students when such intervention is warranted, students need to conduct their searches as a sequence of activities and to understand the underlying search "concepts and strategies that transcend individual products" (Neuman, 1995b, p. 297). In his studies of the use of database software by social studies classes, Ehman et al. (1991, cited in Bialo & Sivin-Kachala, 1996) concluded that to ensure effective and efficient searching instructors must provide an overall structure for student tasks as well as "clear expectations with a sequence of activities." In addition, explaining and modeling essential elements of the problem-solving process and offering students opportunities to practice these elements within a framework of supervision were deemed both appropriate and necessary.

In her dissertation study, Pitts (1995) found that her informants' lack of mental models for information seeking compromised the entire research process and the learning from the research task. She concluded that the mental models students did have related to the library and its resources, which actually kept them from appreciating either the types of information available or how that information was organized. Thus, students employing an outmoded model of media center resources assumed that their failure to find relevant titles in one electronic resource meant that the information on the topic was simply unavailable in that setting. Antiquated mental models of the library as a self-contained warehouse of materials also appeared to hamper students in Oberman's (1995) study, who failed to realize the possibilities for information access that exist in the contemporary media center. McNally (2003, personal conversation) also found the lack of mental models for the process, task, and environment hampered search success.[3]

Basic and Information Literacy: Ineffective Strategies and Skill Deficiencies

According to Nahl and Harada (1996), "a growing body of research" in the use of information-seeking skills among elementary and secondary school students shows that these youngsters consistently demonstrate a "lack of general information seeking strategies" (pp. 199–200) for selecting appropriate search terms, especially when they are searching complex and abstract rather than concrete topics for which there are no direct and obvious matches (Moore & St. George, 1991; Walter, 1996, cited in Kafai & Bates, 1997). Other studies show that children lack skills in generating alternative search terms and synonyms (Fidel et al., 1999; Moore & St. George, 1991; Nahl & Harada, 1996; Neuman, 1995a; Solomon, 1993); handling variant spellings (Solomon, 1994), abbreviations (Chen, 1993), and homonyms (Solomon, 1994); and using available thesauri (Moore & St. George, 1991). Walter, Borgman, and Hirsh's (1996) and Chen's (1993) studies highlighted language skill deficits as creating problems, noting particularly the discrepancies between the terms youngsters frequently use and those that indexers typically assign as subject headings. A related problem observed by Irving (1990) was the "particular difficulty" children had in "developing questions that were both sufficiently specific and efficiently expressed" (p. 87).

Chen (1993) noted the failure of students to extend searches beyond the terms originally chosen and to use subject headings and tracings as keys to appropriate alternatives. Students in Newman's (1995a) study also noted failure to "switch" approaches or employ other terms when their searches got "stuck" or when their search terms produced an insufficient number of "hits." These results were confirmed by student search behavior in Fidel et al. (1999), who noted that students frequently changed their topics rather than do the intellectual work of finding suitable alternatives to describe the topics originally chosen. This would seem to support Eaton's (1991, cited in Fidel et al.) finding that successful searches may rely on the searchers' abilities to change and detach themselves from unsuccessful strategies and then to continue the original search in a different manner. It also suggests that the invitational (open) mood identified by Kuhlthau (1993b) as essential to keeping the information-gathering phase of the ISP going demands a degree of cognitive flexibility not usually acknowledged.

Noting the difficulties that students have traditionally had in using print resources, Neuman (1995a) found that these carried over into "electronic" library materials as well. For example, Neuman reported that students often fail to identify classification numbers and other kinds of information on computer screens that would assist them in continuing their searches; similarly, Edmonds, Moore, and Balcom (1990) documented the difficulties youngsters had in following online instructions.

Deficits in basic literacy skills have also been identified as limiting student effectiveness in online searching. For example, in many studies, difficulties related to reading skills (Irving, 1990; Chen, 1993), alphabetizing (Edmonds, Moore, & Balcom, 1990), spelling (Chen, 1993; Irving, 1991; Kafai & Bates, 1997; Nahl & Harada, 1996; Solomon, 1992, 1993, 1994), and vocabulary (Solomon, 1994) all proved confounding for students attempting to search electronically. Irving's (1990) students also encountered difficulties in scanning online texts to find the main idea within a screen of information, a difficulty that Fidel et al. (1999) mention as a problem for students in their study as well. In the same vein, Kafai and Bates (1997) noted student problems in extracting information from child "unfriendly" Web sites, defined by the students as those that employed "big words and lots of text without pictures" (p. 108). Neuman (1995a) particularly noted that the sophistication, complexity, and specificity of information obtained through electronic resources frequently exceeded the reading comprehension levels of the students as well as their needs and concluded that this problem creates "serious conceptual obstacles to students' effective use of these resources for learning" (p. 6).

The Complexities of Design and Interface

The complexity of the information systems and their patterns of organization are difficult for novice searchers to manage, both conceptually and mechanically. Irving (1990, 1991) found that children lacked understanding of the design of online systems as well as more basic concepts related to searching such as how the computers are used in information retrieval. Although children observed by Keil (1979) and Borgman et al. (1995) were able to make sense of hierarchically arranged topics presented online, student searchers in Neuman's (1995a) study experienced difficulties with file arrangement. In addition, they frequently failed to select databases appropriate for their topics or use them in an appropriate order.

Many youngsters found extremely troublesome the creation of search protocols to which the systems they searched could respond (Kafai & Bates, 1997; Nahl & Harada, 1996). Novice searchers also experienced difficulties with the mechanics of the computer itself. Other problems involved the use of search commands (Fidel et al. 1999; Irving, 1990), keyboarding (Chen, 1993; Marchionini, 1989; Solomon, 1994) and typing (Chen, 1993; Kafai & Bates, 1997). Although, as Neuman (1995a) noted, experience with computers will eventually alleviate these kinds of difficulties and, in fact, enables students to master more "sophisticated searching techniques" (p. 108), those with minimal computer skills and online experience may require considerable practice.

Kafai and Bates (1997) found that students were more "receptive to learning" about "differences between search engines" after they had actually encountered search failures (p. 100). However, it should also be noted that where mechanical difficulties frustrate the search, the "extensive cognitive energy required" to overcome the difficulties involved in simply getting to the information may leave little energy, "time or patience to perform advanced cognitive operations on that information" (Neuman, 1995, p. 12). Under these conditions, it is easy to understand why sometimes children conclude that it is finding, downloading, or copying down the information rather than its analysis, synthesis, and use that are the major goals of the research task or project (Irving, 1990).[4]

A possible obstacle to information seeking online noted by Broch (2000) is screen "clutter." Because pop-up advertisements on commercial and other sites tend to "reduce the amount of space available for information," users are forced to scroll down or follow a series of links, some of which take users to online booksellers or other Web businesses. Denning, Shuttleworth, and Smith (1998) assert that scrolling and links make "the navigation task more complex for the user . . . and may be particularly cumbersome or disorienting for children" (Broch, 2000). Of course it is also true that adults and children have different "tastes" when it comes to Web page design. The adults interviewed by Lazarus and Mora (2000), for example, preferred "succinct, uncluttered information, whereas younger users want Web sites that have fast-moving imagery and sound."

Although at least some of the difficulties that students encounter clearly relate to the idiosyncrasies of specific online resources, the good news is that most of the student-centered problems can be overcome through instructional intervention and careful planning on the part of teachers and library media specialists. It is clear that students also need to develop skills related to the mechanics of searching. These would include some knowledge of the mechanics of online systems (including search commands and basic keyboarding moves). Of equal importance for students is an awareness of how information is organized and represented in online search environments, so that they can select databases appropriate for their topics/subjects and that yield information in a useful format (e.g., titles, abstracts, extracts, or full text).

The rest of this chapter presents a brief review of the research literature related to the problems students encounter in electronic searching and some strategies that library media specialists can use in improving student chances for achieving search success.

Lack of Topic Knowledge to Support Information Seeking

Research related to online searching underscores the importance of domain knowledge and generally holds that students who "jump into" online searches without taking time to develop some familiarity with topic-related concepts and a facility with topic-related vocabulary (Fidel et al. 1999; Irving, 1991; Solomon, 1993, 1994) severely compromise their chances of a successful search experience (Gross, 1997; Hirsh, 1997; Loerke, 1994). Because background knowledge enables students "to recall more concepts and integrate these concepts more readily into their cognitive structure" (Chi, Hutchinson, & Robin, (1989, cited in Borgman et al., 1995, p. 666), "building adequate content knowledge [is] a critical first step in successful information searching" (p. 206), regardless of whether the research tasks are self-selected tasks or imposed by others.

The lack of background knowledge sets the stage for a variety of problems. For example, Solomon (1993), Moore and St. George (1991), and Irving (1985) found that children who lacked knowledge of their topics were unable to pose appropriate research questions or select appropriate search terms. These findings underscore the emphasis Chen and Kuhlthau (1994, cited in Nahl & Harada, 1996) place on identifying "descriptors and alternative subject headings" (p. 200) as prerequisites to a successful search process. Research indicates that when children lack essential frameworks, they experience difficulties in identifying an interest to pursue and later in narrowing, focusing, or refining their topics (Kuhlthau, 1993b; Oberman, 1995; Scott & Van-Noord, 1996). For this reason, Kuhlthau in particular recommends that students explore their topics thoroughly before beginning the tasks of collecting sources and gathering information. Domain knowledge as a preliminary to successful information seeking was also addressed by Neuman (1995a), whose research indicated that a student's understanding of the topic not only determines the types of the resources that the student most needs but also the relevance of the information and resources eventually located.

Irving's research indicates that timing the teaching of subject knowledge alongside online searching is one way to ensure that students know enough about the topics to undertake initial searches. Widely appreciated in other kinds of instruction, this strategy has been successfully applied to searching tasks described by Ruggiero (1988, cited in Bodi, 1992) and Mark and Jacobson (1995). Hayes (1994, cited in Mark & Jacobson) for example, found that getting students to consider all the areas that could be covered within particular topics made students more aware of "how broad" their topics actually were.

Problems for Concrete Thinkers

It is clear from the research that difficulties in accessing and using online information sources are related to cognitive development. Whereas Oberman (1995) noted problems that students experienced in dealing with abstractions, Walter, Borgman, and Hirsh's (1996) study found that "the only topics that were consistently easy for children to find were concrete subjects that were [also] easy to spell" (p. 108). Related to concrete operational thinking is the assumption many youngsters make that the title of a book or article reveals its content in a straightforward way. Yet many books and magazine articles carry "catchy" titles that give no hint as to what they are "about." The obscurity of titles was a problem for searchers in a study by Kafai and Bates (1997); and as Hirsh's (1998) informants used titles as indicators of relevance, their ability to evaluate retrieved items was seriously diminished. Finally, Neuman (1995a) has noted the inappropriateness of many online resources for student learners. As newcomers to "the subject matter areas they are in school to master," Neuman explains, students frequently need basic texts, which provide an overview of a subject rather than "cutting edge research results" (p. 6) of the sort generally retrieved from database or Internet sources.

Too Much Information or Just "Enough"

Since information overload frequently leads adults to the premature abandonment of online searches (Wiberley & Daugherty, 1988, cited in Oberman, 1995), it is fair to assume that less experienced information seekers will find excessive search output intimidating as well. In point of fact, managing search results has indeed proved to be a daunting task for many students (Liebscher & Marchionini, 1988). Oberman's (1995) insightful comment that resources available online make it possible to bring "the information to the user, not the user to the information" was realized when the sheer volume of search "hits" made selecting relevant items difficult or where students faced the prospect of reading through long texts online (Irving, 1991). Interestingly, searchers observed by Fidel et al. (1999) frequently stopped with the first screen they encountered, using it as a sort of index or abstract of the site, rather than scrolling through successive screens in search of the information they needed. Schacter, Chung, and Dorr's (1998) students reacted in much the same way. Information overload and students' strategies to cope with it have been documented in studies by Akin (1998), Gordon (2000), and Agosta (2001) as well.

Of course, how much information is too little, too much, or just right depends in large part on the learning style and the cognitive level of the information seeker, the demands of the task, and the information context. In considering information seeking online, Kuhlthau (1999) notes the changes created by access to the Internet: "What is enough [information] may have been a fairly straightforward notion when a person could gather all there was to know on a problem or topic in a contained collection. The concept of enough is quite a different matter in the present information environment" (p. 6). In point of fact, "enough" will be an individual determination based on "what is enough to make sense for oneself within a context and to accomplish the task at hand" (p. 6)" and should be considered at each stage of the information search process (ISP). In a very real sense, the ability to assess for oneself "what is enough" is an important information skill that children will have to learn and relates directly to the ability to bring closure to a search task. To a certain extent, the concept of enough may help to answer the question often heard in the classroom and library: "How many sources do I need to use?" Depending on the situation, the concept may turn out to be liberating for both instructor and learner.

Lack of Time for Skill Development and Searching

Irving (1990, 1991) and others have noted the importance of class scheduling for online searching, because children need time for learning how to search, for practicing search techniques, protocols, and procedures, and for applying newly acquired searching skills to research tasks. Irving (1991) found that a once-a-week schedule of class sessions was insufficient to provide students the time needed to become competent searchers. Not only did this sort of scheduling magnify the impact of system failures and mechanical difficulties, but the intervals between class periods also increased student forgetfulness of procedures and strategies, often necessitating the repetition of instruction done previously.

Time was also an issue for students in the Pew Research Center (2001) study. These youngsters reported that even when there was access to computers in labs, libraries, and classrooms, their involvement in curricular activities in the classroom left little school time for online research. Sometimes equipment was a problem as well. One middle school girl complained: "[W]hen I go to school, it takes a long time to get online, and by that time, the project you're trying to do is already half over. It's no use anyway." The time issue surfaced as well in Broch's (2000) review of search engines designed for children's use. Specifically, Broch discussed the time it takes students to review the potentially large number of "hits" that sometimes result when searching online.

Finally, students in Bilal's study (2000) complained about the slow response of the Yahooligans! Web search engine. According to Bilal, the time issue for youngsters was exacerbated by their lack of research skills as well as by the search engine's complexity. This confirms the importance of technology instruction as an essential literacy skill. Informants in Todd and Kuhlthau's (2003) recent study of Ohio school students, for example, reported that instruction in Internet information evaluation "enables them to save time in the research process by not having to deal with junk information" (p. 11).

Social and Institutional Barriers to Information Seeking: The Digital Divide

Inequities in educational opportunities due to community socioeconomics directly affect students' access to information in print and online sources (Kozol, 2000; Neuman & Celano, 2001) and to the use of the Internet for school research tasks. As discussed in Chapter 5 in a section on information needs and children, the disparities between those with easy access to computers and the Internet and those without persist, with children from low-income homes having less access to personal computers than students from high-income families. The Pew Research Center (2001) study also indicated that because not all students have computers at home, teachers are reluctant to make Internet-based assignments. In order to improve Internet access to students, an increasing number of high schools have created after-school programs, particularly in schools serving low-income students. In addition, many communities are providing Internet access and technology training through local agencies such as community technology centers, libraries, and churches. Lazarus and Mora's (2000) informants appear to want the sorts of support that these kinds of centers are designed to provide: "coaches and mentors to guide them in finding what they want on the Web, suggesting sites or activities to get started, helping use a tutorial, and the like" (p. 21). These initiatives may eventually help to level what remains a very unequal educational playing field for many American youngsters.

> For the more than 4 million children who are without a phone in the home, the implications of the digital divide are even more evident. Despite the rapid increase in computer use and Internet access during the late 1990s, there is still a formidable gap that separates the haves from the have-nots.
>
> —Wilhelm, Carmen, & Reynolds, 2002

Another aspect of the "divide" relates to online content. For example, a significant barrier to information seeking for some students is the predominance of English as the language of the Internet. In fact, Lazarus and Mora (2000) report that fully 87 percent of the content on the Web is in the English language, and only 2 percent of the sites surveyed were multilingual even though 32 percent of Americans speak a language other than English. They also found that even where sites have some bilingual sections, the links they offer take information seekers to English-language sites. Moreover, Lazarus and Mora report that some "areas on Yahoo! Español, such as education, family, government, and jobs, did not contain the same amount of useful (practical and local) information in Spanish" (p. 23). On the other hand, these researchers also found some "sophisticated multilingual Web sites that offer online learning tools . . . students can listen to English word pronunciations; they can practice grammar and receive immediate feedback" (p. 24).

The fact that the Internet is primarily text based makes successful information retrieval online a problem for all children but especially for those for whom English is a second language. Minority adults and youngsters in Lazarus and Mora's (2000) study spoke of needing

> an environment where they can get literacy support or help with English if they need it. They want a place where others in the community are doing the same thing and where they can count on coaching and support to build their confidence, answer their questions, and guide them in new directions. . . . [It appears that] the circumstances through which people get information is as important as the medium.

Implications for Instruction and Intervention

The research related to student searching provides some insights into the skills students need and the kinds of lessons that may be the most valuable in helping students reap the positive outcomes that so much of the literature assures us can be gained by accessing electronic resources. Given the range of problems that children have encountered in searching online, Chen's (1993) observation that "merely emphasizing the mechanical aspects of online technology will probably not serve students very well" (p. 38) seems particularly appropriate. Rather, librarians must apply their knowledge of information and search techniques, curricular goals, instructional design, and student abilities in planning instruction and guiding students in seeking information. In addition, they must create and sustain a climate for searching success while also documenting problems so that their own instructional strategies, and perhaps even the systems themselves, can be redesigned to reflect a more student-centered, child-friendly focus. These are complex responsibilities indeed.

Fortunately, lessons learned from recent research studies provide many clues to student information needs in electronic environments and can help library media specialists develop curricular strategies. Indeed, it is clear that we cannot expect students to pick up the information skills they need without instructional intervention (Entwistle, 1981; Nahl & Harada, 1996), no matter how computer savvy they may appear. In addition, the work of Irving (1990, 1991), Kuhlthau (1993b, 1997), McNally and Kuhlthau (1994), Fidel et al. (1999), and others repeatedly underscores the need for library media specialists to play an active role in assisting youth in information seeking and learning from information sources.

Perhaps the biggest challenge for library media specialists lies in planning and implementing a coherent program of instruction that not only meets the needs of students with vastly diverse computer skills, search experience, and interests but that also encourages "deep" as opposed to "surface" understandings of the processes involved (Entwistle, 1981). Tailoring instruction to fit skills levels will be increasingly complex as the range of student experience with computers and Internet searching continues to widen. Sitting through instruction on basic computer operations will be every bit as frustrating for experienced "surfers" as advanced instruction would be for already angst-ridden novices. The basis of any instruction at whatever level must be the enactment of active learning, which requires learners to relate new information to what they already know; link abstractions to experience; and evaluate the ideas they encounter in light of their relevance and utility (Entwistle, 1981).

Studies related to student use of electronic resources and online searching suggest that essential elements of a dynamic and effective information skills curriculum include instruction about the information search process; an emphasis on the presearch phase of the process; the exploration of the research topic; instruction on critical strategies for evaluating Web-based information; attention to basic literacy skills; attention to searching strategies; and emphasis on information handling skills and information use.

Process Models as Structures for Learning

A process approach to the teaching of research, particularly as provided in models created by Kuhlthau (1991, 1993b, 1994), Eisenberg and Berkowitz (1990), Irving (1985), Stripling and Pitts (1988), Pappas and Tepe (1997), and others, constitutes useful structures within which online searching activities can be planned and implemented. Kuhlthau's model is valuable in its specific emphasis on gaining a view of the topic through exploration as a prerequisite for data collection. In addition, its consideration of affective, behavioral, and cognitive aspects of information seeking make it is a useful tool for teachers and librarians in helping students plan and cope with the frustration and stress as well as the high cognitive demands created by the use of electronic resources. Eisenberg and Berkowitz's (1990) Big6 Skills, which has been successfully applied to searching in electronic environments, would be particularly useful in matching database to topic at the stage of information-seeking strategies, which research indicates has been a problem for student searchers in the past. However, it is well to note that in the final analysis students will have to create their own mental models as frames for independent problem solving online. Providing students with an overview of the options would be a place to start in engaging students in this important activity.

Presearch Activity as a Key to Search Success

It is seems evident that the activities that precede actual searching are more than simply opening moves in the analysis of the research task at hand. Over and over again, studies of electronic searching portend the importance of presearch planning (Nahl & Harada, 1996), question creation, search term generation, and strategy selection. In addition, providing a presearch "space" in the overall project makes good instructional sense in that it allows students to capitalize on what they already know and make personal connections with important issues or aspects of the topics before proceeding. Instructors can help students learn to become planners by conducting activities that stimulate thinking about the topic and the research process and that provide activities that allow students to practice making research decisions. Presearch planning is also a useful strategy for library media specialists. For example, Irving (1990) found brainstorming to be valuable for both librarians and students in that these activities helped the instructors consider the informational dimensions of the research task, the kinds of resources that would be needed, and the "range of topics in which the students were interested" (p. 64). Graphic organizers, and other types of "visual representations," which allow students to "see" facts from a content area in meaningful patterns (Clarke, Martell, & Willey, 1994, p. 70), have also been found helpful to students in exploring possible search topics, formulating search questions, and in selecting search terms when used as a part of the presearch planning (Irving, 1990) process. In fact, Irving concluded that these activities enhanced the opportunities for successful searching and for information seeking in general. Indeed, the generation of "alternative terms" was itself "a valuable exercise" in exploring student "understanding of the subject matter" (p. 88).

The importance of creating a focus or narrowing a topic has proven to be even greater as a presearch strategy, since in online environments the possibility of retrieving literally thousands of items is a distinct possibility. According to Creanor et al. (1995), "The sheer volume forces users to think more precisely about the topic and about their own needs, to make qualitative decisions on the nature of the material at every step, [and] to rely on their own judgment to a much greater extent" (p. 5) than was necessary before.

Creation of focused questions assumes that children can discern the difference between broad and narrow topics or questions and objective and subjective questions (Oberman, 1995). Activities that provide practice for students in recognizing the difference might include presenting students with a list of focused and unfocused research questions and asking them to identify and discuss them as alternatives to a topic, then to select broad and narrow search terms based on the questions as a group exercise. The identification of key words, which is an important strategy in creating search protocols or "strings," can be facilitated by providing practice in main idea identification (e.g., underlining the nouns in a passage, crossing out useless words, and identifying key concepts) and the selection of key words. The expansion of this key word list through the use of synonym finders and the matching of search terms with subject headings or descriptors are also useful presearch activities.

Once children have a general understanding of the topic and have generated some key words to use in searching particular aspects, they will need assistance in constructing effective search statements and browsing techniques. Although Boolean searching can be a difficult concept for young children to grasp initially, library media specialists and teachers have found creative and "concrete" activities to allow children to conceptualize the strategy and practice this skill. For example, one teacher in Irving's (1990) study successfully presented the concepts of the AND,OR,BUT NOT operators by having the class divide and regroup itself according to eye and hair color. This makes particularly good sense in light of the research findings by Sein and Bostrom (1989) that concrete thinkers who may have low visualization skills find analogic models more effective as instructional aids than abstract visualizations.

For teachers and librarians, presearch activities provide time and opportunity to assess student knowledge of the topics, their general skill levels, and their mental models of the ISP. Instructors can also use the presearch "space" for activities that alert students to the many pitfalls that may await them in accessing information online and to make students aware of the range and levels of assistance that the library media specialist can provide. Providing students with information on the strengths and limitations of available databases as well as Internet resources is important, since, as Fidel et al; (1999) found, students sometimes have unrealistic expectations about both the resources and the library media specialist. For example, students researching topics assigned for homework believed that the librarian knew exactly where the information was and could lead them directly to it. Using presearch activities to help students plan in advance may alert students to the realities of the information universe in addition to reducing the "cognitive load" (Marchionini, 1987, p. 70) for novice searchers.

Loranger (1994) has said that good thinkers "make plans for learning." However, research indicates that preplanning of sequential activities is not a part of the repertoire of novice searchers (Grover et al., 1996; Marchionini, 1989), who often tend to rely instead on system feedback. For example, high school students in Fidel et al.'s (1999) study believed "there was no need" for planning the search in advance as they expected to follow whatever leads and links presented themselves as a result of inputting their original search terms.

The Basics of Online Searching

Studies on online searching have produced a laundry list of skills that students must develop to ensure that they can become effective and efficient searchers; not surprisingly, among the most important of these are basic literacy skills related to reading, spelling, and writing, and language. While the lack of such skills may not hamper initial searching activities of youngsters who have access to iconographic interfaces and other types of "kid-friendly" OPAC software, computer software, and Web sites, the lack of such skills will create barriers as the complexity of search tasks increases. The abilities to read for comprehension, to scan a paragraph for the main ideas, and to see the relationships between ideas and concepts on a given topic are the precursors to the ability to generate keywords as search terms; understanding synonyms and the ability to handle alternative word forms are also essential to search success.

Reinforcement of good study skills is also a prerequisite to successful searching and effective use of retrieved information. There is some research evidence to show that note taking is a valuable way to extract information from a text and is preferable to reading or underlining because it "requires greater cognitive effort and a deeper level of processing" (Loranger, 1994, p. 354) and serves as an aid to the recall of information. In fact, "according to Anderson and Armbruster (1984), the very act of writing aids in the processing of new information because it focuses attention" (pp. 354–355).

Research on searching behavior of students from elementary through high school demonstrates their need for instruction in the critical appraisal of Internet sources. Specifically, Hirsh (1998) has identified the "need to learn to analyze and challenge the authority of documents found on the Internet" (p. 54). A strategy that Jacobson and Ignacio (1997) found useful in raising student awareness of evaluative criteria such as authority, accuracy, and the like was to have students design Web pages themselves.

Search Strategies

Initially, instruction on searching was dependent on instructional materials provided by system designers and vendors (Huston & Oberman, 1989). Over time, researchers have compiled an impressive literature on the information-seeking behavior of adults. Among the most helpful have been studies that examined the ways in which end-users go about seeking information in online environments. In an often-cited study by Bates (1989), it was found that in actual search situations end-users rarely followed a linear course but invoked an iterative "berrypicking" process that evolved and changed as their searches unfolded. Recent research on information seeking and children by Borgman et al. (1995) suggests that searches conducted by children on their own also tend to follow nonlinear patterns. However, Kafai and Bates (1997) have noted that student searchers need assistance and support with their search process, particularly "with scanning text and using hypertext links" (p. 107). The problem for novice searchers, as Neuman (1995a) suggests, is that they often lack either the domain knowledge or the cognitive flexibility to allow them to change their perspective, their focus, or their direction without some assistance. This problem can be complicated by the reluctance many children have to ask for assistance, particularly as they approach adolescence. For this reason, young searchers might welcome and benefit from the instruction that includes the "idea tactics" that Bates (1979b) has suggested (see Chapter 6).

Use of Student Journals: Are They Worth the Time and Effort for Students and Librarians?

The use of teacher/librarian-monitored journals to chronicle student experience and track projects and problems has been effective in helping all ages of students from primary school to college (Mark & Jacobson, 1995). Kuhlthau (1991, 1993b), for example, found that journals provide a means for the recording of students' thoughts, problems, and concerns. In addition, a student's journal becomes a permanent artifact of the process and a resource that can be used as a springboard to the next project and consulted as a tutorial for review before the next project begins. Students later used these notations as a basis for evaluating the process and the product. Teachers and librarians can also use journals as venues within which to pose questions that will stimulate student thinking. Hayes (cited in Mark & Jacobson, 1995, p. 29) found that relating questions to specific aspects of Kuhlthau's ISP was particularly useful. Appropriate questions might include: Does the focus relate to the reading and to the topic? Should the focus be narrowed further (or broadened)? Do terms and keywords relate directly to the focus? As the work and instruction continue, teachers can pose other types of questions to check for student understanding. Mark and Jacobson (1995) also recommend the use of student journals and class sessions devoted to presearch discussion of research topics. While journaling and discussion are time-consuming, Hayes found that their use 'improved [both the] focus of the student's first drafts" and the "quality of the final papers" (p. 29).

Mark and Jacobson (1995) noted the use of journals takes time and may lengthen the project. However, they also report that teachers' responses in student journals promote "a stronger focus and can prevent a disappointing final product" (p. 28). In addition, student complaints recorded in journals can pinpoint weaknesses in the collection, in instruction, and in programming. A view of library resources and insights on instruction and intervention strategies from the perspective of students can be powerful tools for improving the quality of services in the school library.

The Library Media Specialist: Instructional and Service Roles

The needs of students involved in online searching should at last put to rest vestigial models of librarianship that claim that collecting and organizing informational materials, creating an information environment, and teaching the skills necessary for library use encompass all dimensions of the school media specialist's job. Current research confirms the need for a variety of instructional strategies and skills and the need to develop new kinds of assistance and services. In point of fact, roles for school librarians to play in supporting students in searching online will appropriately include instruction, facilitation, advising/counseling, and occasionally, information provision. Since in online environments student access to resources is reduced where personal assistance is not provided (Edmonds, Moore, & Balcom, 1990, p. 31), there may be ethical issues involved for library media specialists who fail to anticipate the degree of assistance that student searchers need.

Within the context of online searching and electronic resources, library media specialists should count on providing instruction in the mechanics of searching, pre-search planning (such as identifying key words and creating search questions), selecting search strategies and databases, and managing search results. In addition, librarians can help students in reviewing lists of citations, interpreting output, assisting with the redesign of the search when necessary, and helping students make relevance judgments (e.g., using criteria such as depth of information, length, reading level, and up-to-dateness in addition to "aboutness") (J.B. Smith, 1987). Finally, research indicates that students may need encouragement and assistance with "end game" activities, which involve organizing and using the information obtained (Irving, 1990, 1991).

Just as an improved knowledge of information and use in electronic environments creates new kinds of activities and levels of interaction for library media specialists, new instructional models may be needed in teaching students the skills they need to navigate technological waters. According to Neuman (1995a), collaborative searching involving both the school media specialist and students and peer mentoring can be effective additions to the librarians' repertoire of instruction strategies. On the other hand, Nahl and Harada (1996) found that students need direct instruction and activity for learning the skills required to conduct successful searches and that written instructions may not be as effective an instructional approach as face-to-face interaction. Irving (1990) came to the same conclusion in noting that the children in her study proved reluctant "to read manuals and detailed handouts before searching computerized files" (Norton & Westwater 1986, cited by Irving, p. 14).

An unanticipated dilemma for librarians brought by the proliferation of OPACs, word processing, CD-ROM workstations, Internet terminals, copiers, and printers has also been cited by both practitioners and researchers: the increasing percentage of the media specialist's day devoted to technological troubleshooting and the concomitant reduction of time available for instruction (Mary Jane McNally, conversation with author, January 1997; Chelton, 1997). Time spent clearing paper jams, rebooting frozen computer screens, and monitoring Internet use is time not spent on enacting the instructional role so carefully articulated in LIS literature over the past quarter of a century. While no one would wish to reinstate a "retro" view of the librarian as custodian of resources and general school factotum, it is increasingly evident that the responsibility for riding herd on technological bulls is an exercise best undertaken by library aides under the careful supervision of the librarian. If not, the profession stands to lose much of the instructional momentum that has been building over the past decades. The expertise of the librarian in making the resources educationally useful and instructing students in the skills they will need to survive in the marketplace and college is simply too important to have it dissipated in the "bittiness" of media center odd jobs.

The problems that await student learners in seeking information in online environments argue for librarians to anticipate, diagnose, and remediate student skills. In turn, "this type of diagnostic learning requires information-searching experiences that are introduced, reinforced, and expanded upon across grade levels and content areas rather than presented as 'one-shot' instruction" (Nahl & Harada, 1996, p. 206) sessions. It also argues for documenting instructional intervention as a part of a coordinated program of information skills and the creation of carefully articulated lesson plans that provide for the assessment of student and class progress (Markuson, 1986, p. 39).

Current research indicates the importance of knowledgeable library media specialists—professionals who not only understand the techniques for online searching but also possess an understanding of the possibilities and idiosyncrasies of online resources. Because online searching of bibliographic records yields citations and abstracts for which the full texts may ultimately be desired, knowing how the documents can be obtained quickly and cheaply requires librarians to keep current of the possibilities for interlibrary loans and online resources. Neuman's (1997) research in particular illuminates a central issue in online and electronic environments: that is, matching the database of resources to the information needs of the students. The truth is that school library media specialists must stay ahead of the learning curve in understanding both the technical aspects and the instructional implications of new electronic resources in order to keep pace with a rapidly accelerating technological context (Bruce, 1994).

While it would appear that children's difficulties with electronic resources result from cognitive and skill deficits, an equally cogent argument could be made that their problems are created by the failure of database designers to create accessible, user-friendly information systems. While waiting for systems to improve, library media specialists must plan programs of intervention that will provide a level of support for young searchers seeking information in potentially "disabling" information systems. The children will be well served if school librarians seize every opportunity they have to suggest to vendors and designers the need for improving the systems designed for student use.

Teacher–Library Media Specialist Partnerships for Collaboration and Staff Development

Research has extended our understandings of the importance of collaboration between librarians and teachers in integrating electronic resources into curricular units (Heeks, 1997; Irving, 1991). Interestingly, Heeks (1989, cited in Irving, 1990) reports that collaboration between teachers and library media specialists on student assignments "helps to make [student] searches result in more relevant retrieval" (p. 14). However, successful integration assumes that teachers themselves understand the process of information seeking, the range of electronic resources available, and the characteristics of these resources, as well as the potential difficulties online searching pose for students. In fact, Irving (1990) found than many teachers lacked knowledge of the research process and of information skills generally.

In the mid-1990s Barron (1994) noted the continuing phenomenon of technophobia (p. 48) among school staff. This problem is bound to diminish as time passes. Indeed, the greater a teacher's facility online, the more likely it is that electronic resources will be incorporated within research tasks in meaningful ways. For example, Means and Olson (1994) found that student access to electronic databases caused teachers in the study to create more complex assignments. On the other hand, ignorance of process approaches to information seeking and use may persist even among more technologically adept faculty members. Fidel et al. (1999) report that teacher-designed online searching tasks in their study were fill-in-the-blanks activities that amounted to little more than electronic scavenger hunts. For this reason, library media specialists may have to "educate" some teachers to the benefits of using a "model" for research and assist teachers in creating assignments that facilitate rather than finesse the important learning opportunities such projects can provide.

In addition, there may be a tendency by some teachers to require that students use electronic resources exclusively, without realizing that such resources are most valuable when they are "integrated" (Markless & Lincoln, 1986, cited in Irving, 1990, p. 14) with "books, magazines, newspapers, video and audio tape, slides, posters, museums, historic sites, [and] field trips" (p. 7), or when students are searching for very specific kinds of information. Teachers should also be encouraged to design assignments that build in a degree of flexibility to make allowances for the additional time that may be needed to conduct electronic searching and to anticipate the instabilities of many information systems at certain times of the day (Neuman, 1997).

Although many search strategies are generic and can be applied to information-seeking tasks in print as well as online resources (Irving, 1990), some aspects of electronic resources are unique. Assignments that are planned to capitalize on the unique problems of such resources and the possibilities they engender for learning should be encouraged. In fact, Mark and Jacobson (1995) have suggested modifying student assignments to take advantage of learning opportunities offered by electronic resources. For example, they suggest that teachers require the use of some specific electronic resources to reveal their advantages and their limitations. These researchers also recommend that students submit printouts of searches, justify their choices of relevant materials, and demonstrate an understanding of the differences between academic and technical journals, popular magazines, and ideological tracts. According to Mark and Jacobson, without asking students to think critically about the relevance, utility, and authority of the resources they consult, the requirement to use any given number of sources on a topic is meaningless.

Notes

1. The Department of Commerce asserts that the K–12 years are critical "in generating student interest in" information technology and the career opportunities now possible for students with the requisite skills and access to computer technology (Twist, 2004).

2. Todd (1998) cites Burbules (1997) in describing

the Net as an indiscriminate mix of five types of information, where quality, importance and reliability of information is difficult to determine. These types are: Information: factual, clearly sourced; bears all the traditional hallmarks of reliability and quality. Misinformation: information judged to be false, out of date, or incomplete in a misleading way. Malinformation: potentially dangerous or damaging information, inappropriate information; information people feel uncomfortable with in openly accessible circulation. Messed Up Information: poorly organized and presented information; sloppy design; problematic navigation. Useless Information: (recognizing one person's trash is another person's treasure) information that appears to serve little informing purpose.

3. It is perhaps instructive to note here research on the mental models that library media specialists have of electronic resources such as databases and the effect these models have on the structure and goals of lessons they plan for students. In a study by Tallman and Henderson (1999), school librarians' acknowledgment of the need to change their mental models did not automatically translate into new strategies for subsequent lessons. Research findings such as this give credence to a claim by Dixon (1994) that "worldwide, school is a puffer belly locomotive chugging incongruously through a high-tech landscape" (quoted in Todd, 1998, p. 16).

4. In a recent article, Everhart (2003) discusses the problem presented by student plagiarism in an electronic world and some policies that school librarians might adopt to reduce cheating. Quoting Minkel, Everhart reports that when they have access, 94 percent of middle and high school students use the World Wide Web for their research projects, and for 71 percent of these students, the Web is "the main source." For many of these students, cheating has become "irresistibly easy and pervasive." "Plagiarism can take many forms," Everhart tells us, "copying without referencing the information, citing improperly, and even purchasing term papers online" (p. 43). Indeed, research by McGregor and Streitenberger (1998, cited in Everhart) indicates that direct instruction in quoting, paraphras-

ing, and citing sources is needed to limit student copying. That is the bad news. The good news is that where teachers and librarians provide instruction on research ethics and the mechanics of citing, support for students in searching for information, authentic research projects, and time to undertake those projects, student research (and ethical behavior) improve (Gordon, 1999, cited in Everhart). Dutilloy (2003) describes a comprehensive approach to the problem of plagiarism by the United Nations International School in New York City, where attitudes to using another's work have cultural as well as ethical dimensions. The school has devised and publicized school policies and penalties related to student plagiarism, instructional intervention on information seeking and citation form, and staff development for teachers on plagiarism and on the design of appropriate assignments. Dutilloy concludes:

> At UNIS, all community members are involved in the development of a plagiarism-free school—the administration, by supporting new policies and enforcing them; the teachers, by creating assignments that encourage independent thinking; and the SLMSs, by providing tools to avoid plagiarism. To encourage and enhance these attitudes, SLMSs must maintain effective communication with all departments. (p. 45)

8 Assessment and Information Skills Instruction

The claim that American public schools are no longer graduating students capable of competing in the global workplace has led to widespread demands for "school improvement" from worried parents, taxpayers, and politicians. Site-based management, charter schools, magnet schools, teacher accountability, and school choice vouchers are just a few ways suggested for the restructuring of public school systems; while basic skills, literature or resource-based instruction, outcomes-based education, early childhood education, national guidelines for curricular content, student achievement, and teacher certification have all been advanced as potential answers to demands for instructional reform. One example of this sort of activity is a current project aimed at the creation of national certification standards to reward excellence for experienced teachers and school librarians.

There is little consensus or research to support the educational efficacy of any of these remedies; indeed, many educators have criticized those who seek a single model for public education that will cure the nation's disparate educational ills or promise "a quick-fix" solution to the complex problems involved in educating children in today's sociopolitical climate. Many educators believe that the nationalization of curriculum and curricular objectives is not the answer and claim that performance norms, as exemplified in standardized tests, which have been used as a sort of "national yardstick" of achievement for decades, have in fact not served well the needs of educational systems trying to cope with student diversity, technological change, and public ambivalence. Eisner (1993), for one, has challenged educators to "create schools that excite both teachers and students and provide the conditions that improve the quality of teaching" (p. 23), rather than instituting a spate of national standards, which themselves imply a parity across school districts that does not at present exist. Howe (1993) opines that "tests have become the tail that wags the dog in the public discussion of educational change in the United States" (p. 9).

Nonetheless, critics continue to invest time and effort in seeking national solutions for problems experienced at the local level. Of course, criticisms aimed at public education in the United States are hardly new; in fact, since the launching of *Sputnik* in 1957, every decade has witnessed similar demonstrations of what amounts to a national educational angst (Madaus & Tan, 1994). As Madaus and Tan have succinctly explained, the 1960s produced criticisms related to the civil rights movement; in the

158

1970s, they related to a decline in the SAT scores; in the 1980s, they related to the publication of *A Nation at Risk*; and in the 1990s, they related to competition in the international marketplace. What makes the most recent round of criticism so compelling is that it comes at a time when the schools are struggling to deal effectively with increasingly diverse school populations amid concerns for educational equity in an economic climate that demands not only that schools educate students "better" but that they do it for "less" (Craver, 1995, p. 13). Given a situation that many consider a crisis of national confidence in public education, it is perhaps not surprising that the methods by which academic achievement and student progress are assessed have also come under scrutiny. In some places, new assessment methods have also been instituted as a way to push school reform agendas, with the idea that if assessment changes so must instruction and ultimately school culture.

Educational Assessment: The Standardized Testing Imperative

For years, the public has relied on standardized achievement tests to take the educational pulse of virtually every school district in the country. The appeal of this type of testing, which has grown in popularity since its introduction in the early part of the 20th century, lies not only in its comparatively low cost and the administrative ease with which it can be accomplished but in the apparent capacity of such tests to quantify educational achievement across students, across subject area content, across grade levels, and across school districts. So complete has public confidence in the results of standardized tests grown over time that most states have implemented testing programs (O'Neil, 1992), and results that were once employed in creating programs of remediation are now being used in making all kinds of educational decisions, from the placement of individual students in alternative programs to their promotion and graduation. Policy decisions in terms of the allocation of resources among school districts have in many instances also been determined by rankings based on student scores (Madaus & Tan; 1994).[1] Indeed, Madaus and Tan and Killaghan (1992, cited in Madaus & Tan, p. 4) assert that bureaucratic rather than educational motives frequently drive interest in standardized test scores.

Why have American educators and parents set such store by standardized test results? One answer surely lies in their apparent reliability—that is, the consistency of test results across situations, time, and context. The fact that standardized tests produce numbers, which at least on their face seem so objective, straightforward, and unambiguous, partially explains their appeal as well. However, critics of this type of testing have become increasingly vocal, calling into question the practice of using single-measure "IQ" tests as predictors of ability and challenging, convincingly, the fairness of test items on the grounds of gender, culture, and socioeconomic status. While in at least some cases test-makers have made an effort to create instruments that are more culturally "fair" (Neuman, 1994), Neuman argues that such efforts do not ameliorate the deleterious effects of using assessment models that both encourage instructors to "teach to the test" (O'Neil, 1992, p. 15) and skew instructional attention in the direction of basic skills as opposed to problem solving and critical thinking. Indeed, Neuman (1994) suggests that the short-answer format of most tests reinforces the notion that "knowledge consists simply of identifying the one and only correct answer to a question formulated by someone else" (p. 68). In her view, defining learning in this way stands in direct opposition to constructivist theories, which hold that learning is a complex activity in which students create their own understandings. Herman (1992) suggests that the "narrowing" of the curriculum to basic skills and the recall of facts and the kinds of instructional practices that accompany test preparation for this level of intellectual engagement are actually detrimental to learning and particularly harmful "in schools serving at-risk and disadvantaged students, where there is the most pressure to improve test scores" (p. 74). For this reason, some critics believe that standardized testing may actually exacerbate inequities "for minorities and non-English speakers" (Madaus & Tan, 1994, p. 5).

Outcomes-Based Education

A major initiative in schools across the country has been the adoption of variations of a model for curricular reform based on the "outcomes" rather than "inputs" or objectives of instruction. According to Grover (1994), outcomes-based education focuses attention on the student as a learner and provides a " 'comprehensive approach to teaching and learning and to instructional management that has its origin in mastery learning and competency-based education' " (Burns & Wood, 1990, quoted in Grover, p. 174). Outcomes differ from the behavioral objectives, which created a focus for instruction in the 1970s and 1980s, in their concern for ensuring that students actually acquire the skills they have been taught; in addition, the "skills" that students are to "master" are less involved with the subject content than they are with critical thinking and problem solving. Since outcomes-based educational strategies necessarily call for the assessment of "student progress toward the stated outcomes" (p. 174), the evaluation techniques used to chart this project must be redesigned. In fact, a variety of new assessment models that build in opportunities for the remediation and enrichment deemed necessary for the achievement of skill mastery are clearly required. Grover also suggests "multi-dimensional" assessment strategies that "accommodate the various learning styles" (p. 175) and multiple intelligences of students.

New Models for Student Assessment

Attempts to answer the challenges posed by new instructional initiatives such as outcomes-based education and literature-based instruction as well as the many concerns educational critics have voiced have sparked a number of innovative "alternatives" to standardized testing models, which will undoubtedly continue to shape school efforts to assess student achievement for years to come. A major difference between "alternative assessment" measures and more "traditional" paper-and-pencil testing procedures is that the former allow students to show what they have learned in a variety of different ways. For example, alternatives frequently promoted in addition to formal tests include portfolios of a student's written and graphic work; student projects of various kinds; student journals and "learning logs" that record their responses, thinking, and activities; and oral and dramatic presentations of their work. An important element in this form of assessment is the active involvement of students in planning and designing rubrics as well as self and peer evaluation as part of the learning process. Indeed, as Maeroff (1991) suggests, with alternative assessment, "students, under the tutelage of their teachers, are trained to provide evidence of their own learning" (p. 274).

Although the creation of alternate models for evaluating students are many and varied, all share an intent to substitute for the indirect means represented by the usual types of test questions some form of direct measurement of learning through the "performance" of what has been learned (Grover et al., 1996). One of the advantages of alternative assessment models, which are increasingly finding support in school districts across the country (Maeroff, 1991), often cited in the literature is that such methods are not add-ons, "busy work," or "gotcha games" (p. 274) that interrupt the flow of ongoing classroom instruction; instead, they are classroom activities that, because they are actually "embedded in instruction" (p. 276), grow directly out of the curriculum rather than appearing as a single, stressful, end-of-term event. For this reason, they can be used formatively, to serve as a basis for improving instruction as the activities proceed. Moreover, a number of assessment alternatives also propose to measure student learning-in-progress as it continues over time. In fact, the "test" activities themselves can have a positive impact on student performance (Chapman, 1991; Quellmalz & Burry, 1983, cited in Herman, 1992) when conducted within the framework of ongoing classroom activity, because they provide students an additional opportunity "to practice the knowledge and skills learned" (Grover et al., 1996, p. 2). Used in this way, "the line between curriculum and assessment" (Krechevsky, 1991, p. 45) practically disappears.

Alternative assessment techniques also provide an additional dimension to many traditional types of assessments in that they aim specifically to measure critical thinking and process skills as well as student acquisition of subject knowledge or "content." As Neuman (1994) notes,

> [T]his focus on the student's direct and purposeful involvement is consistent with current cognitive theory, which holds that deep understanding occurs only when learners actively construct their own knowledge rather than passively absorbing facts and ideas presented by others (Grady, 1992; Wiggins, 1989; Wolf et al., 1991). (pp. 69–70)

Indeed, as Grover et al (1996) note, types of alternate assessment models that require the performance of the learning tasks are more likely than are traditional kinds of testing methods to tap critical thinking and the other complex processes that are inevitably involved in information seeking. Finally, Frazier and Paulson (1992) argue that the opportunities that assessment alternatives provide allow students to gain practice in self-evaluation and encourage "ownership, pride, and high self-esteem" (p. 64), all of which are related to school success and achievement.

In addition to focusing attention on critical thinking and active participation on the part of the student learner, alternative assessment models give back to the educator in the classroom the professional responsibility for student learning (Grady, 1992; Perrone, 1991; Wiggins, 1989, all cited in Neuman, 1994) in ways that allow for a more individualized approach to instruction. Many leaders in education have advocated the importance of this approach to instructional design. For instance, Eisner (1993) has argued that assessment must take into account "where [a] student started, the amount of practice and effort expended, the student's age and developmental level, and the extent to which his or her current work displays progress" (p. 23).

Authentic Assessment

What is authentic assessment, and how does it differ from alternative and performance assessment strategies? The goals and strategies of alternative and authentic assessment are very similar in that they both aim to allow the presentation of "a reliable picture of a student's understandings" (Stripling, 1994a, p. 79). That is, they measure how well objectives have been mastered by allowing students to demonstrate what they know in ways that allow teachers to assess the effectiveness of their instruction. The difference between the alternative and authentic forms of assessment is that in the latter students are asked to enact the specific skills in question, instead of answering questions related to that skill or performing specific behaviors in contrived contexts (Meyer, 1994).

To a great extent the success of authentic assessment lies with teachers who have the ability to make the connections between an academic subject and real-world applications at levels that are appropriate and consistent in terms of a student's development and background knowledge. In addition, authentic assessments of student performance necessarily presuppose and demand an "authentic" curriculum and one that allows students access to the same sorts of information and resources that would be "available in real-life, problem-solving situations" (Stripling, 1994a, p. 80). Other conditions that support authentic curriculum are frameworks for collaboration among students; teachers and community members; student discretion in what work will be used in assessing learning; and flexibility in terms of time limits for completion of products and processes.

Authentic Assessment Models

Data collection for authentic assessment requires teachers to evaluate student learning on authentic tests, "questionnaires, interviews, ratings, observations, performance samples, and work products" (Crittenden, 1991)" (Stripling 1994a, p. 79). Assessment models usually considered within an authentic assessment model comprise a variety of evaluative instruments and approaches, including one or a combination of locally produced and standardized tests, student-created portfolios, student performances and exhibitions, and personal contacts between the students and their instructors.

Authentic Tests

To be authentic, tests must provoke or stimulate problem solving, critical thinking, and writing. In addition, they must (1) allow students to demonstrate their strengths through the employment of multiple measures, including the student's self-assessment; (2) apply reasonable real-world standards in the assignation of grades; and (3) allow for different approaches to learning. According to Stripling (1994a), authentic tests should also be enjoyable activities in themselves. Reliability for "authentic tests" needs to be established through a pretesting of the test items, and through the creation of scoring rubrics, so that the outcomes of the testing can be used to inform future instruction.

Authentic Portfolios

Valencia (1991) notes that portfolios not only allow teachers to track student cognitive, affective, social, and motivational progress but also make teachers more "sensitive to processes of learning" in ways that allow them to "select and create measures of students' talents and weaknesses so that appropriate instructional opportunities can be provided" (p. 680). At the same time, authentic portfolios hold the possibility of increasing the time students spend in reading and writing and provide the vehicles for monitoring more closely and accurately their progress in developing literacy skills.

Two types of portfolios have been described in the literature. The first represents a compilation of student work carried out over time, with items students select to meet goals they themselves establish in collaboration with the teacher. Students are usually asked to write an introduction to the portfolio that reflects their own evaluation as well as evaluation of the instructor. A second portfolio model, suggested by Gardner (1991, cited in Stripling, 1994b), documents the thinking and activity involved in the creation of major projects and may contain records of original brainstorming sessions, early and current drafts, written critiques by instructors and peers, "works by others that particularly inspired or influenced the project," student self-assessments, instructor evaluation, and student thoughts on future projects (p. 106). The arrangement of portfolio documents (e.g., finished pieces, drafts, revisions, journals) is usually an individual matter decided on by the student, who may choose to present items by topic, by format, by achievement level, or chronologically (Stripling, 1994a).

Authentic Performances

As options to more traditional assessment measures, authentic performances and exhibitions, defined as "prepared demonstration[s] of student learning" (Stripling, 1994b, p. 106), are suitable when activities do not lend themselves to paper-and-pencil assessments nor to portfolios. These might include musical activities, speech and debate exercises, or physical expression in athletics, dance, or drama (especially the recreation or reenactment of historical events).

Student Profiles

Project Spectrum, a joint educational initiative created by educators from Harvard University and Tufts University in 1984, uses the creation of student profiles to assess the strength and weaknesses of student skills. Based on Howard Gardner's (1983) multiple intelligences theory and "the theory of development in non-universal domains" of David Feldman (p. 44), a program of activities is created for individual students that capitalizes on their strengths and develops areas where skills need to be improved (Krechevsky, 1991). Student profiles log the linguistic and mathematical aspects of student progress as well as the "mechanical, spatial, bodily, musical, social and scientific abilities" (p. 44) in "a short description of the child's participation in the project's activities" (p. 46).

Personal Contacts

Personal contacts, observations, conferencing, and diagnostic interviews allow students and teachers to explore student achievement interactively and can provide an index of student strengths and weaknesses, an opportunity for support for student thinking, and a forum for the discussion of student ideas. Observation is a particularly valuable way of assessing interactions between and among individuals and between groups and to monitor the activity and operation of student participation in group projects (Stripling, 1994a). Interviews can be formal and informal and may involve students and teachers, or peers.

Alternative/Authentic Assessment Models: Difficulties and Disadvantages

A number of difficulties often accompany efforts to implement alternative and authentic assessment models. Staff development and support are almost always necessary since new ways to measure achievement usually necessitate changes in instructional strategies and lesson plans (Herman, 1992, p. 77). Maeroff (1991) has addressed these issues, identifying preparation and training time, expense, complexity, and imprecision as some of the costs of implementing various forms of alternative assessment. She goes on to voice a concern that lies at the heart of many of the arguments against attempts to adopt alternative assessment models; because they lack a comparative aspect, they do not allow parents and teachers to chart a child's progress against the achievement level of his or her peers. Indeed, "psychometricians have raised serious questions about establishing the validity, reliability, generalizability, and comparability of assessments conducted according to methods that are so individualized and dependent upon human judgment (Koretz et al., 1992; Linn, Baker, and Dunbar, 1991; Moss, 1992)" (Neuman, 1994, p. 71). In point of fact, alternative assessment strategies may not be suitable for all assessment needs, and critics have also noted that non-norm-referenced assessments are open to inequities and misrepresentations. In addition, while creative efforts at assessment abound, research on the evaluation that results is minimal at the present time. For these reasons, Maeroff hopes "that alternative assessment is not rushed onto the battlefield of testing so hastily as to produce in its unperfected form friendly fire that harms the very children who are supposed to be the beneficiaries" (p. 276).

Determining the Value of the School Library

The concern for evaluating every aspect of the educational enterprise has increased pressure on school media specialists to demonstrate their contributions to their schools as well as the impact of an "Information Age" information skills curriculum on student achievement. Thus, librarians who were at one time preoccupied with creating collections of a certain size and programs reaching a certain number of students are refocusing their attention on the learning that results from their instructional programs. The rest of this chapter will trace the evolution of school library evaluation, present the research findings related to library and information skills instruction, and discuss their implications for school librarians and library programming.

Traditional Approaches to School Library Evaluation

Three major approaches to library evaluation characterize the research literature in school librarianship: library standards; library use measures; and library skills achievement measures. As has typically been true with innovations in educational assessment, evaluation methods employed by researchers and librarians reflect passions and preoccupations in educational vogue at various times and over time. During the 1940s and 1950s, which in many respects constituted the formative years of school librarianship, the primary interest of the profession lay in establishing a well-stocked central facility staffed by certified library personnel. For this reason, a good deal of assessment attention turned to comparisons between individual schools or school districts and national or state library standards as measures of a quality library "presence" (Gallivan, 1974). Once most schools had installed centralized facilities for school resources, and libraries opened their doors to students and school staff, librarians tended to follow the public library model, often employing circulation and library visits as estimates of library use. Since the 1960s, however, there have been a number of research efforts to show the impact of library programming on the acquisition of "library skills," library use, student attitudes, and student achievement. The efforts to assess the "value" of the library and its impact on student learning have largely employed scores on the "library skills" portion of standardized tests. This shift in evaluation strategies in many ways demonstrates *Information Power's* (AASL & AECT, 1988) emphasis on the teaching role of the library media specialist.

Library Standards

As originally conceived, library standards in terms of collection size, staff, and facilities were thought to be essential to ensure the quality and value for public libraries (Joeckel, 1943). Indeed, over time a number of researchers have shown that library collection size was related to exemplary library programs (Greve, 1974; Loertscher, Ho, & Bowie, 1987) and that the presence of certified staff was also positively related to programming excellence (Loertscher, Ho, & Bowie, 1987) and higher levels of library service (Loertscher & Land, 1975). Although useful, at least initially, in supporting budgetary requests, employing standards as evaluation measures has been problematic in that a causal linkage between such standards and the improvement of library services has never been established definitively (Baker & Lancaster, 1991). For one thing, the findings of "standards" studies are often ambiguous in that they have meant different things to different people at different times. To some, evaluation standards represent the "ideal" in terms of collections and services; to others they represent the "minimum" required to open a library's doors. Another problem is that standards tend to become obsolete quickly. This is particularly true in and across school settings, where communities change, enrollments fluctuate, curricula shift, and instructional approaches and innovations wax and wane. Furthermore, library standards represent types of "input" measures, which focus on materials but do not assess the value of these materials relative to instructional approach nor student learning. In some cases, the invocation of standards has even created problems, especially where maintaining numerical minimums discourages librarians from discarding outdated or inappropriate resources and equipment.

Measures of Library Use: Circulation and Library Visits

From time to time, counting the circulation and library contacts in the aggregate and per student has been advanced as an appropriate approach to assessment in some school libraries. Although such data are relatively easy to gather and document, they do not necessarily indicate use of information nor indicate why some resources are chosen over others. Indeed, they reveal next to nothing about the value of a collection to the curricular needs of a particular school nor the ability of the resources to match the developmental levels of particular students. In addition, in some school settings, there may be constraints on the independent use of the library due to library policies, library hours, or other situational factors that have little or nothing to do with the range and value of library services and collections. Nor do library contacts always reflect a positive attitude toward the library and library materials, or their use or their usefulness, especially where children are compelled to come to the library as part of regularly scheduled "library skills" classes. Finally, where teachers require students to check out a prescribed book or a number of books for classroom or recreational use, circulation statistics can often be misleading.

The first edition of the American Library Association's *Information Power* (1988) suggested that libraries attempt to document library use and utility through patterns of planning and teaching. Quantitative measures such as the number of students and teachers served, the number and frequency of group activities in the library, the number of collaborative projects, the extent of collaborative planning, and student use of library resources to meet classroom objectives were all advanced as alternatives to tracking the circulation of library materials. More recently, professionals and researchers have argued that these approaches are themselves too indirect to support persuasive arguments of program value. Berkowitz (1994), for example, argues that such measures do not reveal anything about what students learn as a result of information skills instruction nor document the impact of that instruction on students' success as learners (p. 36).

Berkowitz suggests instead that library media specialists use a more broad-based assessment plan that demonstrates how the use of "library resources help[s] to advance the district and school goals" and the "achievement, attitudes, and behaviors" of students (p. 37). According to Berkowitz, such approaches constitute measures of performance that hold the possibility for more clearly establishing the value of a school library to both staff and students. However, in Berkowitz's view, it is *only* outcomes in terms of student learning that will ensure that libraries continue to receive administrative support and adequate funding. Therein lies the greatest challenge: How can library media specialists validate their intuitive understandings that library programs contribute to student learning? Ultimately, as Berkowitz points out, school librarians and researchers alike must find ways to make the effectiveness of information skills instruction both "describable and visible" (p. 33).

> Children and teachers need library resources—especially books—and the expertise of a librarian to succeed. Books, information technology and school librarians, who are part of the school's professional team, are basic ingredients for student achievement.
>
> —Laura Bush, 2002

Measuring Student Achievement

Although research efforts in library and information science continue to grow in number and sophistication, studies designed to show the value of information skills instruction for student learning are only just beginning to yield a cohesive body of results to which librarians can point as justification for their programs. Since the 1980s, much of the research has been fragmented (Aaron, 1982; Eisenberg & Brown, 1992; Kuhlthau, 1987). With the exception of recent studies by Lance and his colleagues, Todd & Kuhlthau (2003), and research based on Kuhlthau's (1993a) ISP, few studies have been either theory-based or replicable, while the use of natural settings where variables are hard to control have yielded results that are not generalizable beyond a specific context. Indeed, in the early 1990s Ken Haycock (1992) complained that in too many cases, studies addressed issues that were of peripheral interest. And while scholars and practitioners concede that student achievement is the appropriate yardstick for assessing value, particularly as the teaching role of the library media specialist has become the standard for school librarianship, until recently few studies were able to show that such links actually exist (Eisenberg & Brown, 1992; Vandergrift & Hannigan, 1986).

Library Collections and Student Achievement

Among the earliest of the research efforts "to evaluate the effectiveness of elementary school libraries" were studies by Mary Gaver (1963), which found a positive relationship between the presence of school libraries and student achievement. In her studies, Gaver attempted to determine the impact of centralized library facilities on student reading and library skills by surveying 271 schools in 13 states. Findings of the study revealed that students experienced "higher educational gain in schools with school libraries" (Gallivan, 1974). In another study, Willson (1965) used survey instruments developed by Gaver to compare reading achievement and library skills proficiency of sixth graders in 12 schools, to assess the impact of a library program administered by a professional librarian. Willson's study found that students with access to a central library and organized instruction achieved higher scores on skills and reading as measured on the Iowa Test of Basic Skills than those who lacked such programs.

A study that sought to link the presence of an active library professional, library materials, and student learning was conducted by educators in Colorado schools in 1992. Results of this research verified "the importance of the library media specialist's instructional role" and the expenditure of funds to maintain school library collections and staff in "promoting academic achievement" (Lance, Welborn, & Hamilton-Pennell, 1992). Lance and his colleagues sought to remedy the methodological shortcomings (data collection, interpretation) critics noted in this research in a second Colorado study (Lance, Rodney, & Hamilton-Pennell, 2000a) as well as in a series of school library studies conducted in Alaska (Lance et al., 2000), Pennsylvania (Lance, Rodney, & Hamilton-Pennell, 2000b), Oregon (Lance et al., 2001), Texas (E.G. Smith, 2001) and New Mexico (Lance et al., 2003). These studies confirm that student competency test scores improve in schools where school library programs are clearly developed, where students have access to information technology, where libraries are run by qualified professionals, where librarians and teachers collaborate to integrate technology into the curriculum, where librarians provide in-service training in technology integration, and where independent use of the library is encouraged and supported. Similar studies are currently under way in additional states.

Another major study, *Student Learning Through Ohio School Libraries*, was undertaken in selected schools in Ohio during the 2002–2003 academic year. Two major researchers in the field of school libraries, Ross Todd and Carol C. Kuhlthau, directed the research, which was funded by a grant from the federal Institute for Museum and Library Service (IMLS). In essence, the study aimed to "provide comprehensive and detailed empirical evidence of how school libraries help students learn, and to provide recommendations for further research, educational policy development, and tools for the school librarian to chart how their school library impacts learning" (Ohio Educational Library Media Association, 2002). Of particular interest as well was the study's effort to ascertain the value of libraries in student learning from the students' point of view, and as such is the "first comprehensive study based on students' evaluation of their media centers" (Whelan, 2004). Students surveyed in the Ohio study reported that the information skills instruction they received in the library "helped them with using and accessing information for their research assignments" (Todd, quoted in Whelan), as well as helping them to do better on classwork and tests. African-American youngsters in the study also reported getting help for their reading in the school library. Overall, students reported that access to and instruction in educational technology was especially valued (Todd & Kuhlthau, 2003).

Reading Achievement and Library Skills Instruction

Longitudinal studies in school libraries were conducted by both Thorne (1967) and Yarling (1968). Thorne used a purposive sample of two schools, randomly selecting 640 students for a two-year study. Pretest and posttest reading comprehension instruments were used to determine the effects of augmented library services on reading comprehension. Thorne found that augmented services resulted in significant gains in reading comprehension and knowledge of library skills. Thorne also noted gender differences in terms of achievement. Girls improved their library skills to a greater degree than did boys, while the boys' reading comprehension scores advanced more than did those of the girls.

Yarling's (1968) study, on the other hand, compared groups of children within and between two elementary schools over three years. One school had a library, and one did not. As a result of exposure to a program that ostensibly provided practice in library location skills, index use, and a variety of study techniques, students in the school with a library performed significantly better on tests in library skills and language competence than groups in the same school tested previously and as compared with groups in the control school. During the same period, the control groups did not show a significant increase in their achievement on the same instruments.

Curriculum Integration

It is widely assumed that teaching information literacy skills within the context of ongoing classroom activities increases student learning. A number of researchers have investigated the relationship of instructional design, library use, and achievement. In a study in the late 1980s, Nolan (1989) looked at the effects of type of instructional design on patterns of student use of the media center. This researcher found that students for whom research skills instruction was delivered within the context of curricular tasks tended to use the library more, had better attitudes about the library, and had higher expectations as to its accessibility and utility than did students taught library skills in stand-alone lessons.

More recently, Todd, Lamb, and McNicholas (1993, cited in Todd, 1995) have reported research that also suggests that an integrated information skills approach to teaching and learning can have a positive effect on a variety of learning outcomes, including improvement of student test scores, recall, concentration, focus on the task, and reflective thinking. In a second study, Todd (1995) compared the effectiveness of a "conventional approach" to information skills instruction and an "integrated approach" on student achievement, attitudes, and motivation. The study itself was undertaken in a culturally diverse girls' Catholic secondary school in Australia. Study participants were divided into treatment groups and control groups, with the former receiving instruction in a six-step process model for information seeking "explicitly aimed at the development of information skills as a basis for the meaningful learning of science" (p. 134). The lessons were planned and taught collaboratively by the science teachers and the library media specialist. Students in the control group received the same science instruction but without an integrated program of library skills instruction. Science concepts were measured on annual science test scores given at midyear and on end-of-year exams. Information literacy skills were assessed through the use of a problem-solving technique Todd devised to show student use of the information process model. Results of Todd's study indicate that students in the treatment group achieved significantly higher scores on both science content and information skills than those in the control groups. Thus Todd concluded that

within the specific research context, and for the specific students involved, integrated information skills instruction appears to have had a significant positive impact on students' mastery of prescribed science content and on their ability to use a range of information skills to solve particular information problems. (p. 37)

While Todd calls for additional studies to test his conclusions in other settings with other students, his study is particularly significant in that it ties information skills instruction, and an integrated process-oriented instructional program, to student achievement within the context of the regular school curriculum.

Standardized Tests

Since the 1980s, a number of researchers have used standardized tests to measure the impact of library skills instruction on student performance (Berkowitz, 1994, p. 34) and to test the relationship between school libraries, instructional programs, and student learning (Table 8.1). For example, Didier (1982) looked at the relationship between elementary school students' reading achievement (measured by standardized test scores) and study skills and library skills instruction. The seventh graders in Didier's study demonstrated higher levels of achievement in reading and study skills and use of newspapers than students in the control group, who had limited exposure to media centers or professional library staff. In a study two years later, Gifford and Gifford (1984) randomly selected and assigned 26 students in selected classes in one school to control and experimental groups. These researchers used a posttest design to determine the effect of a two-week program of bibliographical instruction on library use and ease of use by students. Dependent measures in this study were the use of specific library resources (e.g., card catalog, newspapers, magazines, vertical file, dictionaries, fiction, and nonfiction) and number of times students requested assistance in the library. Findings revealed that the experimental group, which, together with the control group, had been given assignments that required the use of the library, asked for less help and used some specific types of resources significantly more often than did students in the control group.

Gilliland's (1986) informal study of groups of California seniors found that test scores on the "study-locational portion of a state-wide mandated test rose appreciably after students had completed an exercise in which they reviewed basic library skills" (p. 67). The exercise, the Senior Library Review, was a worksheet activity that "require[d] students to participate actively, to act and think independently," to use reading and writing skills, "to use some higher order thinking skills such as analysis, and problem solving skills that would result in a product that they could use to write a paper or speech"(p. 67).

Dewees (1987) employed an experimental research design to compare groups of randomly assigned students in fifth-grade classes in a single elementary school. The experimental group received six weeks of process-oriented instruction, which culminated in the production of a research paper. Student learning was assessed on a standardized achievement test. Results indicated that the experimental group scored significantly higher on the research skills portion of the test. Brodie (1988) also employed standardized test scores as measures in a study that compared student knowledge of library skills and the amount of library use by two groups of youngsters involved in special programs for gifted fourth- and fifth-grade students. In this study, Brodie found that "students in the experimental group experienced a significant difference in the use of the media center . . . and for use of six types of library materials: fiction, nonfiction, reference, encyclopedias, periodicals, and audiovisual materials" (Bracy, 1990, p. 128).

Table 8.1
Summary of Major Research Findings Related to Library and Information Skills Instruction and Student Achievement

- School libraries have a positive effect on student achievement (Gaver, 1963; Greve, 1974; Hall-Ellis & Berry, 1995; Lance, Rodney, & Hamilton-Pennell, 2000a, 2000b; Lance, Welborn, & Hamilton-Pennell, 1992)

- Library skills instruction has a positive effect on student achievement in reading comprehension (Didier, 1982; Gaver, 1963; Thorne, 1967; Yarling, 1968), language skill development (Didier, 1982; Yarling, 1968), and knowledge of library skills (Gaver, 1963; Thorne, 1967; Yarling, 1968)

- Integration of library skills and classroom curriculum resulted in an increase in library use (Nolan, 1989) and higher achievement in information gathering skills and chart and graph reading (Becker, 1970)

- Instruction in library resources resulted in more independence and increased use of specific types of library resources (Brodie, 1988; Didier, 1982; Gifford & Gifford, 1984)

- Library skills instruction resulted in more positive attitudes about the library and its usefulness (Nolan, 1989) and higher test scores on locational skills (Gilliland, 1986), research skills (Dewees, 1987), and study skills (Didier, 1982)

- Where school libraries are well funded and librarians participate in the instructional process, academic achievement is higher (Hall-Ellis & Berry, 1995; Lance, Welborn, & Hamilton-Pennell, 1992; E. G. Smith, 2001)

- An integrated approach to library and information skills instruction has a positive effect on student learning related to test scores, recall, concentration, focus on the task, and reflective thinking (Todd, Lamb, & McNicholas, 1993)

- Library skills instruction using a six-step process model can have a positive impact on student learning of science content (Todd, 1995)

- School libraries and school librarians help students become better learners by providing resources in a variety of media to support curricular tasks and leisure reading; instruction in the search process, problem solving, and technology; by engaging students with information and assisting with research projects; by promoting reading; and by individualizing and personalizing instruction (Todd & Kuhlthau, 2003)

Standardized Testing and Higher-Order Thinking

According to Jackson (1994), the content of standardized measures used to assess library skills is usually based on curricular guides and textbooks in general use across the United States. A multiple-choice structure for test items is the form most often employed in these instruments. The fact that "the cognitive skill most [easily and therefore] frequently" (p. 25) tested through multiple-choice questions is recall has made problematic their use in assessing student thinking in terms of analysis, synthesis, and evaluation skills. In a review of the *Iowa Test of Educational Development (ITED)* (1989), the *Tests of Achievement and Proficiency (TAP)* (1990), and the *Comprehensive Tests of Basic Skills, fourth edition (CTBS4)* (1989), Jackson found that although test items aim to address process skills involving identification of information problems, evaluation of sources, note taking, analysis of information, and synthesis of ideas and information use, their employment of a limited number of short-answer test items does not address the complexities of information seeking as it has been described in the work of Irving (1985), Kuhlthau (1993b), and other LIS theorists. In particular, Jackson notes the failure of these tests to assess information retrieval, search strategies, or the complex "process of narrowing or broadening a topic" (p. 30) or selecting a research thesis and creating researchable research questions.

Outcomes-Based Education: Implications for Library Media Programs

Research in library and information skills instruction has generally shown that a positive relationship exists between library programming and student achievement; and, at least in a general way, the types of measures used can tell us that programs studied are or are not effective. Less frequently, however, do such measures offer insights into how learning can be enhanced or how programs can be improved. In many instances, the types of skills tested are not those that contemporary librarians regard as the most important. For example, despite the fact that for many years educators have known that "being able to locate information was of little intellectual benefit to students" (Henne, 1966, cited in Jackson, 1994, p. 26), library skills questions that ask students to identify specific reference sources or demonstrate location and access skills are still being used as measures of student competence. In addition, changes in the structure of library and information skills instruction, particularly the redefinition of literacy to include information-seeking skills, a process approach to information skills instruction (Kuhlthau, 1993b), and the "critical thinking curriculum" (Callison, 1994, p. 43), argue for the development of new approaches to information skills assessment.

When applied within the context of the school library, Grover (1993, 1994) sees assessment as part of the overall program requiring the library media specialist to diagnose the information needs of student learners and the information skills necessary for them to achieve their curricular goals; apply customized learning opportunities; and assess the outcomes of these interventions. Given the challenges of assessing a multidimensional program of instruction and an information skills curriculum focused on developing critical thinkers and problem solvers, librarians are faced with a question: What kinds of measures can be devised that will provide such information? One answer clearly lies with alternative assessment measures described above and now a part of contemporary educational reform efforts in many states (Grover, 1994; Maeroff, 1991). Indeed, processes that underlie contemporary models of information seeking, and teaching a process approach to library skills instruction, are difficult to measure using paper-and-pencil tests. But as Berkowitz (1994) notes, librarians must find and use "measures of effectiveness," such as those tested by Todd (1995), which can show that information skills instruction results in student achievement and an improvement in test results in content areas. In addition, Berkowitz urges librarians to arrange for the systematic collection of data, to document and establish criteria and standards for achievement, and to share the results with others in the school and the community.

The assessment of information-seeking skills based on learner outcomes assumes the expertise of a master teacher. As Grover (1994) asserts: "[T]he library media specialist must be able to diagnose or analyze the information skills level of individuals or groups, prescribe or recommend appropriate learning activities, teach or assist with the implementation of work for teaching information skills . . . and a framework for assessing instruction" (p. 187). Grover has suggested a multimodal menu of strategies for librarians and teachers to use in gathering data on student progress, including observation, interviews, journals, projects, formal tests, self- and peer-evaluation, and portfolios. Information obtained through these means can be used to plan "additional learning activities" (p. 187), class groupings, and peer tutoring pairs. A major strength of these assessment models is the opportunity they provide for students to reflect on their own work, skills, or progress, as well as on the work of their peers.

Relationship of Alternative Assessment Models and the Process Approach Curriculum

Neuman (1994) notes the basic compatibility of the move to create alternatives to traditional methods of assessment with contemporary library information skills curricula in that "library media center programs are grounded in many of the same assumptions that undergird alternative assessment" (p. 72). This affinity should not be surprising as both initiatives draw on constructivism as a theory base and focus on the processes of learning. Nor has this new approach to information skills instruction, with its emphasis on collaboration and instructional intervention, gone unnoticed in the education community. As Theodore Sizer, creator of the "Coalition of Essential Schools," has observed, "One good way to start designing an Essential school is to plan a library and let its shadow shape the rest" (1990, quoted in Stripling, 1994b, p. 105).

It is interesting to note that the techniques for data collection (e.g., observation, interviewing, and analyzing student projects) as suggested by Kuhlthau (1993b) and others are fundamentally the same as those used in alternative assessment approaches. Moreover, these techniques mirror approaches to "qualitative inquiry," which is achieving greater acceptance in the fields of education and school librarianship (Neuman, 1994). For this reason, Neuman suggests that library media specialists have a role to play in the creation of an " 'assessment culture' " (Wolfe et al., 1991, quoted in Neuman, p. 73) that relies on "new understandings of learning and intelligence, new standards of evidence," and "sensitivity and rigor in the application of [assessment] alternatives" (p. 73).

The Library Media Specialist and Alternative Assessment

Stripling (1994a, 1994b) clearly considers alternative assessment as *the* model for the future and sees a central role for school librarians in helping to anticipate the changes

Figure 8.1
Stripling's (1994b) Taxonomy of Assessment Involvement for
Library Media Specialists

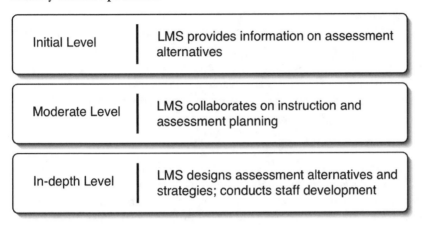

Initial Level	LMS provides information on assessment alternatives
Moderate Level	LMS collaborates on instruction and assessment planning
In-depth Level	LMS designs assessment alternatives and strategies; conducts staff development

that the implementation of new assessment models will require. "If the primary goal of education is to cultivate thoughtfulness and understanding and if the school library media center is at the core of that effort, then the school library media specialist must lead in changing assessment techniques" (1994b, p. 106). And "since learning theory shows that students learn far more by 'doing' than by any other method," librarians can "provide the logical information laboratory for practice within an educational setting" (Markuson, 1986, p. 39).

Stripling (1994b) posits a three-level taxonomy of involvement for library media specialists in the initiation and progress of authentic assessment (see Figure 8.1). At the Initial Level, the school media specialist does not play a role in instructional design of projects but can provide information on the use of assessment alternatives, perhaps developing a professional collection of materials and resources upon which school staff can draw. In addition, the media specialist can facilitate discussion on assessment alternatives and create collections that support students involved in the creation of "alternative" projects.

At the Moderate Level, library media specialists collaborate in planning instruction and assessment and otherwise provide professional assistance by teaching production techniques (e.g., word processing video production) and monitoring student performance practices. At the highest or "In-depth" Level, Striping (1994a) suggests that library media specialists are intimately involved in designing "authentic assessment strategies" (p. 92) with teachers, in helping students select their work for inclusion in their portfolios, in providing assistance with evaluating student products, and conducting in-service instruction to staff on alternate assessment techniques and strategies. In creating evaluative measures for alternative projects, Stripling suggests that rubrics be developed that allow comments on the overall framework of the project (clarity and achievement of goals and the organization of information), reflection (student assessments and depth of comments), content, style (originality, creativity, and personal connection or "voice"), and presentation (fluency and form).

Conclusion

Clearly there is a need for more research, not only in terms of the effectiveness of library skills instruction but also into the impact library programs can have on the contexts for learning. Information skills instruction based on a process approach to information seeking and inquiry learning certainly addresses the need for improving critical thinking and problem-solving skills that have purchase in real-world contexts. However, Herman (1992) notes that "changes in assessment are only part of the answer to improved instruction and learning. Schools need support to implement new instructional strategies and to institute other changes to assure that all students can achieve the complex skills that these new assessments strive to represent" (p. 77). Most particularly, library media specialists and teachers together must provide assignments and activities that demand critical thinking and problem-solving skills.

Note

1. The emphasis on standardized testing peaked in the early years of the new millennium in the federal mandate for higher achievement and greater accountability embedded in the No Child Left Behind Act passed in 2001. Briefly, this legislation calls for states to create educational standards, implement annual progress testing (for students in grades 3–8), and impose penalties on schools whose students fail to meet state minimums. The program emphasizes literacy and reading, early childhood education, and staff development for K–3 teachers in reading instruction. The impact of the No Child Left Behind initiative's emphasis on standardized testing has led to changes in curriculum and instruction and has left library media specialists to cope as they can to find their own roles in helping bring about the goals that the law was designed to achieve.

9 Information Seeking as a Social Encounter

> Our students may not remember whether or not you found the information they were seeking in the library, but they will never forget how you treated them.

This sign, observed on the desk of one school media specialist, sums up a concern that makes manifest the social nature of library activities. The simplicity of this idea and the commonsense aspect of such a message tend to obscure its importance, and perhaps it is for that reason that the relational aspects of library-student interactions have so seldom been addressed in the scholarly literature on school librarianship. Indeed, it is fair to say that most of the interest in the area of school media research targets the cognitive aspects of information seeking and the cognitive dimensions of teaching and learning.

The Cognitive Approach to Information Seeking and Learning

The contemporary emphases on the development of mental models and on information seeking as a cognitive task have proved extremely valuable in providing direction for school librarians in creating meaningful programs of instruction. It seems likely that the excitement generated by the advances in our understanding of the information search process, and concomitant pressures related to information literacy issues, have made inquiries into the relational nature of teaching and the service aspects of the school library media program appear peripheral, if not totally irrelevant. However, Frohmann (1992) and others have cautioned against reducing to "a narrative of mental events" the "complexities of real practices, conduct, accomplishments and actions of information seeking, information use, and 'information processing' " (p. 375). In addition, a number of other scholars have attempted to incorporate a concern for the affective experience of information users into their research and models. For example, Nahl-Jakobovits and Jakobovits (1993) have noted the "serious affective information needs" students have, related to their own abilities in accessing library resources. Specifically, these researchers found that students "fear making mistakes," are often "intimidated by the complexity of search tools," and lack "confidence in their ability to find information" (p. 83). Kuhlthau's (1993b) research has also brought attention to the anxieties experienced by many students at the initial stages of the ISP and stresses the importance of providing support for students experiencing the dip in confidence during the initiation and exploration phases of the research activity. However, Kuhlthau's emphasis is squarely on those uncertainties that are directly related to information and information tasks rather than those arising from or in librarian-student interactions or from aspects of the social context. Even those studies that have included "attitudes" toward the library as measures of its value (e.g., Todd, 1995) have as their primary focus the relationship between student attitudes and the library's resources or a particular instructional approach and only secondarily on the social experiences that contribute to the creation of those attitudes.

Although no one would deny the centrality of the teaching role for library media specialists, the "information specialist" or intermediary role, acknowledged in *Information Power* (AASL & AECT, 1988, 1998), is one of the three major responsibilities of the contemporary school librarian. For this reason, it is entirely appropriate that school librarians act as information "agents" for school staff, administrators, and students. Enacting the role of informational "intermediary" requires a service orientation; but, as Chelton (1999) notes, the pressures to inculcate information literacy skills and promote the informational "independence" of students have sometimes led to a reluctance on the part of library professionals to provide the kinds of service support that are frequently available to users in public libraries. Rather than providing information, Chelton asserts, the school librarian "defines her role as helping people find information on their own." Yet given the increasing complexities of the information universe, one questions, with Liesener (1985), the efficacy of predicating all efforts at information seeking in school libraries on a "self sufficiency" (p. 17) model. This is particularly the case where, as in Chelton's (1999) study, there is "little follow up by library staff to see if users" actually find the information being sought (p. 283).

Social Aspects of Information-Seeking and Information Skills Instruction

Contemporary trends in teaching emphasize the "active" and "constructed" nature of learning and the importance of interaction among students and between students and teachers (Bruner, 1975, 1977; Vygotsky, 1978); indeed, an increasing awareness and valuing of group processes and social engagement as an essential part of the instructional context is often cited in the educational research literature. For example, the importance of "affective bonds" between adults and students has been recognized by Winograd and Gaskins (1992, p. 232), who claim that "the need for a supportive, trusting advocate is particularly important for students experiencing academic difficulties." Suggesting that schools need to become as concerned about being "high touch" as they are about being "hi-tech" (p. 232), Mann (1986, cited in Winograd & Gaskins) argues that reaching out to less successful students and providing personal contact constitute an essential part of all successful intervention programs. Delpit (1995) and others note that this may be especially true for some minority students. All too often, however,

> [E]ven advocates of systemic change . . . often leave off of their agenda any recognition of the importance of having schools see students as people.
> —Howe, 1993

"even advocates of systemic change . . . often leave off of their agenda any recognition of the importance of having schools see students as people" (Howe, 1993, p. 130). Howe continues, "[I]f educators pay careful attention to human relationships and foster a sense of the school as a community, schools can become places where students and teachers want to be" (p. 134).

The interactive nature of the school librarian's role has been marked in a study of achievement effects by Ryan (1991, cited in Bialo & Sivin-Kachala, 1996), who identified social interaction among students and among students and teachers/librarians as one of the three characteristics essential for the creation and maintenance "of the most effective learning environments" (p. 54). Kulleseid (1986) has also noted the contribution of the librarian's interpersonal skills to the successful modeling and facilitation of student-student and teacher-student interactions. Gehlken's (1994) examination of library programs in three exemplary schools in South Carolina also noted the importance of "proactivity and commitment in meeting student needs." Indeed, Gehlken observed: "in every case, student samples overwhelmingly identified the single most important service provided by the library media program as help from the media specialist." Students surveyed by Todd and Kuhlthau (2003) felt the same way. "It wasn't really the library," reported one student, "it was the librarians that helped me" (p. 22).

Kuhlthau's (1996) intervention model, which describes tutoring and counseling activities for librarians in supporting students in seeking information, clearly assumes high-level communication and interactional skills. This model is based on Vygotsky's (1978) belief that the most effective teaching activities are interactions that are planned to support student achievement at a level of functioning higher than could be managed if they were left to struggle along on their own.

Swain's (1996) extension of Kuhlthau's (1993a) research provides further insights into the role of social interaction in information seeking. In particular, Swain noted the importance of social relationships developed between students and library staff members who provided assistance in relieving the stresses and anxieties the students experienced in selecting their topics, using library tools, and conducting their searching activities. Unhappily, even in the few studies where the social aspects of library service and instruction constitute part of the data, as, for example, in Nahl-Jakobovits and Jakobovits' (1993) finding "that students fear talking to librarians," they are often ignored by practitioners and seldom pursued further by researchers.

Furthermore, issues of identity construction, which are usually considered of paramount interest and importance in other contexts, have seldom been the object of interest in school library research. Recently, however, a number of scholars have expressed a concern for this important aspect of librarianship, and their explorations of service interactions provide evidence that there is often more "at stake" in library encounters than simply the "transfer" of information. If, as Ken Haycock (1992) suggests, interactional skills are essential elements in the librarian's professional tool kit, and if media specialists wish to implement programs that are truly user-centered, then the social experiences of students in school libraries should be studied and the findings used, where necessary, to rethink and reshape professional attitudes and behavior. The rest of this chapter reviews some of the salient studies related to interactional aspects of the library experience in the hope that insights they provide will raise sensitivity and spark discussion among both researchers and practitioners.

Interpersonal Interactions in the School Library Context

Writing in the *School Library Media Quarterly* in 1982, Betty Martin was one of the first to recognize the relational nature of teaching and learning in the library. Specifically, she considered the value of interpersonal relationships with students, school administrators, faculty, parents, and community members in creating trust, communicating clearly, building influence, and solving problems essential to the creation of exemplary library programs. According to Martin, self-acceptance, self-confidence, the ability to exhibit warmth, a sense of caring, and sensitivity to the feelings of others are all characteristics fundamental for establishing a context of support for information-seeking activities. In providing assistance, Martin admonished readers to attend "to the affective domain, valuing each person as unique, then showing individuals that you know their worth, and accepting them, recognizing their accomplishments, and helping them to develop self esteem" (p. 54). Strategies Martin suggested for librarians to use in making library visitors feel welcome included taking an interest in their interests; respecting their rights and needs in terms of acceptance and valuing; and taking care to "avoid interrupting, shaming, name calling, commanding, moralizing, lecturing, arguing, or criticizing" (p. 56).

Martin (1982) also called attention to the variety of paralinguistic (e.g., voice tone, rate of speech, modulation) and nonverbal behaviors (e.g., gestures, expressions, posture, personal distance, style of dress, etc.) that have a bearing on the ways librarians relate to their users. In fact, she acknowledged that "nonverbal messages may be more powerful in communicating feelings than verbal ones" (p. 54). Nahl-Jakobovits and Jakobovits (1990) and N.P. Thomas (1996) have also urged librarians to attend to textual "messages" directed at library users in the form of signs, notes, rules, and directions. Stating "rules" or prohibitions in positive rather than negative ways, personalizing library messages, and minimizing the punitive aspects of library texts are suggested as techniques that contribute to the creation of welcoming and confirming library environments.

Library Encounters as Communicative Action

Recent research studies by Mokros, Mullins, and Saracevic (1995), Radford (1996), and Chelton (1997), address issues identified by Martin (1982) and others as barriers to "exemplary library program[s]" (p. 56). These three studies draw on communication theory as explained in the work of Erving Goffman (1967) and Watzlawick, Beavin, and Jackson (1967) to investigate interaction in a variety of library contexts. Within this framework, an act of communication includes not only the expression of the report, or informational content, at hand but also the "relational content," the feelings participants have about themselves, each other, and the situation in which they are involved. For this reason, the manner in which words are spoken (e.g., whether deferential and respectful or deprecatory and demeaning) is at least as powerful as the meaning of the words themselves.

According to interactionists, social identity, the sense of who one is in relation to social others, arises in knowing how we regard ourselves and how we are ourselves regarded in social situations (Goffman, 1967). For this reason, the "selves" of interactants are potentially "at risk" in every social engagement. An essential dimension that this work contributes to an understanding of the instructional context is that there are always relational aspects embedded within each informational encounter. Interactionists would argue that the "self" needs of library users are at least as important as their information needs.

Acknowledging the role of communication in creating meaning, context, and the self, Mokros, Mullins, and Saracevic (1995) studied interactions between librarians and students involved in an online searching activity in an academic library. In the view of these theorists, library activities that are undertaken with such frequency that they are enacted routinely and "unconsciously" are nonetheless charged with relational messages about who is in control of the activity and the nature of the relationship between the interactants (e.g., parity or asymmetry) within the activity. Through an analysis of videotapes created in a number of reference encounters, researchers concluded that the opening moments of service interactions are particularly significant in setting the stage for all the activities that follow. Mokros and colleagues' study revealed that in some cases the librarians' own presentation and control needs resulted in experiences for the library users that were disconfirming. Considered as confirmational for both librarians and users in the study were those interactions that demonstrated, through words and gestures, a sense of parity in terms of status and marked interactants as coparticipants in a shared research activity.

Radford (1996) explored the dimensions of approachability in a study among high school and college students in three academic libraries, all of whom were engaged in a reference activity that required the use of library resources. Citing the uncertainty and anxiety Kuhlthau (1993b) identified as common experiences for users in the initial and exploratory phases of a research task, and the important role that librarians can play in mediating the experience for users as they contemplated the complexities of the contemporary library, Radford sought to determine what barriers might exist for users in seeking reference assistance. Her results indicated that the librarians in her study exhibited nonverbal "gestures," such as eye contact, manner, and deference, to which library users were extremely sensitive. In addition, the students Radford interviewed revealed that they used these nonverbal cues in assessing the "approachability" of the librarians and planned their information-seeking strategies accordingly. In short, they avoided some reference librarians and sought assistance from others on the basis of whether or not they thought a librarian seemed open and friendly. Significantly, the students in Radford's study considered that obtaining the desired information in a reference interaction, while important, was not as important as having their relational needs met. This led Radford to conclude that library users "may still leave the interaction with a negative impression of the librarian and of the library experience in general" (p. 125) regardless of the informational outcome of a library visit.

The "negative attitudes" identified by Radford's (1996) informants included "(a) having no time, (b) unhelpful, (c) uncaring, (d) sour, (e) abrupt, and (f) impatient" (p. 130). These kinds of behaviors seem to reflect those described in a study by Mellon (1990, cited in Chelton, 1997) in which high school students reported that librarians tended to respond only to direct questions, made disparaging remarks about the kinds of questions that students posed, and made them feel stupid. Recent research conducted by the Pew Research Center (2001) indicates that the "bad attitude" of librarians has led many students to abandon libraries altogether in favor of information seeking on the Internet.

In her dissertation research, Chelton (1997) confirmed the multidimensional nature of the school media specialist's job and the many kinds of interactions that take place in high school libraries. Drawing on the work of Kuhlthau (1993a), Radford (1996), and Mokros, Mullins, and Saracevic (1995), Chelton used communication frameworks to explore these interactions, particularly as they involved issues of identity construction of the adolescents she observed. In her study, Chelton (1997, 1999) noted in particular many library interactions she observed in which the adults assumed "authority" positions in enforcing school and library rules. She then considered the ways in which these manifestations of authority might interfere with a librarian's ability to support information seeking predicated on a participatory, interventionist model.

The adolescents Chelton (1997) interviewed expressed, sometimes poignantly, sometimes angrily, their sensitivity to deference issues and the disrespect many had themselves encountered in all kinds of service settings. The specific behaviors about which the youngsters complained included being ignored, watched, and stereotyped. These same students identified listening skills, courteous behavior, niceness, helpfulness, and promptness as important elements in positive service encounters. It is especially important to note here that although the students themselves identified "respect" as their primary information need in library interactions, the adults Chelton interviewed failed to recognize this aspect of their encounters with students. Thus, while the adolescents appeared to want "an identity-confirming, emotional connection to adult service providers" (p. 179) in the library as elsewhere, the librarians tended to view student needs as primarily informational in nature and isomorphic with the questions that the students asked! This is a significant disconnect and may well explain the differences in how library interactions are perceived by students and librarians.

Confirming a similar finding by Mokros, Mullins, and Saracevic (1995), Chelton (1997) argued that the opening "moves" of a library interaction, when the participants greeted or failed to greet each other, established the nature of the relationship (e.g., who is in control of the interaction), signaled the deference with which students would be treated, and defined the "situation" or interactional context as potentially productive or adversarial. Chelton concluded that where expectations created in these interactional openings are negative, the chances for productive encounters are severely limited.

An important aspect of Chelton's research is the concern it expresses with regard to the impact of "everyday" types of library interactions and routine activities on the selves of the youngsters involved. Thus, Chelton argues:

> Helping an adolescent to use the photocopy machine, or checking out a book or asking to see a pass may seem mundane and tedious to someone who does it constantly. The young person receiving the service, however, is neither mundane nor tedious, but rather, another person who wants an emotional connection (Scheff, 1990). Providing library service without it is otherwise a very empty and possibly meaningless activity. (1997, p. 208)

The fact that in some cultures the relational "work" to establish a basis for further interaction must precede information tasks (Bialo & Sivin-Kachala, 1996; Delpit, 1996; Salvatore, 2000) appears to suggest as well that the social aspects of service are especially important for school librarians serving multicultural/multiethnic school communities. In light of the research findings of Bialo and Sivin-Kachala and Salvatore, some students may see direct inquiries by the librarian, which constitute the warp and woof of the traditional reference interview and which frequently characterize the opening moves in other kinds of school library interactions, as overly inquisitive, if not downright intrusive and rude.

Self-Esteem Needs and the Library Media Center

The psychological dimension of library-student interaction created a focus for the dissertation work of Diane McAfee Hopkins (1989). In particular, Hopkins's work considered the contributions that library programming and services could make to the development of feelings of self-worth in student users and the importance of establishing a positive atmosphere in the school library. Hopkins's research identified the provision of appropriate library materials, maintaining the accessibility to a variety of resources, and the creation of a welcoming physical setting as contributing to students' feelings of being valued in the library. In fact, Hopkins's research found students also experienced a sense of affirmation and acceptance through participation in library activities that fostered cooperation and independence (McAfee, 1981, cited in K. Haycock, 1992). Irving (1990) also noted the importance of this kind of library activity in her observation that learning to obtain "information personally" created a "tremendous sense of independence" (p. 86) and was an important by-product of information skills instruction; while students in Nahl-Jakobovits and Jakobovits's (1990) study found "deeply rewarding" those "required course-integrated library research" tasks that led them to "an enlarged conception of their capacity to learn and succeed" (p. 80). Finally, esteem needs appear to be implicated in Todd and Kuhlthau's (2003) conclusion that "students value professional, respectful and courteous interactions and appear to engage more readily with library services when their needs are met in a supportive, constructive, and pleasant manner" (p. 15).

How We Describe Library Users Matters

Chelton (conversation with author, August 24, 1997) has argued that the ways in which adolescents are discussed in the media and popular culture create stereotypes and expectations, frequently negative, which are then reflected in treatment adolescents receive in service interactions. This theme appears in a recent article by Marcus (2002). This author identifies titles such as *Unglued and Tattooed: How to Save Your Teen from Raves, Ritalin, Goth, Body Carving, GHB, Sex and 12 Other Emerging Threats; Parenting Your Out-of-Control Teenager; Yes, Your Teen Is Crazy*; and *Now I Know Why Tigers Eat Their Young: Surviving a New Generation of Teenagers* as not only pejorative, in the sense that they condition service providers to view all adolescents with suspicion, but also grossly insensitive to youngsters who are successfully navigating the often turbulent waters of adolescence.

The idea that the words we choose in describing library users also have unintended consequences in terms of library services has been the subject of an interesting study by Tuominen (1997). Drawing on communication theory, Tuominen applied a discourse analytic lens to the vocabulary that Kuhlthau (1993b) and others have employed in studies related to information seeking in libraries. Discourse analysis acknowledges the constitutive and value-laden character of language and argues that the terms we use actually create a reality that we think they only describe. Tuominen suggests that characterizing the library user as "uncertain," "anxious," "confused," and "unfocused," while at the same time identifying the librarian as an "expert," "rational," "problem solver," and "teacher," creates a context for relational asymmetry that may actually stymie the delivery of services. This is especially the case where successful service interventions are predicated on a model of shared responsibility and cooperation between users and librarians. Tuominen also argues that when anxiety is considered as a personal characteristic of the library user rather than as an outcome of the interaction

Table 9.1
Summary of Research Insights Related to Social Interactions in the Library Context

- Information seeking is affective and social as well as cognitive and informational

- The relational aspects of a library encounter may be as important as the informational aspects

- Students have self needs and want to feel respected and valued in library encounters

- The opening moments of a library interaction establish the relational nature (adversarial, participatory; expert, novice; superior, inferior) of the encounter

- Approachability and negativity are expressed in verbal and nonverbal actions and are "read" by students and used in planning their information-seeking activities

- The ways in which users are characterized in the research literature and library practices can promote asymmetry in interactions and inhibit participatory information activities

- The pejorative characterizations of teenagers in and by the media create narratives that, if unchallenged by library professionals, can condition attitudes that reduce service provision for teens in libraries

between the library user and aspects of the system and the environment, librarians are released from the responsibility to examine the very practices that make libraries and information seeking intimidating for many people.

Table 9.1 summarizes the research findings related to social interaction in the library context. Taken together this research underscores the importance of students' experiences in library activities. Considering the interactional issues related to instruction and service encounters serves to confirm, in a very real sense, not only the complexities of the librarians' tasks but also the significant roles that librarians can play in creating opportunities for positive encounters between their students and the school. Librarians devoted to helping students achieve educational and life goals must pay serious attention to this very important aspect of school librarianship. As C.A. Haycock (1991) reminds us, in the final analysis we are in the business of teaching kids, not content (p. 15).

Epilogue

Over time, many have commented on the lack of communication between research scholars and practicing library media specialists. Durrance (1988), for example, asserts that "researchers most often write for other researchers and librarians for other librarians, to the extent that these are really two sets of literatures, one based on practice the other on research (p. 161). Although it may be true that researchers and librarians represent different constituencies, they are surely bound together in their shared concern for improving the quality and effectiveness of library instruction. To achieve this goal, scholars and library media specialists must rely on each other, for in a very real sense, it is in practice that theories are verified, and it is theory that makes practice credible. To improve the quality of both, the exchange of ideas, insights, and information between researchers and practitioners is vital.

This book is an effort to build a bridge between the researcher and the practitioner, if in fact a gap between them exists. In sharing with practicing library media specialists the lessons learned from research studies and with researchers some "tales" from the field, it is hoped that both practice and research will be informed and enriched. Most scholars and practitioners agree that there is an enormous need for continued research in the areas of school librarianship and information skills instruction. Longitudinal studies are urgently needed to determine to what extent instruction in information skills prepares students for the business of living in an information-rich world. As Kuhlthau (2003) states, "information seeking is a primary activity of life" (p. 13). Future studies should also include testing of the many process models now being implemented, pursuing further theories related to learning styles, gender issues, social status, culture, ethnicity, exceptional students, and studying the relationship of technology to learning. Of special interest as well would be studies of independent information-seeking activities of students outside the confines of school-related information tasks.

Two significant recent events bode well for enriching our knowledge of information seeking and learning within the context of school libraries. The first is a research retreat, Treasure Mountain 10, held at the Elms Resort in Excelsior Springs, Missouri, in June 2002. This retreat brought together scholars in library media education and 20 masters and doctoral students interested in conducting and improving research methodology in school librarianship at both professional and academic levels.

The second was the establishment at Rutgers of the Center for International Scholarship in School Libraries (CISSL) in April 2003 (http://www.cissl.scils.rutgers.edu). Spearheaded by center directors Carol C. Kuhlthau and Ross Todd, CISSL's mission involves research, future leadership, professional education, and the dissemination of research findings. In launching CISSL, Kuhlthau called for renewed attention to the need for additional research into best practice, and promised the creation of a forum to involve scholars and librarians across the "world in a more coordinated, collaborative and cross-cultural approach to research" in school librarianship, particularly research that links school libraries and student learning.

Determining the kinds of information students need and want as they go about their daily activities and school tasks, and gaining knowledge of their preferred formats for communication and information resources, will assist librarians in designing services and instruction to support student information seeking in a context broad enough to encompass the global aspects of the larger information universe.

According to Hooten (1989):

> [C]hildren and youth need access to information to find answers to problems, to pursue independent discovery of who they are and who they want to become, to obtain information that can assist them to overcome their weaknesses and enhance their strengths, and to allow them to build life long information-seeking patterns. (p. 268)

Because they have access to all the students in their schools, library media specialists are in a position to make real differences in the lives of every one of these children. Vandergrift and Hannigan (1986) have acknowledged this aspect of school librarianship and the role librarians can take in helping students "develop the kind of educated imagination that empowers them to consider alternatives and to construct possible models of a better and more humane world" (p. 171). The challenges that such a responsibility provides are striking.

The task of helping students build information literacy skills for lifelong learning reminds us that we are in the business of educating students for the long haul. However, we must also be concerned about the short term—that is, helping students meet their immediate goals—only some of which will involve their school assignments. Common sense would argue that unless we are successful in the latter, students' abilities and motivation to achieve the former will be seriously compromised.

Library media specialists cannot make a contribution to education if clerical tasks and technological troubleshooting divert attention and resources from their primary instructional responsibilities or if they are marginalized in their schools. On the contrary, cooperation and collaboration for teaching and learning require investments of time and energy in building relationships that further our instructional goals. As librarians, we need teachers to provide the instructional context for the integration of information skills—and in helping to educate information-literate students, teachers need the expertise and knowledge that librarians possess.

A review of the research relating to instruction and learning in the modern media center reminds us that to accept the responsibility for teaching library and information skills is not for the faint of heart. The job requires sometimes on alternate days, sometimes at the same moment, the wisdom of Solomon, the patience of Job, and the communication skills of a Ronald Reagan—not to mention, creativity, stamina, a sense of humor, sensitivity, and an ethic of care. Perhaps because the complexities of the job require of library media specialists the best they have to give and draws upon all of their talents, abilities, and energies, and because the work itself is vital to our students, the professional life that school librarianship offers can be as rewarding and fulfilling as any in the educational spectrum.

References

Aaron, S.L. (1982). Review of Selected Doctoral Dissertations about School Library Media Programs and Resources January 1972–December 1980. *School Library Media Quarterly, 10,* 210–240.

AASL. (1960). *Standards for School Library Media Programs.* Chicago: American Library Association.

AASL & AECT. (1975). *Media Programs: District and School.* Chicago: American Library Association.

———. (1988). *Information Power: Guidelines for School Library Media Programs.* Chicago: American Library Association.

Agosto, D.E. (2001). Propelling Young Women into the Cyber Age: Gender Considerations in the Evaluation of Web-Based Information. *School Library Media Research, 4.* Available on the Internet at http://www.ala.org/aasl/SLMR/vol4/gender/gender/html (Accessed January 23, 2003).

———. (2002). Bounded Rationality and Satisficing in Young People's Web-Based Decision Making. *Journal of the American Society for Information Science and Technology, 53,* no. 1, 16–27.

Akin, L. (1998). Information Overload and Children: A Survey of Texas Elementary School Students. *School Library Media Quarterly.* Available on the Internet at http://www.ala.org/aasl/SLMQ/overload.html (Accessed January 23, 2003).

American Library Association. (1945). *School Libraries for Today and Tomorrow: Functions and Standards.* Chicago: American Library Association.

———. (1998). *Information Power: Building Partnerships for Learning.* Chicago: American Library Association.

Anderson, J.A. (1988). Cognitive Styles and Multicultural Populations. *Journal of Teacher Education, 39,* no. 1, 2–9.

Anderson, P.H. (1985). *Library Media Leadership in Academic Secondary Schools.* Hamden, CT: Library Professional Publications.

Armstrong, M., & Costa, B. (1983). Computer Cat at Mountain View Elementary School. *Library Hi Tech, 1,* no. 3, 47–52.

Aversa, E.S., & Mancall, J.C. (1989). *Management of Online Search Services in Schools.* Santa Barbara, CA: ABC–CLIO.

Baker, L., & Brown, A.L. (1984). Metacognitive Skills and Reading. In P.D. Pearson (Ed.), *Handbook of Reading Research* (pp. 353–394). New York: Longman, 1984.

Baker, S.L., & Lancaster, F.W. (1991). *The Measurement and Evaluation of Library Services.* Arlington, VA: Information Resources Press.

Barron, D.D. (1994). School Library Media Specialists and the Internet: Road Kill or Road Warriors? *School Library Media Activities Monthly, 10,* no. 9, 48–50.

Bates, M.J. (1979a). Information Search Tactics. *Journal of the American Society for Information Science, 30,* no. 4, 205–214.

———. (1979b). Idea Tactics. *Journal of the Association for Information Science, 30,* no. 5, 280–289.

———. (1989). The Design of Browsing and Berrypicking: Techniques for the Online Search Interface. *Online Review, 13,* no. 4, 407–423.

Baughman, J.C. (2000). *School Libraries and MCAS Scores.* Preliminary Edition. Boston: Graduate School of Library and Information Science. Available on the Internet at http://web.simmons.edu/~baughman/mcas-school-libraries/ (Accessed February 1, 2004).

Baumbach, D.T. (1986). Information Skills for the Information Age: The State of Our States. In S.L. Aaron & P.R. Scales (Eds.), *School Library Media Annual* (Vol. 4, pp. 278–285). Littleton, CO: Libraries Unlimited.

Baxter, S.J., & Smalley, A.W. (2003). *Check It Out! The Results of the School Library Media Program Census. Final Report.* Saint Paul, MN: Metronet. Available on the Internet at http://www.metronet.lib.mn.us/survey/index.cfm (Accessed February 10, 2004).

Becker, D.E. (1970). Social Studies Achievement of Pupils in Schools with Libraries and Schools without Libraries. Ph.D. diss., University of Pennsylvania.

Belkin, N.J. (1980). Anomalous State of Knowledge for Information Retrieval. *Canadian Journal of Information Science, 5,* no. 13, 133–143.

Belkin, N.J., Oddy, R.N., & Brooks, H.M. (1982a). Information Retrieval: Part I. Background and Theory. *Journal of Documentation, 38,* no. 2, 61–71.

———. (1982b). Ask for Information Retrieval: Part II. *Journal of Documentation, 38,* no. 3, 145–164.

Belmont, J.M. (1989). Cognitive Strategies and Strategic Learning: The Socio-Instructional Approach. *American Psychologist, 44,* no. 2, 142–148.

Benton Foundation. (1996). *Buildings, Books, and Bites: Librarians and Communities in the Digital Age.* Available on the Internet at http://www.benton.org/publibrary/index.html (Accessed February 1, 2004).

Berkowitz, R.E. (1994). From Indicators of Quantity to Measures of Effectiveness: Ensuring Information Power's Mission. In C.C. Kuhlthau, M.E. Goodin, & M.J. McNally (Eds.), *Assessment in the School Library Media Center* (pp. 33–42). Englewood, CO: Libraries Unlimited.

Berkowitz, R.E., & Serim, F. (2002). Moving Every Child Ahead: The Big6 Success Strategy. Multimedia Schools. Available on the Internet at http:////www.infotoday.com/Mmschools/May_02/berkowitz.htm (Accessed January 29, 2003).

Bialo, E.R., & Sivin-Kachala, J. (1996). The Effectiveness of Technology in Schools: A Summary of Recent Research. *School Library Media Quarterly, 25,* no. 1, 51–57.

Bilal, D. (1998). Children's Search Processes in Using World Wide Web Search Engines: An Exploratory Study. *Proceedings of the ASIS Annual Meeting, 35,* 45–53.

———. (2000). Children's Use of the Yahooligans! Web Search Engine: 1. Cognitive, Physical and Affective Behaviors on Fact-Based Search Tasks. *Journal of the American Society for Information Science, 51,* no. 7, 646–665.

———. (2001). Children's Use of the Yahooligans! Web Search Engine: II. Cognitive and Physical Behaviors on Research Tasks. *Journal of the American Society for Information Science and Technology*, *52*, no. 2, 118–136.

———. (2002a). Children's Use of the Yahooligans! Web Search Engine. III. Cognitive and Physical Behaviors on Fully Self-Generated Search Tasks. *Journal of the American Society for Information Science and Technology*, *53*, no. 13, 1170–1183.

———. (2002b). Perspectives on Children's Navigation of the World Wide Web: Does the Type of Search Task Make a Difference? *Online Information Review*, *26*, no. 2, 108–117.

Bilal, D., & Watson, J.S. (1998). Children's Paperless Projects: Inspiring Research Via the Web. In *Proceedings of the 64th IFLA General Conference, August 16–21, 1998, Amsterdam, The Netherlands* (pp. 101–107, Booklet 3). Amsterdam, The Netherlands: Xerox.

Bird, J., & Libby, J. (1978). Stimulating High-Order Thinking with Database Searching. *Indiana Media Journal*, *15*, no. 2, 15–19.

Bishop, K. (2001). *Inquiry-Based Learning: Lessons from Library Power*. Worthington, OH: Linworth.

Bishop, W.W. (1986). Training in the Use of Books. In L.L. Hardesty, J.P. Schmitt, & J.M. Tucker (Eds.), *User Instruction in Academic Libraries: A Century of Selected Readings* (pp. 69–85). Metuchen, NJ: Scarecrow Press.

Bloom, B. (1956). *Taxonomy of Educational Objectives*. New York: David McKay.

Bobotis, N.C. (1978). Relationship of Modes of Instruction and Bilingualism to Achievement in Library Skills. Ph.D. diss., University of New Mexico.

Bodi, S. (1992). Collaborating with Faculty in Teaching Critical Thinking: The Role of Librarians. *Research Strategies*, *10*, no. 2, 69–76.

Bogen, J.E. (1969). Some Educational Aspects of Hemispheric Specialization. *UCLA Educator*, *17*, 24–32.

Bondy, E. (1984). Thinking about Thinking: Encouraging Children's Use of Metacognitive Processes. *Childhood Education*, *60*, no. 4, 234–238.

Borgman, C.L. (1986). Why Are Online Catalogs Hard to Use? Lessons Learned from Information-Retrieval Studies. *Journal of the American Society for Information Science*, *37*, no. 6, 387–400.

Borgman, C.L., Gallagher, A.L. Krieger, D., & Bower, J. (1990). Children's Use of an Interactive Catalog of Science Materials. In D. Henderson (Ed.), *Proceedings of the 53rd ASIS Annual Meeting* (Vol. 27, pp. 55–68). Medford, NJ: Learned Information.

Borgman, C.L., Hirsh, S.G., Walter, V.A., & Gallagher, A.L. (1995). Children's Searching Behavior on Browsing and Keyword Online Catalogs: The Science Library Catalog Project. *Journal of the American Society for Information Science*, *46*, no. 9, 663–684.

Bowie, M.M. (Comp.). (1986). *Historic Documents of School Libraries*. Fayetteville, AR: Hi Willow Research Publishing.

Bracy, P. (1990). Completed Research Pertinent to School Library Media Programs. In J.B. Smith (Ed.), *School Library Media Annual* (Vol. 8, pp. 126–134). Littleton, CO: Libraries Unlimited.

Breivik, P.S. (1989). Politics for Bridging the Gap. *Reference Librarian*, no. 24, 5–16.

———. (1991). Literacy in an Information Society. *Community, Technical, and Junior College Journal*, *61*, no. 6, 28–29, 32–35.

Breivik, P.S., & Senn, J.A. (1994). *Information Literacy: Educating Children for the 21st Century*. New York: Scholastic.

Bretzing, B.H., Kulhavy, R.W., & Caterino, L.C. (1987). Notetaking by Junior High Students. *Journal of Educational Research*, *80*, no. 6, 359–362.

Brien, D.P. (1995). The Teaching and Learning Processes Involved in Primary School Children's Research Projects. E.D.D. diss., University of New South Wales.

Broch, E. (2000). Children's Search Engines from an Information Search Process Perspective. *School Library Media Research*. Available on the Internet at http://ala.org/aasl/SLMR/vol3/childrens/childrens_main.html (Accessed January 29, 2003).

Brodie, C.S. (1988). Library Programs for the Gifted and Talented: Differentiated Versus Traditional. Ph.D. diss., Texas Women's University, Denton, TX.

Brown, J.S., Collins, A., & Duguid, P. (1989). Situated Cognition and the Culture of Learning. *Educational Researcher, 18,* 32–42.

Bruce, B.C., & Leander, K.M. (1997). Searching for Digital Libraries in Education: Why Computers Cannot Tell the Story. *Library Trends, 45,* no. 4, 746–770.

Bruce, H. (1994). Media Center Automation: A Watershed for the School Media Specialist. *School Library Media Quarterly, 22,* no. 4, 206–212.

Bruffee, K.A. (1984). Collaborative Learning and the "Conversation of Mankind." *College English, 46,* no. 7, 635–652.

Bruner, J. (1975). *Toward a Theory of Instruction.* Cambridge, MA: Harvard University Press.

———. (1977). *The Process of Education.* Cambridge, MA: Harvard University Press.

———. (1980). *Beyond the Information Given.* New York: Norton.

———. (1986). *Actual Minds, Possible Worlds.* Cambridge, MA: Harvard University Press.

Buckland, M.K. (1983). *Library Services in Theory and Context.* New York: Pergamon Press.

Burdick, T.A. (1996). Success and Diversity in Information Seeking: Gender and the Information Search Styles Model. *School Library Media Quarterly, 25,* no. 1, 19–26.

———. (1997). Snakes and Snails and Puppy Dog Tails: Girls and Boys Expressing Voice in Information Research Projects. *Journal of Youth Services in Libraries, 11,* no. 1, 28–36.

Bush, Laura. (2002). Press release. Available on the Internet at http://www.laurabush foundation.org/release_060402.html (Accessed February 4, 2004).

Butler, P. (1933). *An Introduction to Library Science.* Chicago: University of Chicago Press.

Buzan, T. (1991). *Use Both Sides of Your Brain.* New York: Dutton.

Callison, D. (1986). School Library Media Programs and Free Inquiry Learning. *School Library Media Quarterly, 15,* no. 6, 20–24.

———. (1990). A Review of the Research Related to School Library Media Collections: Part I. *School Library Media Quarterly, 19,* no. 1, 57–62.

———. (1994). Expanding the Evaluation Role in the Critical-Thinking Curriculum. In C.C. Kuhlthau, M.E. Goodin, & M.J. McNally (Eds.), *Assessment in the School Library Media Center* (pp. 43–57). Englewood, CO: Libraries Unlimited.

———. (1995). Expanding the Evaluation Role in the Critical-Thinking Curriculum. In Fifteenth Anniversary Task Force, Library Instruction Round Table, American Library Association (Comp.), *Information for a New Age: Redefining the Librarian* (pp. 153–169). Englewood, CO: Libraries Unlimited.

———. (2000). Key Instructional Term: Motivation. Available on the Internet at http://www.crinkles.com/keyWords.html (Accessed January 29, 2003).

Carey, J.O. (1997). From Library Skills to Information Literacy: Implications for Teaching and Learning. Presentation at Treasure Mountain Research Retreat. Portland, OR, April.

———. (1998). Library Skills, Information Skills, and Information Literacy: Implications for Teaching and Learning. *SLMQ Online.* Available on the Internet at http://www.ala.org/ala/aasl/pubsandjournals/slmrb/slmrcontents/volume11998slmgo/carey.htm (Accessed February 10, 2004).

Carey, S. (1985). *Conceptual Change in Childhood*. Cambridge, MA: MIT Press.

Carr, D.W. (1990). Qualitative Meanings in Cultural Institutions. *Journal of Education in Library and Information Science*, *31*, no. 2, 98–112.

Carroll, F.L. (1981). *Recent Advances in School Librarianship*. Oxford: Pergamon Press.

Carson, C.H., & Curtis, R.V. (1991). Applying Instructional Design Theory to Bibliographic Instruction: Microtheory. *Research Strategies*, *9*, no. 2, 60–76.

Carvin, A. (2000a). Beyond Access: Understanding the Digital Divide. Keynote Address, NYU Third Act Conference, May 19, 2000. Available on the Internet at http://www.benton.org/Divide/thirdact/speech.html (Accessed January 23, 2003).

———. (2000b). Mending the Breach: Overcoming the Digital Divide. Available on the Internet at http://www.edu-cyberpg.com/Teachers/andycarvin1.html (Accessed February 11, 2004).

Cecil, H.L., & Heaps, W.A. (1940). School Library Service in the United States: An Interpretive Survey. New York: Wilson. In M.M. Bowie (Comp.), *Historic Documents of School Libraries*. Fayetteville, AR: Hi Willow, 1986.

Chelton, M.K. (1997). Adult-Adolescent Service Encounters: The Library Context. Ph.D. diss., Rutgers, The State University of New Jersey.

———. (1999). Structural and Theoretical Constraints on Reference Service in a High School Library Media Center. *Reference & User Services Quarterly*, *38*, no. 3, 275–287.

Chelton, M.K., & Thomas, N.P. (1999). Introduction: Why a Special Issue on Youth Issues? In M.K. Chelton & N.P. Thomas (Eds.), Special Issue: Youth Issues in Information Science. *Journal of the American Society for Information Science*, *50*, no. 1, 7–9.

Chen, S.-H. (1993). A Study of High School Students' Online Catalog Searching Behavior. *School Library Media Quarterly*, *22*, no. 1, 33–40.

Clark, L.A., & Halford, G.S. (1983). Does Cognitive Style Account for Cultural Differences in Scholastic Achievement? *Journal of Cross-Cultural Psychology*, *14*, no. 3, 279–296.

Clarke, J., Martell, K., & Willey, C. (1994). Sequencing Graphic Organizers to Guide Historical Research. *The Social Studies*, *85*, no. 5, 70–78.

Clarke, P.S. (1973). Reading Interests and Preferences of Indian, Black, and White High School Students. Ph.D. diss., North Texas State University.

Claxton, C.S. (1990). Learning Styles, Minority Students, and Effective Education. *Journal of Developmental Education*, *14*, no. 1, 6–8, 35.

Clements, D.H., & Nastasi, B.K. (1988). Social and Cognitive Interaction in Educational Computer Environments. *American Educational Research Journal*, *25*, no. 1, 87–106.

Clements, D.H., Nastasi, B.K., & Swaminathan, S. (1993). Young Children and Computers: Crossroads and Directions from Research. *Young Children*, *48*, no. 2, 56–64.

Coleman, J.G. (1989). Library Media Personnel: The Essential Ingredient. In J.B. Smith (Ed.), *School Library Media Annual* (Vol. 7, pp. 46–56). Englewood, CO: Libraries Unlimited.

Collins, A., Brown, J.S., & Newman, S.E. (1989). Cognitive Apprenticeship: Teaching the Crafts of Reading, Writing, and Mathematics. In L.B. Resnick (Ed.), *Knowing, Learning, and Instruction*. Hillsdale, NJ: Lawrence Erlbaum.

Comer, J.P. (2001). Schools That Develop Children. *The American Perspective Online*, *12*, no. 7 (April 23). Available on the Internet at http://www.prospect.org/print/V12/7/comer-j.html (Accessed January 24, 2003).

Cooper, L.Z. (2002). A Case Study of Information-Seeking Behavior in 7-Year-Old Children in a Semistructured Situation. *Journal of the American Society for Information Science and Technology*, *53*, no. 11, 904–922.

Cottrell, J.R., & Eisenberg, M.B. (2001). Applying an Information Problem-Solving Model to Academic Reference Work: Findings and Implications. *College & Research Libraries, 62*, no. 4, 334–347.

Craver, K.W. (1989). Critical Thinking: Implications from Research. *School Library Media Quarterly, 18*, no. 1, 13–18.

———. (1995). Shaping Our Future: The Role of School Library Media Centers. *School Library Media Quarterly, 24*, no. 1, 13–18.

Creanor, L., Durndell, H., Henderson, F.P., Primrose, C., Brown, M.I., Draper, S.W., & McAteer E. (1995). *A Hypertext Approach to Information Skills: Development and Evaluation.* Glasgow, Scotland: University of Glasgow Series, TLT Publications.

Csikszentmihalyi, M. (1990). *Flow: The Psychology of Optimal Experience.* New York: Harper & Row.

Davies, R.A. (1974). Educating Library Users in the Senior High School. In J. Lubans (Ed.), *Educating the Library User* (pp. 39–52). New York: Bowker.

Davis, R.C. (1986). Teaching Bibliography in Colleges. In L.L. Hardesty, J.P. Schmitt, & J.M. Tucker (Comps.), *User Instruction in Academic Libraries: A Century of Selected Readings* (pp. 35–45). Metuchen, NJ: Scarecrow Press.

Delpit, L.D. (1995). *Other People's Children: Cultural Conflict in the Classroom.* New York: New Press.

Denning, R., Shuttleworth, M., & Smith, P. (1998). Interface Design Concepts in the Development of a Web-Based Information Retrieval System. *Bulletin of the American Society for Information Science, 24*, no. 4, 17–20. Available on the Internet at http://www.asis.org/Bulletin/Apr-98/design.html (Accessed March 12, 2003).

Dervin, B. (1983). *An Overview of Sense-Making Research: Concepts, Methods, and Results to Date.* Seattle: School of Communications, University of Washington.

———. (1989). Users as Research Inventions: How Research Categories Perpetuate Inequities. *Journal of Communication, 39*, no. 3, 216–232.

———. (1999). The Implications of Connecting Metatheory to Method. *Information Processing & Management, 35*, no. 6, 727–750.

Dervin, B., & Dewdney, P. (1986). Neutral Questioning: A New Approach to the Reference Interview. *Research Quarterly, 35* no. 4, 506–513.

Dervin, B., & Nilan, M. (1986). Information Needs and Uses. In M.E. Williams (Ed.), *Annual Review of Information Science and Technology (ARIST)* (Vol. 21, pp. 3–33). White Plains, NY: Knowledge Industry Publications.

Dewees, K.B. (1987). *The Effect of Teaching Library Skills Using "The Pooh Step-by-Step Guide for Writing the Research Paper" at Lieder Elementary School in the Cypress Fairbanks Independent School District. A Research Report.* Houston, TX: Prairie View A&M University, 1987. (ERIC ED 284 577)

Dewey, J. (1916). *Democracy and Education: An Introduction to the Philosophy of Education.* New York: Macmillan.

———. (1933). *How We Think.* Lexington, MA: Heath.

———. (1934). *Art as Experience.* New York: G.P. Putnam's Sons.

Dewey, M. (1986). The Relation of the Colleges to the Modern Library Movement. In L.L. Hardesty, J.P. Schmitt, & J.M. Tucker (Comps.), *User Instruction in Academic Libraries: A Century of Selected Readings* (pp. 46–54). Metuchen, NJ: Scarecrow Press.

Dickinson, D.W. (1981). Library Literacy: Who? When? Where? *Library Journal, 15*, 853–855.

Didier, E.K. (1982). Relationships between Student Achievement in Reading and Library Media Programs and Personnel. Ph.D. diss., University of Michigan.

———. (1985). An Overview of Research on the Impact of School Library Media Programs on Student Achievement. *School Library Media Quarterly*, *14*, no. 1, 33–36.

Dike, V.W. (1993). School Libraries/Media Centers. *In World Encyclopedia of Library and Information Services* (3rd ed., pp. 743–753). Chicago: American Library Association.

Donham, J., Bishop, K., Kuhlthau, C.C., & Oberg, D. (2001). *Inquiry-Based Learning: Lessons from Library Power*. Worthington, OH: Linworth.

Doyle, C.S. (1994). Information-Literate Use of Telecommunications. *DMLEA Journal*, *17*, no. 2, 17–20.

Draper, S.W., Brown, M.I., Henderson, F.P., & McAteer, E. (1996). Integrative Evaluation: An Emerging Role for Classroom Studies of CAL. *Computers & Education*, *26*, nos. 1–3, 17.

Driver, R., Asoko, H., Leach, J., Mortimer, E., & Scott, P. (1994). Constructing Scientific Knowledge in the Classroom. *Educational Researcher*, *23*, no. 7, 5–12.

Dunn, R., Beasley, M., & Buchanan, K. (1994). What Do You Believe about How Culturally Diverse Students Learn? *Emergency Librarian*, *22*, no. 1, 8–14.

Dunn, R., & Smith, J.B. (1990). Learning Styles and Library Media Programs. In J.B. Smith (Ed.), *School Library Media Annual* (Vol. 8, pp. 32–49). Englewood, CO: Libraries Unlimited.

Durrance, J.C. (1988). Information Needs: Old Song, New Tune. In *Rethinking the Library in the Information Age: Issues in Library Research. Proposals for the 1990s* (pp. 159–177). U.S.D.E. Office of Educational Research and Improvement. Library Programs. Washington, DC: GPO.

Dutilloy, J. (2003). Implementing a Plagiarism Policy at the United Nations International School. *Knowledge Quest*, *31*, no. 4, 44–45.

Dwyer, D. (1994). Apple Classroom of Tomorrow: What We've Learned. *Educational Leadership*, *51*, no. 7, 4–10.

Eadie, T. (1990). Immodest Proposals: User Instruction for Students Does Not Work. *Library Journal*, *115*, no. 17, 42–45.

Edmonds, L., Moore, P., & Balcom, K.M. (1990). The Effectiveness of an Online Catalog. *School Library Journal*, *36*, no. 10, 28–32.

Edyburn, D.L. (1988). Examining the Successful Retrieval of Information by Students Using Online Databases. *School Library Media Quarterly*, *16*, no. 4, 256–260.

Eisenberg, M.B. (1984). Curriculum Mapping and Implementation of an Elementary School Library Media Skills Curriculum. *School Library Media Quarterly*, *12*, no. 2, 411–418.

Eisenberg, M.B., & Berkowitz, R.B. (1990). *Information Problem-Solving: The Big Six Skills Approach to Library and Information Skills Instruction*. Norwood, NJ: Ablex.

———. (1996). *Helping with Homework: A Parent's Guide to Information Problem Solving*. Syracuse, NY: ERIC Clearinghouse in Information and Technology.

Eisenberg, M.B., & Brown, M.K. (1992). Current Themes Regarding Library and Information Skills Instruction: Research Supporting and Research Lacking. *School Library Media Quarterly*, *20*, no. 2, 103–109.

Eisenberg, M.B., & Spitzer, K.L. (1991). Information Technology and Service in Schools. In M.E. Williams (Ed.), *Annual Review of Information Science and Technology (ARIST)* (Vol. 26, pp. 243–285). Medford, NJ: Learned Education.

Eisner, E. (1993). Why Standards May Not Improve Schools. *Educational Leadership*, *50*, no. 5, 22–23.

Ellis, D. (1989). A Behavioral Approach to Information Retrieval Systems Design. *Journal of Documentation*, *45*, no. 3, 171–212.

Ely, D.P. (1992). Response 1 to Ann Irving. In J.B. Smith (Ed.), *School Library Media Annual* (Vol. 10, pp. 46–47). Englewood, CO: Libraries Unlimited.

Engeldinger, E.A. (1988). Bibliographic Instruction and Critical Thinking: The Contribution of the Annotated Bibliography. *Research Quarterly, 28,* no. 2, 195–202.

Engeldinger, E.A., & Stevens, B.R. (1984). Library Instruction within the Curriculum. *College and Research Libraries, 45,* no. 11, 593–598.

Entwistle, N. (1981). *Styles of Learning and Teaching: An Integrative Outline of Educational Psychology.* Chichester, England: John Wiley and Sons.

Eriksen, E.H. (1968). *Identity, Youth and Crisis.* New York: Norton.

Everhart, N. (2003). Students and Plagiarism. *Knowledge Quest, 31,* no. 4, 43–44.

Farber, E.I. (1986). College Libraries and the University-Library Syndrome. In L.L. Hardesty, J.P. Schmitt, & J.M. Tucker (Comps.), *User Instruction in Academic Libraries: A Century of Selected Readings* (pp. 243–253). Metuchen, NJ: Scarecrow Press.

———. (1995). Bibliographic Instruction, Briefly. In Fifteenth Anniversary Task Force, Library Instruction Round Table, American Library Association (Comp.), *Information for a New Age: Redefining the Librarian* (pp. 23–34). Englewood, CO: Libraries Unlimited.

———. (1998). Technological Idolatry and the Reference Librarian. Available on the Internet at http://library,willamette.edu/publications/movtyp/spring98/evan.htm (Accessed January 27, 2003).

Fidel, R., Davies, R.K., Douglass, M.H., Holder, J.K., Hopkins, C.J., Kushner, E.J., Miyagishima, B.K., & Toney, C.D. (1999). A Visit to the Information Mall: Web Searching Behavior of High School Students. *Journal of the American Society for Information Science, 50,* no. 1, 24–37.

Fitzgerald, M.A. (1999). Evaluating Information: An Information Literacy Challenge. *School Library Media Research, 2.* Available on the Internet at http://www.ala.org/aasl/SLMR/vol2/evaluating.html (Accessed January 23, 2003).

Ford, D.Y. (1996). *Reversing Underachievement among Gifted Black Students.* New York: Teachers College Press.

Frazier, D.U., & Paulson, F.L. (1992). How Portfolios Motivate Reluctant Writers. *Educational Leadership, 49,* no. 8, 62–65.

Freedman, K., & Liu, M. (1996). The Importance of Computer Experience, Learning Processes and Communication Patterns in Multicultural Networking. *ETR & D, 44,* no. 1, 43–59.

Frick, E. (1986). Information Structure and Bibliographic Instruction. In L.L. Hardesty, J.P. Schmitt, & J.M. Tucker (Comps.), *User Instruction in Academic Libraries: A Century of Selected Readings* (pp. 266–275). Metuchen, NJ: Scarecrow Press.

Frohmann, B. (1992). The Power of Image: A Discourse Analysis of the Cognitive Viewpoint. *Journal of Documentation, 48,* no. 4, 365–386.

Gallivan, M.F. (1974). Research on Children's Services in Libraries: An Annotated Bibliography. *Top of the News, 30,* no. 3, 275–293.

Gardner, H. (1983). *Frames of Mind: The Theory of Multiple Intelligence.* New York: Basic Books.

———. (1996). Probing More Deeply into the Theory of Multiple Intelligences. *NAASP Bulletin, 80,* no. 583, 1–7.

———. (1999a). *Intelligence Reframed: Multiple Intelligences for the 21st Century.* New York: Basic Books.

———. (1999b). Project Sumit. Available on the Internet at http://www.pzweb.harvard.edu/SUMIT/MISUMIT.htm (Accessed February 23, 2003).

Garland, K. (1995). The Information Search Process: A Study of Elements Associated with Meaningful Research Tasks. In B.J. Morris, J.L. McQuiston, & C.L. Saretsky (Eds.), *School Library Media Annual* (Vol. 13, pp. 171–183). Englewood, CO: Libraries Unlimited.

Gaver, M.V. (1963). *Effectiveness of Centralized Library Service in Elementary Schools*. New Brunswick, NJ: Rutgers University Press.

Gawith, G. (2002). Information Literacy: Problems and Solutions. Available on the Internet at http://www.theschoolquarterly.coom/info_lit_archive/defn_discussion/00_gg_ipls.htm (Accessed January 29, 2003).

Gedeon, R. (2000). Accessing the Right Brain with Bibliographic Instruction. *Research Strategies, 16*, no. 4, 259–269.

Gehlken, V.S. (1994). The Role of the High School Library Media Program in Three Nationally Recognized South Carolina Blue Ribbon Secondary Schools. Ph.D. diss., University of South Carolina.

Ghikas, M.W. (1989). Collection Management for the 21st Century. In P. Woodrom (Ed.), *Managing Public Libraries in the 21st Century* (pp. 119–135). New York: Haworth Press.

Giese, R.N., Cothron, J.H., & Rezha, R.J. (1992). Take the Search Out of Research: A Guide to "Checking Out" the Library. *The Science Teacher, 59*, no. 1, 32–37.

Gifford, V., & Gifford, J. (1984). Effects of Teaching a Library Usage Unit to Seventh Graders. Paper presented at the Annual Conference of the Mid-South Educational Research Association, New Orleans, LA. (ERIC ED 254 230)

Gillespie, J.T., & Spirt, D.L. (1973). *Creating a School Media Program*. New York: Bowker.

Gilligan, C. (1982). *In a Different Voice*. Cambridge, MA: Harvard University Press.

Gilliland, M.J. (1986). Can Libraries Make a Difference? Test Scores Say "Yes"! *School Library Media Quarterly, 15*, no. 2, 67–70.

Goffman, E. (1967). *Interaction Ritual: Essays on Face-to-Face Behavior*. New York: Pantheon.

Goodin, M.E. (1987). The Transferability of Library Skills from High School to College. Ph.D. diss., Rutgers, The State University of New Jersey.

———. (1991). The Transferability of Library Research Skills from High School to College. *School Library Media Quarterly, 20*, no. 1, 33–41.

Gordon, C. (1999). Students as Authentic Researchers: A New Perspective for the High School Research Assignment. *School Library Media Research, 2*. Available on the Internet at http://www.ala.org/aasl/SLMR/vol2/authentic.html (Accessed January 23, 2003).

———. (2000). The Effects of Concept-Mapping on the Searching Behavior of Tenth-Grade Students. *School Library Media Research, 3*. Available on the Internet at http://www.ala.org/aasl/SLMR/vol3/content.htm (Accessed January 23, 2003).

Gordon, H. (1996). Hemisphericity. In J.G. Beaumont, P.M. Kenealy, & M.J. Rogers (Eds.), *The Blackwell Dictionary of Neuropsychology* (pp. 388–395). Cambridge, MA: Blackwell.

Greve, C.L. (1974). The Relationship of the Availability of Libraries to the Academic Achievement of Iowa High School Seniors. Ph.D. diss., University of Denver.

Gross, M. (1995). The Imposed Query. *Research Quarterly, 35*, no. 2, 236–243.

———. (1997). Pilot Study on the Prevalence of Imposed Queries in a School Library Media Center. *School Library Media Quarterly, 25*, no. 3, 157–166.

Grover, R. (1993). A Proposed Model for Diagnosing Information Needs. *School Library Media Quarterly, 21*, no. 2, 95–100.

———. (1994). Assessing Information Skills Instruction. *The Reference Librarian*, no. 44, 173–189.

Grover, R., Blume, S., Dickerson, J., Lakin, J., & Schumacher, M. (1996). An Interdisciplinary Model for Assessing Learning. Paper presented at the Library Research Seminar I, Tallahassee, FL.

Hagopian, G., Iandoli, A., Wellins, C.L., & Williams, H.B. (1996). Four Phase Study: Impact of Learning Styles on Teaching and Learning in an Urban District. Paper presented at the National Development Council Annual Conference, Vancouver, British Columbia, December.

Hale-Benson, J.E. (1982). *Black Children: Their Roots, Culture and Learning Styles*. Provo, UT: Brigham Young University Press.

Hall-Ellis, S.O., & Berry, M.A. (1995). School Library Media Centers and Academic Achievement in South Texas. *Texas Library Journal*, 71, no. 2, 94–97.

Hanchett, T.W. (1987). The Rosenwald Fund. Available on the Internet at http://www.cmhpf.org/S&RR/McClintockNewellRosen.html (Accessed February 1, 2003).

Hardesty, L.L., Schmitt, J.P., & Tucker, J.M. (Comps.). (1986). *User Instruction in Academic Libraries: A Century of Selected Readings*. Metuchen, NJ: Scarecrow Press.

Harmon, C.T., & Bradburn, F.B. (1988). Realizing the Reading and Information Needs of Youth. *Library Trends*, 37, no. 1, 19–27.

Hartzell, G.N. (1994). *Building Influence for the School Librarian*. Worthington, OH: Linworth Publishing.

Haycock, C.A. (1991). Resource-Based Learning: A Shift in the Roles of Teacher, Learner. *NASSP Bulletin*, 75, no. 535, 15–22.

Haycock, K. (1992). *What Works: Research about Teaching and Learning through the School's Library Resource Center*. Vancouver, BC: Rockland Press.

Heeks, P. (1997). School Libraries. In J. Feather & P. Sturges (Eds.), *International Encyclopedia of Information and Library Science* (pp. 410–412). London: Routledge.

Hensley, R. (1991). Learning Style Theory and Learning Transfer Principles during Reference Interview Instruction. *Library Trends*, 39, no. 3, 203–209.

Herman, J.L. (1992). What Research Tells Us about Good Assessment. *Educational Leadership*, 48, no. 5, 74–78.

Hirsh, S.G. (1997). How Do Children Find Information in Different Tasks? Children's Use of the Science Catalog. *Library Trends*, 45, no. 4, 725–745.

———. (1998). Relevance Determinations in Children's Use of Electronic Resources: A Case Study. *Proceedings of the 61st ASIS Annual Meeting*, 35, 63–72.

———. (1999). Children's Relevance Criteria and Information Seeking on Electronic Resources. *Journal of the American Society for Information Science*, 50, no. 14, 1265–1283.

Hoerr, T.R. (1996). Introducing the Theory of Multiple Intelligences. *NASSP Bulletin*, 80, no. 583, 8–9.

Honebein, P. (1996). Seven Goals for the Design of Constructivist Learning Environments. In B.G. Wilson (Ed.), *Constructivist Learning Environments: Case Studies in Instructional Design* (pp. 11–24). Englewood Cliffs, NJ: Educational Technology Publications.

Hooten, P.A. (1989). Online Catalogs: Will They Improve Children's Access? *Journal of Youth Service in Libraries*, 2, 267–272.

Hopkins, D.M. (1989). Elementary School Library Media Programs and the Promotion of Positive Self-Concept: A Report of an Exploratory Study. *Library Quarterly*, 59, no. 2, 131–147.

Hopkins, D.M., & Zweizig, D.L. (1999). Power to the Media Center (and to the People, Too). The National Library Power Initiative. *School Library Journal* (May), 25, 27.

Howe, H., II. (1993). *Thinking about Our Kids*. New York: Free Press.

Huston, M.M. (1989). Search Theory and Instruction for End Users of Online Bibliographic Information Retrieval Systems: A Literature Review. *Research Strategies*, 7, no. 1, 14–32.

Huston, M.M., & Oberman, C. (1989). Making Communication: A Theoretical Framework for Educating End-Users of Online Bibliographic Information Retrieval Systems. *The Reference Librarian*, no. 24, 199–211.

Hyland, A.H. (1978). Recent Directions in Educating the Library User: Elementary Schools. In J. Lubans, Jr. (Ed.), *Progress in Educating the Library User* (pp. 29–44). New York: Bowker.

Inhelder, B., & Piaget, J. (1958). *The Growth of Logical Thinking: From Childhood to Adolescence*. New York: Basic Books.

Irvine, J.J., & Irvine, R.W. (1995). Black Youth in School: Individual Achievement and Instructional/Cultural Perspectives, In R.L. Taylor (Ed.), *African-American Youth: Their Social and Economic Status in the United States* (pp. 129–142). Westport, CT: Praeger.

Irving, A. (1983). Educating Information Users in Schools. In *British Library Research Reviews* (Vol. 4). London: The British Library.

———. (1985). *Study and Information Skills across the Curriculum*. London: Heinemann.

———. (1990). *Wider Horizons: Online Information Services in Schools*. Library and Information Research Report 80. London: British Library.

———. (1991). The Educational Value and Use of Online Information Services in Schools. *Computers and Education*, 17, no. 3, 213–225.

Jackson, M.M. (1994). Library Information Skills and Standardized Achievement Tests. In C.C. Kuhlthau, M.E. Goodin, & M.J. McNally (Eds.), *Assessment in the School Library Media Center* (pp. 25–32). Englewood, CO: Libraries Unlimited.

Jacobson, F.F. (1997). Introduction. *Library Trends*, 45, no. 4, 575–581.

Jacobson, F.F., & Ignacio, E.N. (1997). Teaching Reflection: Information Seeking and Evaluation in a Digital Library Environment. *Library Trends*, 45, no. 4, 771–802.

Jacobson, F.F., & Jacobson, M.J. (1993). Representative Cognitive Learning Theories and BI: A Case Study of End User Searching. *Research Strategies*, 11, no. 3, 124–137.

Jacobson, T.E., & Mark, B.L. (1995). Teaching in the Information Age: Active Learning Techniques to Empower Students. *The Reference Librarian*, 51–52, 105–120.

Jakobovits, L.A., & Nahl-Jakobovits, D. (1990). Measuring Information Searching Competence. *Research Libraries*, 51, no. 5, 448–462.

Jay, M.E. (1986). The Elementary School Library Media Teacher's Role in Educating Students to Think. *School Library Media Quarterly*, 15, no. 1, 28–32.

Joeckel, C.B. (1943). *Post-War Standards for Public Libraries*. Chicago: American Library Association.

Johnson, L. (1986). Stephens College Library Experiment. In L.L. Hardesty, J.P. Schmitt, & J.M. Tucker (Comps.), *User Instruction in Academic Libraries: A Century of Selected Readings* (pp. 110–120). Metuchen, NJ: Scarecrow Press.

Jonassen, D.H., Myers, J.M., & McKillop, A.M. (1996). From Constructivism to Constructionism: Learning with Hypermedia/Multimedia Rather Than from It. In B. Wilson (Ed.), *Constructivist Learning Environments: Case Studies in Instructional Design* (pp. 93–106). Englewood Cliffs, NJ: Educational Technology Publications.

Joyce, M.Z., & Tallman, J.I. (1997). *Making the Writing and Research Connection with the I-Search Process*. New York: Neal-Schuman.

Julien, H.E. (1999). Barriers to Adolescents' Information Seeking for Career Decision-Making. *Journal of the American Society for Information Science*, 50, no. 1, 38–48.

Jung, C.G. (1923). *Psychological Types*. New York: Harcourt & Brace.

Kafai, Y., & Bates, M.J. (1997). Internet Web-Searching Instruction in the Elementary

Classroom: Building a Foundation for Information Literacy. *School Library Media Quarterly, 25*, no. 2, 103–111.

Kaiser Family Foundation. (2002). See No Evil: How Internet Filters Affect the Search for Online Health Information: A Kaiser Family Foundation Study. Menlo Park, CA. Available on the Internet at http://www.kff.org (Accessed January 27, 2003).

Kansas Association of School Librarians Research Committee. (2001). *The Handy 5: Planning and Assessing Integrated Information Skills Instruction* (R. Grover, C. Fox, & J.M. Lakin, Eds.). Lanham, MD: Scarecrow Press.

Keil, F.C. (1979). *Semantic and Conceptual Development: An Ontological Perspective.* Cambridge, MA: Harvard University Press.

Kelly, G.A. (1963). *A Theory of Personality: The Psychology of Personal Constructs.* New York: Norton.

Kennedy, J.R., Jr. (1986). Integrated Library Instruction. In L.L. Hardesty, J.P. Schmitt, & J.M. Tucker (Comps.), *User Instruction in Academic Libraries: A Century of Selected Readings* (pp. 231–242). Metuchen, NJ: Scarecrow Press.

Kester, D.D. (1994). Secondary School Library and Information Skills: Are They Transferred from High School to College? *The Reference Librarian, 44,* 9–17.

Kleifgen, J.A. (1989). Computers and Opportunities for Literacy Development. *ERIC/CUE Digest,* no. 54. New York: Eric Clearinghouse on Urban Education.

Knapp, P.B. (1966). *The Monteith College Library Experiment.* New York: Scarecrow Press.

———. (1986). A Suggested Program of College Instruction in the Use of the Library. In L.L. Hardesty, J.P. Schmitt, & J.M. Tucker (Comps.), *User Instruction in Academic Libraries: A Century of Selected Readings* (pp. 151–166). Metuchen, NJ: Scarecrow Press.

Kohlberg, L. (1969). *Development of Moral Thought and Action.* New York: Holt, Rinehart & Winston.

Kolb, D.A. (1983). *Experiential Learning.* Englewood Cliffs, NJ: Prentice-Hall.

Kolb, D.A., & Fry, R.E. (1975). Toward an Applied Theory of Experiential Learning. In C. Cooper (Ed.), *Theories of Group Process* (pp. 33–57). London: John Wiley.

Kozol, J. (2000). An Unequal Education. *School Library Journal.* Available on the Internet at http://slj.reviewsnews.com/index.asp?layout-articlePrint&articleID-CA153042 (Accessed January 23, 2003).

Krashen, S. (1993). *The Power of Reading: Insights from Research.* Littleton, CO: Libraries Unlimited.

Krechevsky, M. (1991). Project Spectrum: An Innovative Assessment Alternative. *Educational Leadership, 48,* no. 5, 43–48.

Kuhlthau, C.C. (1985). *Teaching the Library Research Process: A Step-by-Step Program for Secondary School Students.* West Nyack, NY: Center for Applied Research in Education.

———. (1987). An Emerging Theory of Library Instruction. *School Library Media Quarterly, 16,* no. 1, 23–27.

———. (1988a). Longitudinal Case Studies of the Information Search Process of Users in Libraries. *Library and Information Science Research, 10,* no. 3, 257–304.

———. (1988b). Perceptions of the Information Search Process in Libraries: A Study in Changes from High School through College. *Information Processing & Management, 24,* no. 4, 419–427.

———. (1991). Inside the Search Process: Information Seeking from the User's Perspective. *Journal of the American Society for Information Science, 42,* no. 5, 361–371.

———. (1993a). Implementing a Process Approach to Information Skills: A Study Identifying Indicators of Success in Library Media Programs. *School Library Media Quarterly, 22,* no. 1, 11–18.

———. (1993b). *Seeking Meaning.* Norwood, NJ: Ablex.

———. (1994). Assessing the Library Research Process. In C.C. Kuhlthau, M.E. Goodin,

& M.J. McNally (Eds.), *Assessment in the School Library Media Center* (pp. 59–65). Englewood, CO: Libraries Unlimited.

———. (1995). The Process of Learning from Information. *School Libraries World Wide*, *1*, no. 1, 1–13.

———. (1996). The Concept of a Zone of Intervention for Identifying the Role of Intermediaries in the Information Search Process. *ASIS 1996 Annual Conference Proceedings*. Available on the Internet at http://www.asis.org/annual-96/ElectronicProceedings/kuhlthau.html (Accessed January 27, 2003).

———. (1997). Learning in Digital Libraries: An Information Search Process Approach. *Library Trends*, *45*, no. 4, 708–724.

———. (1999). Accommodating the User's Information Search Process: Challenges for Information Retrieval Systems Designers. *Bulletin of the American Society of Information Science*, *25*, no. 3. Available on the Internet at http://www.asis.org/Bulletin/Feb-99/kuhlthau.html (Accessed March 12, 2003).

———. (2001). Rethinking Libraries for the Information Age School: Vital Roles in Inquiry Learning. Keynote Address, The International Association of School Librarianship: Conference and International Research Forum on Research in School Librarianship, Auckland, New Zealand, July 9, 2001. Available on the Internet at http://www.iasl-slo.org/keynote-kuhlthau2001.html (Accessed January 20, 2003).

———. (2003). *Seeking Meaning: A Process Approach to Library and Information Services*. Westport, CT: Libraries Unlimited.

Kuhlthau, C.C., Goodin, M.E., & McNally, M.J. (1996). *The Virtual School Library: Gateway to the Information Highway*. Englewood, CO: Libraries Unlimited.

Kulleseid, E.R. (1986). Extending the Research Base: Schema Theory, Cognitive Styles, and Types of Intelligence. *School Library Media Quarterly*, *15*, no. 1, 41–48.

Kuykendall, C. (2001). Improving Black Student Achievement by Enhancing Student's Self Image. Northwest Regional Educational Laboratory (NWREL). Available on the Internet at http://www.nwrel.org/cnorse/booklets/achieve/ (Accessed February 27, 2003).

Lance, K.C. (2002). What Research Tells Us about the Importance of School Libraries. Proceedings, The White House Conference on School Libraries, June 4, 2002, pp. 17–22. Washington, DC: Institute of Museum and Library Services.

———. (2003). The Importance of School Libraries. Available on the Internet at http://www.laurabushfoundation.org/Lance.pdf (Accessed January 27, 2003).

Lance, K.C., Hamilton-Pennell, C., Rodney, M.J., Peterson, L., & Sitter, C. (2000). Information Empowered: The School Librarian as an Agent of Academic Achievement in Alaska Schools. Executive Summary available on the Internet at http://www.library.state.ak.us/dev/infoemp.html (Accessed January 27, 2003).

Lance, K.C., Rodney, M.J., & Hamilton-Pennell, C. (2000a). How School Libraries Help Kids Achieve Standards. The Second Colorado Study. Denver: Colorado Department of Education. Available on the Internet at http://www.lrs.org/documents/lmcstudies/CO/execsumm.pdf (Accessed January 27, 2003).

———. (2000b). *Measuring Up to Standards: The Impact of School Library Programs and Information Literacy in Pennsylvania Schools*. Pennsylvania Department of Education's Office of Commonwealth Libraries. Gainsburg, PA: Pennsylvania Citizens for Better Libraries. Available on the Internet at http://www.statelibrary.state.pa.us/libraries/lib/libraries/measuringup.pdf (Accessed February 10, 2004).

———. (2001). Good Schools Have School Librarians: Oregon School Libraries Collaborate to Improve Academic Achievement. Salem: Oregon Educational Media Association. Available on the Internet at http://www.oema.net/Oregon_Study/OR_Study.htm (Accessed February 10, 2004).

———. (2003). *How School Librarians Improve Outcomes for Children: The New Mexico Study.* Santa Fe: New Mexico State Library.

Lance, K.C., Welborn, L., & Hamilton-Pennell, C. (1992). *The Impact of School Library Media Centers on Academic Achievement.* Denver: State Library and Adult Education Office, Colorado Department of Education.

Large, A. (2001). Focus Groups with Children: Do They Work? *Canadian Journal of Information and Library Science, 26,* nos. 2–3, 77–89.

———. (2002). Gender Differences in Collaborative Web Searching Behavior: An Elementary School Study. *Information Processing & Management, 38,* no. 3, 427–443.

Large, A., & Beheshti, J. (2000). The Web as a Classroom Resource: Reactions from the Users. *Journal of the American Society for Information Science, 51,* no. 12, 1069–1080.

Large, A., Beheshti, J,. & Breuleux, A. (1998). Information Seeking in a Multimedia Environment by Primary School Students. *Library and Information Science Research, 20,* 343–376.

Large, A., Beheshti, J., & Rahman, T. (2002). Design Criteria for Children's Web Portals: The Users Speak Out. *Journal of the American Society for Information Science and Technology, 53,* no. 2, 79–94.

Lavoie, D.R., & Good, R. (1988). The Nature and Use of Prediction Skills in a Biological Computer Simulation. *Journal of Research in Science Teaching, 25,* no. 5, 335–360.

Lazarus, W., & Mora, F. (2000). Online Content for Low-Income and Underserved Americans: The Digital Divide's New Frontier. Available on the Internet at http://www.childrenspartnership.org. (Accessed February 2, 2003).

Lazear, D. (1991). *Seven Ways of Knowing: Teaching for Multiple Intelligences.* Palatine, IL: Skylight.

Lenox, M.F., & Walker, M.L. (1993). Information Literacy in the Educational Process. *The Educational Forum, 57,* 312–342.

Lewis, R.W. (1989). Elementary School Children Express Their Need for Catalog Information. *Journal of Youth Services in Libraries, 2,* no. 2, 151–156.

Lieberman, M. (1989). *Reports on the Fairfax County Area III Geometry and Algebra Projects, 1988 and 1989.* Available from the Excel office, 200 W. Station St., Barrington, IL 60010.

Liebscher, P., & Marchionini, G. (1988). Browse and Analytical Search Strategies in a Full-Text CD-ROM Encyclopedia. *School Library Media Quarterly, 16,* no. 4, 223–233.

Liesener, J.W. (1985). Learning at Risk: School Library Media Programs in an Information World. *School Library Media Quarterly, 14,* no. 1, 11–20.

Limberg, L. (1999). Model School Libraries: Tools or Threats? Reflections on a Development Project in Sweden. *School Libraries Worldwide, 5,* no. 1, 49–65.

Lin, P. (1994). Library Instruction for Culturally Diverse Populations: A Comparative Approach. *Research Strategies, 12,* no. 3, 168–173.

Lindlof, T.R. (1995). *Qualitative Communication Research Methods.* Thousand Oaks, CA: Sage.

Lingren, J. (1981). Toward Library Literacy. *RQ, 20,* no. 3, 233–235.

Loerke, K. (1994). Teaching the Library Research Process in Junior High. *School Libraries in Canada, 14,* no. 2, 23–26.

Loertscher, D., Ho, M.L., & Bowie, M.M. (1987). "Exemplary Elementary Schools" and Their Library Media Center: A Research Report. *School Library Media Quarterly, 16,* no. 3, 147–153.

Loertscher, D., & Land, P. (1975). An Empirical Study of Media Services in Indiana Elementary Schools. *School Library Media Quarterly, 4,* no. 1, 8–18.

Loertscher, D.V. (1985). Collection Mapping: An Evaluation Strategy for Collection Development. *Drexel Library Quarterly, 21,* no. 2, 9–21.

———. (1996). A Farewell Challenge. *School Library Media Quarterly, 24,* no. 4, 192, 194.

Loranger, A.L. (1994). The Study Strategies of Successful and Unsuccessful High School Students. *Journal of Reading Behavior, 26,* no. 2, 347–360.

Lubans, J. (1974). *Educating the Library User.* New York: Bowker.

Madaus, G.F., & Tan, A.G.A. (1994). The Growth of Assessment. In C.C. Kuhlthau, M.E. Goodin, & M.J. McNally (Eds.), *Assessment in the School Library Media Center* (pp. 1–24). Englewood, CO: Libraries Unlimited.

Maeroff, G.I. (1991). Assessing Alternative Assessment. *Phi Delta Kappan, 73,* no. 4, 273–281.

Mancall, J.C., Aaron, S.L., & Walker, S.A. (1986). Educating Students to Think: The Role of the School Library Media Program. *School Library Media Quarterly, 15,* no. 1, 18–27.

Mancall, J.C., Lodish, E.K., & Springer, J. (1992). Searching across the Curriculum. *Phi Delta Kappan, 73,* no. 7, 526–528.

Marchionini, G. (1987). An Invitation to Browse: Digital Text Systems for Novice Users. *The Canadian Journal of Information Science, 12,* nos. 3–4, 69–79.

———. (1989). Information-Seeking Strategies of Novices Using a Full-Text Electronic Encyclopedia. *Journal of the American Society for Information Science, 40,* no. 1, 54–66.

———. (1991). Psychological Dimensions of User-Computer Interfaces. *Eric Digest.* Syracuse, NY: ERIC Clearinghouse on Information Resources.

Marchionini, G., & Teague, J. (1987). Elementary Students' Use of Electronic Information Services: An Exploratory Study. *Journal of Research in Computing in Education, 20,* no. 2, 139–155.

Marcus, D.L. (2002). Her Parents Look at Her as a Problem. *Knowledge Quest, 30,* no. 5, 19–21.

Mark, B.L., & Jacobson, T.E. (1995). Teaching Anxious Students Skills for the Electronic Library. *College Teaching, 43,* no. 1, 28–31.

Markuson, C. (1986). Making It Happen: Taking Charge of the Information Curriculum. *School Library Media Quarterly, 15,* no. 1, 37–40.

Martin, B. (1982). Interpersonal Relations and the School Library Media Specialist. *School Library Media Quarterly, 11,* no. 1, 43–44, 53–57.

Martin, L.A. (1984). *The Organizational Structure of Libraries.* Metuchen, NJ: Scarecrow Press.

Martinez, M.E. (1994). Access to Information Technologies among School-Age Children: Implications for a Democratic Society. *Journal of the Association for Information Science, 45,* no. 6, 395–400.

Maslow, A.H. (1970). *Motivation and Personality.* New York: Harper and Row.

McCarthy, B. (1987). *The 4MAT System: Teaching Learning Styles with Right/Left Mode Techniques.* Barrington, IL: Excel.

———. (1990). Using the 4MAT System to Bring Learning Styles to Schools. *Educational Leadership* (October), 31–46.

———. (1996). *About Learning.* Barrington, IL: Excel, Inc.

McClure, C.R., & Hernon, P. (Eds.). (1991). *Library and Information Science Research: Perspectives and Strategies for Improvement.* Norwood, NJ: Ablex.

McDonald, F.B. (1988). Information Access for Youth: Issues and Concerns. *Library Trends, 37,* no. 1, 28–42.

McGill-Frantzen, A., Allington, R., Yokoi, L., & Brooks, G. (1999). Putting Books in the Classroom Seems Necessary But Not Sufficient. *Journal of Educational Research, 93,* 67–74.

McGregor, J.H. (1994). Information Seeking and Use: Students' Thinking and Their Mental Models. *Youth Services in Libraries, 8,* no. 1, 69–76.

McKenzie, J. (1997). The Research Cycle. Available on the Internet at http://www.fno. org/oct97/researchcycle.htm (Accessed January 29, 2003).

McNally, M.J. (2004). Analysis of Students' Mental Models: Using the Internet in an Authentic Learning Situation. Ph.D. diss., Rutgers, The State University of New Jersey.

McNally, M.J., & Kuhlthau, C.C. (1994). Information Search Process in Science Education. *The Reference Librarian, 44,* 53–60.

Means, B., & Olson, K. (1994). The Link between Technology and Authentic Learning. *Educational Leadership, 51,* no. 7, 15–18.

Meho, L.I., & Tibbo, H.R. (2003). Modeling the Information Seeking Behavior of Social Scientists: Ellis' Study Revisited. *Journal for the Association for Information Science and Technology, 54,* no. 6, 570–587.

Mendrinos, R. (1994). *Building Information Literacy Using High Technology: A Guide for Schools and Libraries.* Englewood, CO: Libraries Unlimited.

Mensching, T.B. (1989). Trends in Bibliographic Instruction in the 1980's: A Comparison of Data from Two Surveys. *Research Strategies, 7,* no. 1, 4–13.

Meyer, C.A. (1994). What's the Difference between "Authentic" and "Performance" Assessment? In C.C. Kuhlthau, M.E. Goodin, & M.J. McNally (Eds.), *Assessment in the School Library Media Center* (pp. 99–101). Englewood, CO: Libraries Unlimited.

Mokros, H.B., Mullins, L.S., & Saracevic, T. (1995). Practice and Personhood in Professional Interaction: Exploring Social Identities in the Addressing of Information Needs. *LISR, 17,* 237–257.

Montgomery, P. (1997). Use of Information: The Information Literacy Phenomenon. In A.E. Tepe & J. Calarco (Eds.), *A Handbook for Pathways to Knowledge* (pp. 8–10). Follett's Information Skills Model. McHenry, IL: Follett Software.

Moore, P. (1993). Information Problem Solving: A Wider View of Library Skills. *Contemporary Educational Psychology, 20,* no. 1, 1–31.

Moore, P.A., & St. George, A. (1991). Children as Information Seekers: The Cognitive Demands of Books and Library Systems. *School Library Media Quarterly, 19,* no. 3, 161–168.

Morton, C. (1996). The Modern Land of Laputa: Where Computers Are Used in Education. *Phi Delta Kappan, 77,* no. 6, 416–419.

Moursund, D. (1991). Restructuring Education Part 3: What Is the Information Age? *The Computing Teacher, 19,* 4.

Nahl, D., & Harada, V.H. (1996). Composing Boolean Search Statements: Self-Confidence, Concept Analysis, Search Logic, and Errors. *School Library Media Quarterly, 24,* no. 4, 199–207.

Nahl-Jakobovits, D., & Jakobovits, L.A. (1990). Learning Principles and the Library Environment. *Research Strategies, 8,* no. 2, 74–81.

———. (1993). Bibliographic Instructional Design for Information Literacy: Integrating Affective and Cognitive Objectives. *Research Strategies, 11,* no. 2, 73–88.

Nastasi, B.K., Battista, M.T., & Clements, D.H. (1990). Social-Cognitive Interactions, Motivation and Cognitive Growth in Logo Programming and CAI Problem-Solving Environments. *Journal of Educational Psychology, 82,* no. 21, 150–158.

National Center for Educational Statistics (NCES). (2000). Internet Access in Public

Schools and Classrooms (1994–2000). Available on the Internet at http://nces.ed.gov/pubs2001/InternetAccess/5.asp (Accessed February 12, 2004).

National Telecommunications and Information Administration (NTIA). (2000). Falling Through the Net: Toward Positive Inclusion. Available on the Internet at http://www.ntia.doc.gov/ntiahome/fttn60/contents00.html (Accessed February 12, 2004).

Neuman, D. (1994). Alternative Assessment: Promises and Pitfalls. In C.C. Kuhlthau, M.E. Goodin, & M.J. McNally (Eds.), *Assessment in the School Library Media Center* (pp. 67–75). Englewood, CO: Libraries Unlimited.

———. (1995a). High School Students' Use of Databases: Competing Conceptual Structures. Paper presented at the annual meeting of the American Society for Information Science, Chicago, IL, October.

———. (1995b). High School Students' Use of Databases: Results of a National Delphi Study. *Journal of the American Society for Information Science, 46,* no. 4, 284–298.

———. (1997). Learning and the Digital Library. *Library Trends, 45,* no. 4, 687–707.

Neuman, S.B., & Celano, D. (2001). Access to Print in Low-Income and Middle-Income Communities: An Ecological Study of Four Neighborhoods. *Reading Research Quarterly, 36,* no. 1, 8–26.

Nofsinger, M.M. (1989). Library Use Skills for College-Bound High School Students: A Survey. *Reference Librarian,* no. 24, 35–56.

Nolan, J.P. (1989). A Comparison of Two Methods of Instruction in Library Research Skills for Elementary School Students. Ph.D. diss., Temple University.

Norris, S.P. (1985). Synthesis of Research on Critical Thinking. *Educational Leadership, 2,* no. 8, 40–45.

Oberman, C. (1995). Avoiding the Cereal Syndrome; Or, Critical Thinking in the Electronic Environment. In Fifteenth Anniversary Task Force, Library Instruction Round Table, American Library Association (Comp.), *Information for a New Age: Redefining the Librarian* (pp. 107–119). Englewood, CO: Libraries Unlimited.

Oliver, R., & Oliver, H. (1997). Using Context to Promote Learning from Information-Seeking Tasks. *Journal of the American Society for Information Science, 48,* no. 6, 519–526.

O'Neil, J. (1992). Putting Performance Assessment to the Test. *Educational Leadership, 49,* no. 8, 14–19.

Ortega y Gasset, J. (1961). The Mission of the Librarian. *Antioch Review, 21,* no. 2, 133–154.

Pack, S. (2000). Public Library Use, School Performance, and the Parental X-Factor: A Bio-documentary Approach to Children's Snapshots. *Reading Improvement, 37,* no. 4, 161–171.

Pappas, M. (1997). *Introduction to the Pathways to Knowledge.* Follett's Information Skills Model. McHenry, IL: Follett Software.

Pappas, M.L., & Tepe, A.E. (1997). *Pathways to Knowledge: Follett's Information Skills Model* (3rd ed.). McHenry, IL: Follett Software.

Parker, E.B., & Paisley, W.J. (1965). Predicting Library Circulation from Community Characteristics. *Public Opinion Quarterly, 29,* no. 1, 39–53.

Pask, G. (1972). A Fresh Look at Cognition and the Individual. *International Journal of Man-Machine Studies, 4,* 211–216.

———. (1975). *Conversations, Cognition and Learning.* Amsterdam: Elsevier.

Pask, G., & Scott, B.C.E. (1972). Learning Strategies and Individual Competence. *International Journal of Mathematics and Mathematical Sciences, 4,* 217–253.

Pearson, P.D. (Ed.). (1984). *Handbook of Reading Research.* New York: Longman.

Peck, K.L., & Dorricott, D. (1994). Why Use Technology? *Educational Leadership, 51,* no. 7, 11–14.

Pew Research Center. (2001). *The Internet and Education: Findings of the Pew Internet & American Life Project*. Available on the Internet at http://www.pewinternet.org/reorts/reports (Accessed January 24, 2003).

Pfau, D.W. (1967). Effects of Planned Recreational Reading Programs. *The Reading Teacher, 21*, no. 1, 34–39.

Pipher, M. (1994). *Reviving Ophelia: Saving the Selves of Adolescent Girls*. New York: Putnam.

Pitts, J.M. (1995). Mental Models of Information: The 1993–94 AASL/Highsmith Research Award Study. *School Library Media Quarterly, 23*, no. 3, 177–184.

Platzner, M., & Vandergrift, K. (n.d.). Notes on Creating a Visual Interpretive Analysis. Available on the Internet at http://www.scils.rutgers.edu/kvander/syllabus/creation.html (Accessed February 11, 2004).

Pointer, J.M.G. (1979). A Descriptive Study of an Elementary School Library Program Emphasizing Personal Reading Development. Ph.D. diss., United States International University.

Polette, N. (1991). *Research without Copying*. O'Fallon, MO: Book Lures.

Prince Edward Island Department of Education. (n.d.). *Building Information Literacy*. Available on the Internet at http://www.edu.pe.ca/bil/bil.asp?ch2.s3.gdtx (Accessed February 11, 2004).

Radford, M.L. (1989). Interpersonal Communication Theory in the Library Context: A Review of Current Perspectives. In *Library and Information Science Annual* (Vol. 5, pp. 3–10). Englewood, CO: Libraries Unlimited.

———. (1996). Communication Theory Applied to the Reference Encounter: An Analysis of Critical Incidents. *Library Quarterly, 66*, no. 2, 123–137.

Ranganathan, S.R. (1957). *The Five Laws of Library Science*. Madras: The Madras Library Association.

Rankin, V. (1992). Pre-Search: Intellectual Access to Information. *School Library Journal, 38*, no. 3, 168–170.

Rawski, C.H. (1973). *Toward a Theory of Librarianship: Papers in Honor of Jesse Hauk Shera*. Metuchen, NJ: Scarecrow Press.

Ray, J.T. (1994). Resource-Based Teaching: Media Specialists and Teachers as Partners in Curriculum Development and the Teaching of Library and Information Skills. *The Reference Librarian, 44*, 19–27.

Redding, N. (1994). Assessing the Big Outcomes. In C.C. Kuhlthau, M.E. Goodin, & M.J. McNally (Eds.), *Assessment in the School Library Media Center* (pp. 131–36). Englewood, CO: Libraries Unlimited.

Rodney, M.J., Lance, K.C., & Hamilton-Pennell, C. (2002). *Make the Connection: Quality School Library Programs Impact Academic Achievement in Iowa*. A Research Project by Iowa Area Education Agencies. Bettendorf, IA: Mississippi Bend Area Education Agency.

Rothstein, S. (1955). *The Development of Reference Services through Academic Traditions, Public Library Practice and Special Librarianship*. Chicago: Association of College and Reference.

———. (1994). Reference Services. In W.A. Wiegand & D.G. Davis, Jr. (Eds.), *Encyclopedia of Library History* (pp. 541–546). New York: Garland.

Salmon, L.M. (1986). Instruction in the Use of a College Library. In L.L. Hardesty, J.P. Schmitt, & J.M. Tucker (Comps.), *User Instruction in Academic Libraries: A Century of Selected Readings* (pp. 86–101). Metuchen, NJ: Scarecrow Press.

Salvatore, C.L. (2000). Community, Institutions, and Identity in the Chamorro Speech Community: An Ethnographic Study of How They Shape Information-Seeking Discourses in the Library. Ph.D. diss., University of Texas–Austin.

Sauer, J.A. (1995). Conversation 101: Process, Development, and Collaboration. In Fifteenth Anniversary Task Force, Library Instruction Round Table, American Library Association (Comp.), *Information for a New Age: Redefining the Librarian* (pp. 135–151). Englewood, CO: Libraries Unlimited.

Savolainen, R. (2003). Book Review: Looking for Information: A Survey of Research in Information Seeking, Deeds, and Behavior by D.O. Case. *Journal of the American Society for Information Science and Technology, 54,* no. 7, 695–697.

Schack, G.D. (1993). Involving Students in Authentic Research. *Educational Research, 50,* no. 7, 29–31.

Schacter, J., Chung, K.W.K., & Dorr, A. (1998). Children's Internet Searching on Complex Problems: Performance and Process Analyses. *Journal of the American Society of Information Science, 44* no. 9, 840–849.

Scharrer, E. (2002). Making a Case for Media Literacy in the Curriculum: Outcomes and Assessment. *Journal of Adolescent & Adult Literacy, 46,* no. 4, 354–358. Available on the Internet at http://www.readingonline.org/newliteracies/lit_index.asp?HREF-/new literacies/jaal/12-02/column (Accessed February 6, 2004).

Schiller, A. (1986). Reference Service: Instruction or Information. In L.L. Hardesty, J.P. Schmitt, & J.M. Tucker (Comps.), *User Instruction in Academic Libraries: A Century of Selected Readings* (pp. 189–203). Metuchen, NJ: Scarecrow Press.

Schön, D.A. (1983). *The Reflective Practitioner: How Professionals Think in Action.* New York: Basic Books.

Scott, M., & VanNoord, G. (1996). Conducting Original Research at the High School Level—The Student's Perspective. *The American Biology Teacher, 58,* no. 4, 217–219.

Sein, M.K., & Bostrom, R.P (1989). Individual Differences and Conceptual Models in Training Novice Users. *Human-Computer Interaction, 4,* 197–229.

Shaw, C.B. (1986). Bibliographical Instruction for Students. In L.L Hardesty, J.P. Schmitt, & J.M. Tucker (Comps.), *User Instruction in Academic Libraries: A Century of Selected Readings* (pp. 107–109). Metuchen, NJ: Scarecrow Press.

Sheingold, K. (1986). Keeping Children's Knowledge Alive through Inquiry. *School Library Media Quarterly, 15,* no. 1, 80–85.

Shenton, A.K., & Dixon, P. (2003). A Comparison of Youngsters' Use of CD-ROM and the Internet as Information Resources. *Journal of the American Society of Information Science and Technology, 54,* no. 11, 1029–1049.

Shores, L. (1986). The Liberal Arts College, a Possibility in 1954? In L.L Hardesty, J.P. Schmitt, & J.M. Tucker (Comps.), *User Instruction in Academic Libraries: A Century of Selected Readings* (pp. 121–129). Metuchen, NJ: Scarecrow Press.

Sillars, M.O. (1991). *Messages, Meanings, and Culture: Approaches to Communication Criticism.* New York: HarperCollins.

Slavin, R.E. (1990). *Cooperative Learning: Theory, Research, and Practice.* Needham, MA: Allyn and Bacon.

Small, R.V. (1998). Designing Motivation into Library and Information Skills Instruction. *School Library Media Quarterly.* Available on the Internet at http://www.ala.org/aasl/SLMQ/small.html (Accessed January 23, 2003).

———. (1999). An Exploration of Motivational Strategies Used by Library Media Specialists during Library and Information Skills Instruction. *School Library Media Research, 2.* Available on the Internet at http://www.ala.org/aasl/SLMR/vol2/motive.html (Accessed January 23, 2003).

Small, R.V., & Ferreira, S.M (1994a). Information Location and Use, Motivation, and Learning Patterns When Using Print or Multimedia Information Resources. *Journal of Educational Multimedia and Hypermedia, 3,* nos. 3–4, 251–273.

———. (1994b). Multimedia Technology and the Changing Nature of Research in the

School Library. In C. Truett (Ed.), *School Library Reference Services in the 90's: Where We Are, Where We're Heading* (pp. 95–106). New York: Haworth Press.

Smith, E.G. (2001). Texas School Libraries: Standards, Resources, Services, and Students' Performance. Austin: Texas State Library and Archives Commission. Available on the Internet at http://www.tsl.state.tx.us/ld/pubs/schlibsurvey/index.html (Accessed February 12, 2004).

Smith, J.B. (1987). Higher Order Thinking Skills and Nonprint Media. *School Library Media Quarterly*, *16*, no. 1, 38–42.

Solomon, P. (1992). On the Dynamics of Information System Use: From Novice to? In D. Shaw (Ed.), *Proceedings of the ASIS Annual Meeting* (Vol. 29, pp. 162–170). Medford, NJ: Learned Information.

———. (1993). Children's Information Retrieval Behavior: A Case Analysis of an OPAC. *Journal of the American Society for Information Science*, *44*, no. 5, 245–264.

———. (1994). Children, Technology, and Instruction: A Case Study of Elementary School Children Using an Online Public Access Catalog (OPAC). *School Library Media Quarterly*, *23*, no. 1, 43–51.

Springer, S.P., & Deutsch, G. (1993). *Left Brain, Right Brain*. New York: W.H. Freeman.

Stiggins, Richard J. (1991). Assessment Literacy. *Phi Delta Kappan*, *72*, no. 7, 534–539.

Stoan, S.K. (1984). Research and Library Skills: An Analysis and Interpretation. *College and Research Libraries*, *45*, no. 2, 99–108.

Stripling, B.K. (1994a). Assessment of Student Performance: The Fourth Step in the Instructional Design Process. In C.C. Kuhlthau, M.E. Goodin, & M.J. McNally (Eds.), *Assessment in the School Library Media Center* (pp. 77–97). Englewood, CO: Libraries Unlimited.

———. (1994b). Practicing Authentic Assessment in the School Library. In C.C. Kuhlthau, M.E. Goodin, & M.J. McNally (Eds.), *Assessment in the School Library Media Center* (pp. 103–118). Englewood, CO: Libraries Unlimited.

———. (1995). Learning-Centered Libraries: Implications from Research. *School Library Media Quarterly*, *23*, no. 3, 163–170.

Stripling, B.K., & Pitts, J.M. (1988). *Brainstorms and Blueprints: Teaching Library Research as a Thinking Process*. Englewood, CO: Libraries Unlimited.

Swain, D.E. (1996). Information Search Process Model: How Freshmen Begin Research. In *ASIS 1996 Annual Conference Proceedings*. Available on the Internet at http://www.asis.org/annual-96/ElectronicProceedings/swain.html (Accessed December 2, 1998).

Tallman, J., & Henderson, L. (1999). Constructing Mental Model Paradigms for Teaching Electronic Resources. Chicago: AASL. Available on the Internet at http://www.ala.org/aasl/SLMR/vol2/mental.html (Accessed December 12, 2002).

Tapscott, D. (1998). *Growing Up Digital: The Rise of the Net Generation*. New York: McGraw-Hill.

Taylor, R.S. (1968). Question-Negotiation and Information Seeking in Libraries. *College and Research Libraries*, *29*, no. 3, 178–194.

Teele, S. (1996). Redesigning the Educational System to Enable All Students to Succeed. *NASSP Bulletin*, *80*, no. 583, 65–75.

Thomas, J.W. (1993). Promoting Independent Learning in the Middle Grades: The Role of Instructional Support Practices. *The Elementary School Journal*, *93*, no. 5, 575–591.

Thomas, N.P. (1996). Reading Libraries: An Interpretive Study of Discursive Practices in Library Architecture and the Interactional Construction of Personal Identity. Ph.D. diss., Rutgers, The State University of New Jersey.

———. (2000a). A Multiplicity of (Research) Models: Alternative Strategies for Diverse Learners. *School Library Media Activities Monthly*, *17*, no. 1, 25.

———. (2000b). Teaching "Kids" Not Content: Recreating the School Library Media Center as a Caring Context for Student Learning. *School Library Media Activities Monthly*, *1*, no. 2, 23.

———. (2001a). Learning Styles and the Big6: Combining the 4MAT Approach and the Big6 Skills to Plan Projects for Diverse Learners. *The Big6 Newsletter*, E-2, no. 2.

———. (2001b). Unpacking Library Posters: A Theoretical Approach. *Journal of the Association for Library and Information Science Education*, *42*, no. 1, 42–56.

———. (2003). Design Matters: Relational Projections in Library Environments. In H.B. Mokros (Ed.), *Identity Matters: Communication-Based Explorations and Explanations* (pp. 77–108). Cresskill, NJ: Hampton Press.

Thomas, N.P., Vroegindewey, D. & Wellins, C. (1997). 4MATting The Big Six©: Tailoring Research Assignments to Student Learning Styles. Paper presented at the American Association of School Librarians annual conference, April 4, 1997, Portland, OR.

Thorne, L.M. (1967). The Influence of the Knapp School Libraries Project on the Reading Comprehension and on the Knowledge of Library Skills of the Pupils at the Farrar Junior High School, Provo, Utah. Ph.D. diss., Brigham Young University.

Tierney, R.J., & Cunningham, J.W. (1984). Research in Teaching Reading Comprehension. In P.D. Pearson (Ed.), *Handbook of Reading Research* (Vol. 1, pp. 609–655). New York: Longman.

Todd, R.J. (1995). Integrated Information Skills Instruction: Does It Make a Difference? *School Library Media Quarterly*, *23*, no. 2, 133–139.

———. (1998). WWW, Critical Literacies and Learning Outcomes. *Teacher Librarian*, *26*, no. 2, 16–21.

———. (2002). Press release. Available on the Internet at www.oelma.org/SLPress Release.htm (Accessed March 27, 2003).

Todd, R.J., & Kuhlthau, C.C. (2003). Student Learning through Ohio School Libraries: Background, Methodology, and Report of Findings. Columbus: Ohio Educational Library Media Association (OELMA).

Todd, R.J., Lamb, E., & McNicholas, C. (1993). Information Skills and Learning: Some Research Findings. *Access*, *7*, 14–16.

Tucker, J.M. (1994). Library Instruction. In W.A. Wiegand & D.G. Davis, Jr. (Eds.), *Encyclopedia of Library History* (pp. 364–366). New York: Garland.

Tuckett, H.W., & Stoffle, C.J. (1984). Learning Theory and the Self-Reliant Library User. *RQ*, *24*, no. 1, 58–66.

Tuominen, K. (1997). User-Centered Discourse: An Analysis of the Subject Positions of the User and the Librarian. *Library Quarterly*, *67*, no. 4, 352–371.

Turkle, S. (1984). *The Second Self*. New York: Simon and Schuster.

Turner, P. (1990). Research Reviews from the Treasure Mountain Research Retreat. In J.B. Smith (Ed.), *School Library Media Annual* (Vol. 8, pp. 139–153). Englewood, CO: Libraries Unlimited.

———. (1991). Information Skills and Instructional Consulting: A Synergy. *School Library Media Quarterly*, *20*, no. 1, 13–18.

Twist, K.L. (2003). A Nation Online, But Where Are the Indians? Introduction: New NTIA Report Excludes American Indians. Digital Divide Nework. Available on the Internet at http://digitaldividenetwork.org/content/stories/index.cfm?key=215 (Accessed January 23, 2003).

———. (2004). Disparities Along the Information Age Career Path. Digital Divide Network. Available on the Internet at http://digitaldividenetwork.org/content/stories/index.cfm?key=8 (Accessed January 5, 2004).

Ury, C. (1996). Prepping for College. *School Library Journal, 42*, 48.

Valencia, S.W. (1991). Portfolio Assessment for Young Readers. *The Reading Teacher, 44*, no. 9, 680–682.

Vandergrift, K.E., & Hannigan, J.A. (1986). Elementary School Library Media Centers as Essential Components in the Schooling Process. *School Library Media Quarterly, 14*, no. 2, 171–173.

Vandergrift, K.E., Platzner, R., Hannigan, J.A., Dresang, E., Lewis, A., Brizendine, S., Watson, T.T., & Satchell, V. (2000). A Visual Interpretive Analysis Initiative: Looking and Learning Collaboratively. *Knowledge Quest, 28*, no. 4. Available on the Internet at http://www.ala.org/aasl/Kqerb/Kqcontents_v28_4.html (Accessed January 23, 2003).

Volman, M. (1997). Gender-Related Effects of Computer and Information Literacy Education. *Journal of Curriculum Studies, 29*, no. 3, 315–328.

Von Glasersfeld, E. (1995). *Radical Constructivism: A Way of Knowing and Learning.* London: Falmer Press.

Vygotsky, L. (1978). *Mind in Society: The Development of Higher Psychological Processes.* Cambridge, MA: Harvard University Press.

Walter, V.A. (1994). The Information Needs of Children. In I.P. Godden (Ed.), *Advances in Librarianship* (pp. 111–129). San Diego, CA: Academic Press.

Walter, V.A., Borgman, C.L., & Hirsh, S.G. (1996). The Science Library Catalog: A Springboard for Information Literacy. *School Library Media Quarterly, 24*, no. 2, 105–110.

Watson, J.S. (1998). "If You Don't Have It, You Can't Find It": A Close Look at Students' Perceptions of Using Technology. *Journal of American Information Science, 49*, no. 11, 1024–1036.

Watzlawick, P., Beavin, J.H., & Jackson, D.D. (1967). *Pragmatics of Human Communication: A Study of Patterns, Pathologies and Paradoxes.* New York: Norton.

Wesley, T. (1991). Teaching Library Research: Are We Preparing Students for Effective Information Use? *Emergency Librarian, 18*, no. 3, 23–30.

Wesson, C.L., & Keefe, M.J. (1995). *Serving Special Needs Students in the School Library Media Center.* Westport, CT: Greenwood Press.

Whelan, D.L. (2004). A New Ohio Study Shows How School Librarians Help Students Learn. *School Library Journal*, Feburary 1. Available on the Internet at http://www.schoollibraryjournal.com/article/CA377858 (Accessed February 10, 2004).

Wiburg, K., & Carter, B. (1994). Thinking with Computers. *The Computing Teacher, 22*, no. 1, 7–10.

Wigfield, A., & Asher, S.R. (1984). Social and Motivational Influences on Reading. In P.D. Pearson (Ed.), *Handbook of Reading Research* (Vol. 1, pp. 423–452). New York: Longman.

Wilhelm, T., Carmen, D., & Reynolds, M. (2002). Annie E. Casey Foundation and Benton Foundation Connecting Kids and Technology: Challenges and Opportunities. Available on the Internet at http://www.digitaldividenetwork.org/content/stories/index.cfm?key=244 (Accessed January 23, 2003).

Wilkerson, R., & White, K. (1988). Effects of the 4MAT System of Instruction on Students' Achievement, Retention, and Attitudes. *Elementary School Journal, 88*, 257–368.

Williams, D., & Wavell, C. (2001). *The Impact of the School Library Resource Centre on Learning.* Library and Information Commission Research Report 112. Report on Research Conducted for Resource: The Council for Museums, Archives and Libraries, Aberdeen, Scotland: The Robert Gordon University. Available on the Internet at http://www.rgu.ac.uk/abs/research/page.cfm?pge=6924 (Accessed February 10, 2004).

Willson, E.J. (1965). Evaluating Urban Centralized Elementary School Libraries. Ph.D. diss., Wayne State University.

Wilson, L.R. (1933). The Development of Research in Relation to Library Schools. *Library Journal*, *58*, no. 22, 817–821.

Winograd, P., & Gaskins, R.W. (1992). Metacognition: Matters of the Mind, Matters of the Heart. In A.L. Costa, J.A. Bellanca, & R. Fogarty (Eds.), *If Minds Matter: A Foreword to the Future* (Vol. 1, pp. 225–238). Palatine, IL: IRI/Skylight Publishing.

Winsor, J. (1986). The College Library. In L.L. Hardesty, J.P. Schmitt, & J.M. Tucker (Comps.), *User Instruction in Academic Libraries: A Century of Selected Readings* (pp. 5–16). Metuchen, NJ: Scarecrow Press.

Woronov, T. (1994). Machine Dreams: Six Myths (and Five Promising Truths) about the Uses of Educational Technology. *Harvard Education Letter*, *10*, no. 5, 1–3.

Wozny, L.A. (1982). Online Bibliographic Searching and Student Use of Information: An Innovative Teaching Approach. *School Library Media Quarterly*, *11*, no. 1, 35–42.

Wyer, J. (1930). *Reference Work: A Textbook for Students Of Library Work and Libraries*. Chicago: American Library Association.

Yarling, J.R. (1968). Children's Understandings and Use of Selected Library-Related Skills in Two Elementary Schools, One with and One without a Centralized Library. Ph.D. diss., Ball State University, 1968.

Young, A.P. (1974). Research on Library-User Education: A Review Essay. In J. Lubans (Ed.), *Educating the Library User* (pp. 1–15). New York: Bowker.

Yucht, A.H. (1997). *Flip It! An Information Skills Strategy for Student Researchers*. Worthington, OH: Linworth.

———. (2002). *FLIP It! A Problem-Solving Framework Developed by Alice H. Yucht*. Available on the Internet at http://www.aliceinfo.org/FLPT_focus.html (Accessed February 11, 2004).

Author Index

Subject Index

AASL. *See* American Association of School Librarians (AASL)

Abstract conceptualizers (Kolb), 73, 89

Academic achievement. *See* Achievement, student

Academic libraries: BI traditions in, 5–11; historical development of services in, 2, 5–11

Access to information for children and youth, xii

Access to technology: benefits for students, 140–141; challenges for students, 141–142; ethical issues related to, 153

Accommodation and assimilation. *See* Piaget, Jean

Accountability, xii, 23; and assessment, 164

Achievement, student: assessment of, 166; and critical thinking, 119; and library instruction and services, 23, 24, 104, 164, 166, 169–170; motivation issues, 126–127; social interaction and, 96, 177

ACRL. *See* Association of College and Research Libraries (ACRL)

Action research, 117

Active experimenters (Kolb), 73, 89

Active learning, 17, 28; computer use and, 135, 149–150; definition of, 104, 108, 110; roles for students in, 110

Adams, Charles Francis, Jr., 16

Adams, Herbert Baxter, 5

Ad Hoc Committee on Bibliographic Instruction, 11

Adolescents: gender issues for, 115; information needs of, 83; self needs of, 180; stereotyping, 181. *See also* Affective/emotional domain; Affiliation needs; Self-esteem

Advocacy, 176

AECT. *See* Association for Educational Communications and Technology (AECT)

Affective/emotional domain: implications for information seeking and instruction, 23, 105, 150, 175–178, 182; needs of minority students, 176

Affiliation needs, 39, 181, 182. *See also* Affective/emotional domain; Adolescents; Self-esteem

African-American students: affect and expressive behavior in, 95; inequities in education and library services for in the South, 18, 26n; instructional strategies for, 95–96, 131n; learning style differences, 95

ALA. *See* American Library Association (ALA)

Alternative assessment: definition of, 160; and the process approach curriculum, 172

American Association of School Librarians (AASL), 15, 19, 53, 57, 103

American Indians, 142, 156; difficulties with synthesis tasks, 131n; and the digital divide, 86

American Library Association (ALA), 6, 11, 12, 13, 17, 18, 19, 20

Wirt, William, 18
Worcester (MA) Free Public Library, 12
Worldview, Western and non-Western,
79–80

Zone of proximal development (ZPD)
(Vygotsky), 29, 35, 106–108
ZPD. *See* Zone of proximal development
(ZPD) (Vygotsky)

About the Author

NANCY PICKERING THOMAS is an associate professor in the School of Library and Information Management, Emporia State University. Dr. Thomas, who received her Ph.D. in Communication, Information and Library Studies from Rutgers, The State University of New Jersey, teaches graduate courses in theoretical foundations of service, children's literature and programming, managing the school library media center, and services for special populations. Articles by Dr. Thomas have appeared in *Advances in Library Administration and Organization, JELIS, School Library Media Activities Monthly*, and the *Big6Newsletter*, in addition to a special issue on youth for the *Journal of the American Society for Information Science*, which she co-edited with Dr. Mary Kay Chelton. In 2002, Dr. Thomas co-chaired (with Dr. Daniel Callison, Indiana University–Purdue University Indianapolis) the Treasure Mountain Research Retreat at the Elms, Excelsior Springs, Missouri.